It was ten o'clock when the astonishingly successful lives of Kitty and Jose Menendez came to a violent and horrible end.

They heard the double front doors fly open, and the sound of running feet pounding across the polished parquet floor in the foyer. Jose and Kitty just had time to stand up and turn around before the French doors between the family room and foyer were thrown back. The only light in the room came from the glimmer of the television set, but they could see two men, each of whom carried a huge shotgun, both of the weapons pointed directly at them.

"NO! NO!" Jose cried, beginning to move to his left. But his cry was drowned in a furious barrage of thundering shotgun blasts. . . .

St. Martin's Paperbacks Titles
by Don Davis

THE MILWAUKEE MURDERS
THE NANNY MURDER TRIAL
BAD BLOOD

Bad Blood

THE SHOCKING TRUE STORY BEHIND THE
MENENDEZ KILLINGS

DON DAVIS

ST. MARTIN'S PAPERBACKS

BAD BLOOD

Copyright © 1994 by Don Davis.

Cover photograph of Lyle and Erik Menendez copyright © *Los Angeles Daily News*/Sygma.
Family photograph (inset) copyright © 1990 *Los Angeles Times*.

ISBN: 0-312-95334-8

Printed in the United States of America

St. Martin's Paperbacks edition/March 1994

10 9 8 7 6 5 4 3 2 1

For Irma and Eric

Acknowledgments

Many people extended helping hands in getting this story together. Particular thanks go to J. Stryker Meyer, John Gaines, Mary McBride, and Jim and Valerie Alvord in San Diego; Vasily Safos and Cynthia Avila in Los Angeles; and Jill Hill. My editor, Charlie Spicer, his assistant, Tory Foran, and the usual gang of suspects at St. Martin's Press made all the signals flash green at the appropriate moments. Thanks also to my agent, Mark Joly, and Bill Haas at the Scott Meredith Literary Agency, for their continued support. Most of all, this book would never have seen the light of day without the untiring expert help of my favorite research assistant, photographer, editor, and beautiful wife, Robin Murphy.

1

August 20, 1989

Money. That was what it was all about, wasn't it?

Jose and Kitty Menendez had plenty of it, millions of dollars, and the promise of more, much more, on the horizon. It was almost as if someone would bring a wheelbarrow full of cash to the house every day and dump it at the front door. Jose was a sharp, tough executive in the Hollywood entertainment industry, his star still on the rise, and his personal wealth bought his family prestige, security, and exciting lives. They lacked no material things.

On Monday morning he would enter the glass, steel, and concrete Los Angeles jungle once again to ply his trade, but on the balmy Southern California Sunday night of August 20, 1989, he sat with his feet propped on the coffee table, channel surfing through the programs on the huge console television set.

A James Bond movie, *The Spy Who Loved Me,* was playing, but Kitty and Jose had better choices. Fictional spy stuff was not as interesting as the news shows. Science sought their attention, as the magical *Voyager 2* space probe, a dozen years into its mission, was sending back startling pictures of the baby blue planet Neptune. Sports buff Jose Kept up with Pete Rose being banned from baseball for life because of his alleged gambling. And, rich themselves, both could chuckle at Malcolm Forbes, who was observing his seventieth birthday by spending two million dollars to throw a mind-boggling party in Tangier, Morocco. Jose would someday like to have that much money to throw around.

Money. For Jose Menendez, who had come to the United States from Cuba at the age of sixteen, money meant quite a lot. It had bought him respect, acceptance in society, safety, fame, and all sorts of trinkets. He had only to look around him to know he had already succeeded beyond the dreams of most people. And, at the age of forty-five, he had many years left to amass a still larger fortune. Money was how he could measure the distance he had traveled from Havana.

After all, he was pulling in an annual salary and bonus of more than a million dollars as the chief executive officer at one of the nation's major video-distribution and music-retailing companies. He could call a number of stars in the entertainment industry his friends—hell, even his kids played tennis with movie stars!—and merely the address of the family home spoke loudly.

The prestige was not due as much to the spaciousness and beauty of the home at 722 North Elm Drive, but rather to the dirt upon which it sat. The home was in Beverly Hills, a five-square-mile fantasyland that contained some of the most expensive and exclusive real estate in the entire nation. Beverly Hills was not an address, it was a legend, immortalized in countless motion pictures and television shows. Living there meant that Jose Menendez, the Cuban immigrant, was a millionaire who had at last reached the big leagues.

The Menendez clan—Jose, Kitty, and their two handsome, black-haired sons, Lyle and Erik—had moved into the house in October 1988 after Jose shelled out two million dollars in cash as a down payment and a bank fell all over itself to give him a mortgage for another two million. Only a year later, it was valued at five and a half million. The two-story white stucco home, with a decidedly Spanish look about it, was located just off Wilshire Boulevard. Several healthy elm trees grew in front of the house, shadowing the black wrought-iron fence capped with pointed spikes and a locking, electronic gate designed to keep unwelcome intruders away. But the big trees also lent a bit of gloom and mystery to the place, a feeling that could not be dismissed by the row of bright impatiens flowers at the foot of the fence.

Jose had more than an ideal address. He had a beautiful wife who could mingle with the best of them on the cocktail circuit and two strong sons who were tennis wizards, not only on the private tennis court in the backyard, but also in tournament play. Lyle was ready to return to Princeton and continue his Ivy League education. Erik, just graduated from Beverly Hills High School, was set to start at UCLA.

Erik, at eighteen, occupied one of the eight bedrooms in the nine-thousand-square-foot house, and Lyle, twenty-one, lived in the two-story guesthouse at the rear of the property. The boys took pride in knowing the house had at various times belonged to music stars Elton John and Prince. Neighbors who remembered the rock and roll superstars were happy that the place was almost soundproof. In fact, with its history of quick turnovers, the neighbors sniffed that the house was the "rental property" of North Elm.

Kitty and Jose had settled in on Sunday evening, alone. The boys had gone to see a movie in nearby Century City. The couple envied the youthful energy of their sons, who could play tennis all day and party all night. In fact, the family had spent most of Sunday on the tennis court, where Jose, who liked nothing more than to win at everything he did, had to face the bitter recognition, once again, that both of his boys were far superior in their ability to swing a tennis racket. He did not want to be an old man, but some things just had to be accepted. He would never see the sunny side of thirty again, or forty.

Sunday afternoon's tennis marathon had followed an equally exhausting Saturday, when the family chartered a thirty-one-foot boat, the *Motion Picture Marine,* for an all-day shark-fishing expedition. The weather had been somewhat rough, and while Kitty and Jose stayed safely in the stern with the captain, his girlfriend, and a deckhand, Lyle and Erik rode up on the bow, and were drenched by splashing waves.

So tonight was a rest period for Jose, before he had to dive back into the entertainment industry pool, a place that was filled with some pretty nasty sharks of its own. Jose, with no room in his heart for the weak, prided himself on being one of the sharks.

He was casually dressed in shorts and a loose shirt, and Kitty was similarly attired in a comfortable sweat suit. She was seated on the floor at his feet, sorting through the admissions material that had been sent to Erik from UCLA. They hoped Erik might do better as a freshman than Lyle had during his first, brief exposure to Princeton.

Jose was a self-made man who loved and exemplified the American story of a dedicated person rising high enough to make a difference. That was why a picture of Dr. Martin Luther King, bearing the famed quotation *I Have A Dream,* hung on the wall of the family room, amid shelves of books, sparkling sports trophies, and a plethora of photographs of the Menendez family. He lounged back against the comfortable L-shaped white sofa, a man completely at ease. Both he and Kitty were giving themselves a treat after the strenuous weekend, and partially eaten bowls of vanilla ice cream and berries sat on the table, flanking a cassette tape of Michael Jackson's music and a cigarette lighter.

It was ten o'clock when the astonishingly successful lives of Kitty and Jose Menendez came to a violent and horrible end.

They heard the double front doors fly open, and the sound of running feet pounding across the polished parquet floor in the foyer. Jose and Kitty just had time to stand up and turn around before the French doors between the family room and foyer were thrown back. The only light in the room came from the glimmer of the television set, but they could see two men, each of whom carried a huge shotgun, both of the weapons pointed directly at them.

"NO! NO!" Jose cried, beginning to move to his left. But his cry was drowned in a furious barrage of thundering shotgun blasts. The assassins did not speak; they just pulled the triggers of their 12-gauge shotguns, over and over and over.

BLAM! BLAM! The first shots struck Jose and Kitty full force, throwing them aside. BLAM! BLAM! BLAM! BLAM! Fans of fire slashed out of the shotgun barrels and heavy pellets of buckshot ripped through flesh and bone and seat cushions and glass. Kitty's hand was almost severed and she fell to the oriental carpet bleeding heavily. Jose was flipped backward onto the couch. BLAM! BLAM! BLAM! BLAM!

The deafening assault continued without letup as the killers kept pulling the triggers. Buckshot sprayed everywhere, and the room looked as if it were being attacked by hordes of insects that could drill into anything and everything. Blood flew out of the victims in curtains at the impact of the shells, strips of brains and intestines smashed against the floor and walls, and still the frenzied firing continued. BLAM! BLAM! BLAM! BLAM! Acrid smoke rose like a shifting gray cloud, filtering the light that came from the television set and the distant foyer.

Then, the firing stopped, as suddenly as it had begun. The ears of the assailants rang in the silence. One stepped forward and pressed the barrel of his shotgun against the back of Jose Menendez's head, which rested at a strange angle on the sofa, and pulled the trigger. The blast took off most of the victim's face.

Finally the guns were empty, but as their hearing returned, the killers detected the soft, ghastly moans of Kitty Menendez, who was trying to pull her shattered body to the perceived safety of the coffee table. The men looked at each other, amazed. How could anyone survive that attack? One quickly ran back outside to his car, shoved more buckshot into his weapon, and returned to the wrecked room. He leaned over the coffee table and carefully nestled the shotgun muzzle against Kitty's left cheek, almost as if giving her a light caress with the cold steel barrel, and pulled the trigger. The blast tore away her nose and one eye.

Convinced that both were quite dead, the killers calmly collected the spent shotgun shell casings and left the house. This was no robbery. It was cold-blooded murder on a peaceful Sunday night in the middle of Beverly Hills.

Lyle and Erik Menendez were puzzled when they drove up to their home about an hour later, for the front gate, normally locked, was standing open. They pulled the car to the right and parked, got out, then went inside. Erik immediately smelled smoke, as if a fire had been burning somewhere in the big house.

The doors to the dark family room were standing open and, when they walked in, they found a scene from a nightmare. Their father lay sprawled, almost sitting up straight, at a corner of the sofa, and their mother lay dead at his feet, both of them drenched in blood.

They stood rooted to the spot, the carnage of the scene etching itself on their minds as they tried to grasp the enormity of knowing the lives of their parents had been snuffed out. The room looked as if it had been painted in blood.

Erik broke down immediately, wailing in grief at the top of his lungs. Lyle, the older of the two, knew he had to do something, but did not know what. He had never seen his father, who had always been in control of every situation, look so helpless. This did not look like Jose Menendez, but like some bloody and misshapen wax doll propped up in his place. Lyle stumbled out of the room, across the foyer, and up the stairs that looped from the hallway to the second floor. In a bedroom, he found a telephone and punched in the police emergency call number, 911.

The telephone rang at the Beverly Hills police station exactly at 11:47 P.M., and a female dispatcher quickly answered as a huge reel-to-reel tape recorder spun slowly in a corner, catching every word. When the nature of the emergency became apparent, a male dispatcher joined the conversation.

DISPATCHER: Beverly Hills emergency.

LYLE MENENDEZ: Yes, police, uh . . . (unintelligible)

DISPATCHER: What's the problem?

LYLE: We're the sons . . . (caller breaks into unintelligible sobs)

DISPATCHER: What's the problem? What's the problem?

LYLE: (Crying) They shot and killed my parents!

DISPATCHER: What? Who? Are they still there?

LYLE: Yes.

DISPATCHER: The people who . . .

LYLE: No, no.

DISPATCHER: They were shot?

LYLE: Erik, man, don't . . . (unintelligible)

DISPATCHER: They were shot?

LYLE: Yes.

DISPATCHER: (Talking over a background sound of screams and Lyle's shouts of "Erik, shut up!") I have a hysterical person on the phone. Is the person still there?

SECOND DISPATCHER: What happened? Have you been able to figure out what happened?

LYLE: I don't know.

SECOND DISPATCHER: Who shot who?

LYLE: I didn't hear anything. I just came home.

SECOND DISPATCHER: You came home and found who shot?

LYLE: My mom and dad.

SECOND DISPATCHER: You're in bed?

LYLE: No.

FIRST DISPATCHER: Are they still in the house, the people who did the shooting?

LYLE: (A scream) Erik! Get away from them!

SECOND DISPATCHER: OK. (Speaking to first dispatcher) Hang up. (Speaking to Lyle) Let me talk to Erik.

LYLE: (Unintelligible response)

SECOND DISPATCHER: Who is the person that was shot?

LYLE: My mom and dad.

SECOND DISPATCHER: Your mom and dad?

LYLE: (A shriek) My mom and dad!

SECOND DISPATCHER: OK. Hold on a sec. (Pause while dispatcher gives police the address that automatically appeared on his screen. Caller weeps uncontrollably.) OK. We're on our way over there now in an ambulance.

The call had lasted only two and one-half minutes, and one minute after it terminated a police cruiser was at the house. Erik was huddled in a fetal ball on the front curb, crying his heart out. Lyle was nearby.

Three minutes after the first officer walked into the family room and discovered the slaughtered bodies, Jose and Kitty Menendez were declared officially dead.

But their story was just beginning.

2

Jose

Jose Francisco Menendez and Maria Carlotta Llanio Menendez watched the rise of Fidel Castro with dread. Both were well known in Havana, and moved with fluid, aristocratic Latin grace across the Cuban social scene.

Jose was a successful accountant and businessman and a former world-class soccer player who still coached the sport in Havana. Maria was a swimmer of championship caliber who had won gold medals in Central American Olympic games and whose aquatic exploits were enshrined in the Cuban Hall of Fame. But their past deeds, which had helped them gain their fortune and stature, were of little use in a land that was coming apart at the seams. They had one son, two daughters, and no future in Cuba, as the Castro regime gobbled up their property, their money, and their dreams.

Cuba, prior to Castro, had been a vacation haven, a gambling mecca, and a profitable economic sphere of the United States. Glittering hotels lined tropical beaches, American tourists poured money into the sunny paradise with twenty-five hundred miles of shoreline, and Cuban businessmen made millions of dollars from cattle ranches, sugarcane and tobacco plantations, oil, and thousands of other ventures. The nation had one of the highest standards of living in the hemisphere, and the Menendez family was among those who were part of the Cuban moneyed elite.

But the island nation also had a wretched underclass, which watched with desperation as American-made limousines of the aristocracy stacked up nightly outside the private clubs. In a time when Communists were making political gains from Vietnam to Egypt, Cuba had a built-in base for revolution. Fidel Castro tapped into that unrest.

So life on the tropical island had been changing swiftly since 1959, when the rebellion overthrew Fulgencio Batista and the bearded Castro took over, determined to hammer Cuba into a model socialist state. Sweeping economic and social reforms were imposed, and to the horror of businessmen, such as Jose Francisco Menendez, the revolutionary government seized the property of upper- and middle-class Cubans without paying for it, turned vast farms into collectives, and voided all leases and mortgages. With Castro's buddy, an Argentine freebooter named Ernesto "Che" Guevara, as president of the National Bank, it became impossible to make a profit in Cuba.

Within a year, the economy was on the skids. Public works and housing projects dried up, and while the upper class lost property, the lower class faced new taxes and higher food prices. Worse, the Castro government ruthlessly crushed all opposition, with firing squads working overtime to cleanse the political house. Opponents were stripped of their possessions, imprisoned, or executed.

So with Cuba rushing headlong toward economic wreckage, the best and brightest among the Cuban elite began to flee. For a businessman, it made no sense at all to wait patiently for Castro's goons to show up and take everything you and your family had accumulated over a lifetime. The first waves of Cubans to escape to America were the educated, the wealthy, the smart, and the brave, usually landing with only the clothes on their backs, sacrificing everything to reach freedom.

Fidel Castro and Jose Enrique Menendez both came to the United States from Cuba in 1960, one to fulminate on behalf of communism before the United Nations, and the other to keep alive a fierce familial spirit of capitalism. Castro was Cuba's prime minister in his second year as dictator. Menendez was a sixteen-year-old boy who had been shuffled out of the country by his well-to-do family to avoid Castro's reach.

The boy had been born in 1944 and was well entrenched in his parents' beliefs in the accumulation of capital and the joys that money could bring. But this Castro fellow and the charismatic Che Guevara were exerting an astonishing pull on the young people of Cuba. Their allure as swaggering mountain fighters, revolutionaries who had overthrown a dictator, and architects of a new society seemed to ring a bell with the nation's youth. Who could argue with a teenager about the true cost of Castro's promise of a better future for everyone?

So it was decided that, since the future was bleak enough at home, Jose would be better off removed from the temptation of communism. And that meant going to America. The rest of the family would follow soon, staying in Cuba to battle for their businesses as long as possible. But as a Menendez, Jose could not be allowed to slide into the utopian dream of communism.

The family had confidence in the young man's ability to make good in a strange land, for he never backed down from a challenge and had a streak of steel in his Latin personality. His mother remembered taking him out to José Martí Airport in Havana one day in 1954, when he was only ten, to meet his father's flight. According to the *Miami Herald,* the boy strode fearlessly up to a guard and announced, "I am Jose Enrique!" as if everybody in Cuba should know his last name. His arrogance worked and the armed guard stepped aside. It was a trait that would follow him through life. He simply felt he was better than everyone else.

At the age of sixteen, Jose found himself on a flight from that same airport, accompanied by his sister's fiancé, bound for the United States. Their destination was not to be Miami's Little Havana section, or Ybor City in Tampa—in fact, it was not even Florida at all. The fiancé had relatives in a place called Pennsylvania, and that's where the two young men would find shelter in America.

"He used to tell us that when he came to the U.S., he didn't speak much English . . . but he said he made it his goal to run one of the largest companies in America," Erik Menendez recalled for a reporter less than a week after his parents were slain.

The family may have been wealthy and held influence in Cuba, but when Jose arrived in the rolling countryside of Pennsylvania, he was virtually penniless. His first lodging in the small town of Hazelton, halfway between Scranton and Allentown, was in the attic of a farmhouse. Pennsylvania was not exactly overrun with people of Spanish extraction. Instead of a setting with familiar Spanish rhythms and speech, Jose Menendez was dropped into a center of white America, far from home and as lonely as could be.

But like most of the earliest Cuban immigrants, his determination to succeed was written all over his face. He may wash dishes today to bring in spending money, but he knew that a special destiny beckoned. All he had to do was work hard and follow his star.

The year of 1960 was a wonderful time to arrive in the United States, for new ideas swirled everywhere. Harper Lee won the Pulitzer Prize for *To Kill a Mockingbird*, Hitchcock scared everyone with *Psycho*, Broadway saw the opening of *Camelot*, and Chubby Checker introduced the twist, which had the world's young people gyrating in new dance steps. In Greensboro, North Carolina, four young black people refused to leave a dime-store lunch counter when denied service and launched an important new chapter in the battle for racial equality. John F. Kennedy, whom Castro described in his speech to the United Nations that year as "an illiterate and ignorant millionaire," became the thirty-fifth president of the United States.

Jose was charming, athletic, and dashingly handsome, a bit of a rogue with a touch of romantic hero about him, telling the girls of Pennsylvania, in his accented English, about how he had escaped from Cuba. He knew that his family prized education as a route to success, and so he studied furiously in high school, where his teachers later remembered him as an excellent student and a star competitor on the swim team. Success was branded on his soul and he would accept nothing less, even as a young man. Other students, particularly those who could flash the kind of money his family had lost, might be able to buy more things, to go more places, to do more things, but none of them would ever be able to outhustle Jose Menendez. That intense drive to succeed at all costs became his trademark.

"He really couldn't do anything well enough," Lyle Menendez said of his father in early December 1989.

It was with a sting of embarrassment that Jose realized that what he really wanted, an Ivy League education, was beyond his financial grasp. Someday, he promised himself, his own children would attend such fine universities. But for the moment, Jose had to live with reality. College was what was important, as he graduated from high school, any college, no matter the name. Since he had to go the scholarship route because of financial problems, and he could not be too choosy.

All the time his foot was tapping, for he was eager to hit the pavement and start making money. He was even ready to peddle encyclopedias door to door, confident that he could sell anything to anybody if just given the chance. No, said the family, the answer was in the classroom, not on the streets.

As a youngster in Cuba, the energetic Jose had been an excellent athlete, and he brought those skills with him to America. Because he displayed talent as a competitive swimmer, like his mother, he won a scholarship to attend Southern Illinois University in Carbondale, Illinois. Athletics were his ticket in, but he could not sandwich the continuing grind of practices and swim meets into his need to study, so he eventually walked away from the pool to spend more time in the classroom. To his surprise, he found that he enjoyed going to SIU.

In many ways, he was already larger than life, even as an impoverished student, with a powerful, evangelical sort of magnetism emanating from his dark eyes. Friends knew that what Jose wanted, Jose was going to get.

They also knew that there was a special reason that Jose liked Southern Illinois University. Her name was Mary Louise Andersen.

3

Kitty

Jose, the dark-eyed Cuban immigrant, soon found himself head over heels in love with a beautiful, all-American girl from a Chicago suburb. Although their meeting may not have been love at first sight, they quickly became a serious campus couple. Called "Kitty" by her friends and family, the vivacious and daring young Mary Louise Andersen was a friendly target for the smooth Latin moves of the good-looking Jose Menendez, who pursued her with his usual over-powering, relentless determination.

She had been born in 1941, the fourth child of Charles and Mae Andersen, and grew up as a rascally tomboy alongside her two brothers, Milt and Brian, and older sister, Joan. The family lived in a modest, two-story house at 4849 West 91st Place in the village of Oak Lawn, a suburb south of Chicago. The house, with its white aluminum siding, black trim, and composition roof, differed little from the neighboring homes in the eight-square-mile community that had become a collection of European ethnic and cultural backgrounds. Irish, Dutch, German, Italian, Scandinavian, and Slavic families all settled in the little town, where towering maple and elm trees shared space with the giant black oaks from which Oak Lawn took its name. The trees shaded the yards and homes from the stifling heat of summer, and the house on West 91st had a backyard with ample room for the Andersen kids to play.

Even today, with the six-lane boulevards of 95th Street, 103rd Street, Cicero, and Pulaski slicing through the once quiet town, Oak Lawn maintains a bit of small-town charm. The local hardware store owner knows customers by their first names and most recent illness, tuxedo and bridal shops dot the thoroughfares, and there is a large emphasis on marriage and family in the neat rows of houses.

Little Mary Louise attended grammar school in a two-story, dark red brick building that was constructed in 1906, the first school in Oak Lawn, and classes met there for a half-century before it became the headquarters for Oak Lawn's Historial Society. She graduated to Covington Middle School as Oak Lawn was hitting its postwar boom time, and her father's heating and air-conditioning business flourished. Her brothers worked with their father and then started similar businesses of their own.

Divorce is a rather routine thing today, but it was still an unusual event in the 1950s, something that could tear a household apart and scandalize a neighborhood. Mary Louise learned one of life's harsh lessons when her father left home and divorced her mother. All Oak Lawn buzzed with the story.

As a result, she became withdrawn and fearful, hesitant to form close friendships with her classmates. The fact that her father remarried, continued to live nearby, and started another family did not ease her turmoil. In her class photographs from Oak Lawn Community High School, she was unable to manage a smile. Dark, brooding eyes are framed by arching brows, and her dark hair was worn thick and very short. But it was in high school that she made one significant change, dropping the formality of Mary Louise and becoming Kitty.

Few classmates remember her, and she did not stand out in club activities. In the thirteen rows of kids lined up on the bleachers for the Pep Club photo, she sits in the back row, unsmiling. During her senior year, she joined Mr. Tucker's Dramatics Club, one of ninety-six girls to do so. The new nickname and the growing confidence she learned in the drama club, where she could pretend to be somebody else for a while, helped her start climbing out of her personal hell. She decided to go to college and won acceptance at Southern Illinois University. She was determined that when she left Oak Lawn and her broken home behind her, life would improve. The departure for SIU meant a ticket to freedom, and no longer would she be the target of gossip by classmates because of her parents' divorce. At Carbondale, she would re-create herself.

In her freshman year at college, Kitty began working in the university's broadcast department, learning to produce dramas for radio and television, a creative endeavor she loved. Before long she had found a group of new friends, from places other than Oak Lawn, and began to blossom into a personable young woman. She was one of a group of students that created the *WSIU Little Theatre,* a weekly radio drama show that was popular not only on campus, but in the surrounding community.

She had a regular beau who was a dashing upperclassman who often performed the lead in campus plays, but for the most part, Kitty was so busy rehearsing and studying there was little time left for going out on dates.

By her senior year, 1962, Kitty had found enough confidence to compete for the title of Miss Oak Lawn. Crowning a queen was the highlight of a VFW-sponsored pageant that was an excuse for the town to get together for a party. It was a chance for Kitty to show her old classmates, particularly the spiteful girls who had made fun of her, just how far she had soared from little Oak Lawn Community High School. On Saturday night, September 15, shortly after 7:30 P.M., the twenty-year-old Mary Louise Andersen, the grown-up Kitty, was crowned Miss Oak Lawn, winning an assortment of prizes from local merchants. Wearing a strapless gown, Kitty may have been heavier, more rounded than her competition, but the judges also took into consideration her accomplishments at Southern Illinois. It was to Kitty that they presented roses, a trophy, and a glittering tiara.

Back at college, she decided to try for even bigger things. Oak Lawn had been conquered nicely by her coronation, and now she was ready to pursue her dream of directing and producing commercial radio and television programs. Kitty Andersen decided to set her cap for New York City, the heartbeat of broadcasting.

Then, without warning, a freshman caught the eye of the sophisticated senior. He was dark, spoke with an interesting accent, and was swaggeringly sure of himself. She had always been low in self-esteem and here was this *kid* who acted as if he owned the world! His name was Jose Menendez, he was at SIU on an athletic scholarship, and the fact that she was older than he was made absolutely no difference at all to him. Jose told her, when they began to date, that he had big plans for the business world. Anything he wanted, he could get. And Jose wanted Kitty.

She had never known what it meant to be pursued by a man until she found Jose. The handsome Cuban and the beauty queen became inseparable and she was quickly smitten by her exotic lover. She had previously thought of Cubans as television's Ricky Ricardo

types or scraggly bearded revolutionaries who followed Castro. But Jose, well, he was different, and
that was something she liked in a man, for she was not
afraid to be different herself. Soon, Kitty began showing up late for class and falling asleep at the radio
control board.

To the amazement of her chums, the days when
Kitty would slink into a tight black dress and don a
snow white wig over her dark hair to hit the town for
an evening of fast-track entertainment were fading.
After Oak Lawn, Kitty had learned to party hard,
whereas Jose was considered by classmates to be
somewhat dull, a square. No sooner had she started to
carve her own glamorous niche in life than she fell into
a world she had not known existed, so she hid her
wilder side to meet Jose's picture of the ideal American girl.

When they strolled on the campus at Carbondale,
heads would turn. Friends whisepered caution, but
Kitty only smiled, plunged ahead, doing exactly as she
pleased. And his attention in the relationship, conducted with the same dynamic drive he showed in
everything he did, was simply overpowering. "All of a
sudden, she was hit by a bulldozer," a roommate of
Kitty's would recall.

"But he's Cuban!" her astounded girlfriends whispered. "But he's just a boy! He's three years younger
than you!" Such things made absolutely no difference
to the independent Kitty, and it soon became clear
that she and Jose would spend their lives together. As
the product of a broken home, Kitty was determined
to make her own marriage a stable and precious thing,
something that Jose promised that he was equally
ready to do.

When she graduated in the summer of 1963, the *Oak
Lawn Independent* noted that "the daughter of Mrs.
Mae Andersen and winner of the Miss Oak Lawn

contest received her Bachelor of Science Degree in Communications,'' and reported that she was heading for New York to get her advanced degree. What the newspaper did not report was that her Cuban boyfriend was abandoning his own scholarship to go with her.

The relationship was getting serious, not without a bit of a fuss from both families, a case of vexation and racism at both ends. The midwestern Andersens were astonished that, of all the men Kitty could have, she wanted a dark-skinned Cuban teenager to be her husband. The Menendez family thought the girl from a divorced family was beneath their normally elite social stratum, and felt that Jose, only nineteen years old, was simply much too young to wed anyway.

He vehemently disagreed. Writing home to answer a letter of protest from his father, Jose expressed his views in the no-nonsense kind of opinion that would become his trademark. "If I was old enough to be on my own at 16, I'm old enough to be married at 19," he declared.

Without further consultation with either family, they eloped and were secretly married in 1963.

Years later, Kitty would return to Oak Lawn regularly to attend high school reunions. Her new station in life was obvious, making her classmates wonder how shy, withdrawn Mary Louise had gotten so lucky. The general theme after Kitty would depart was "Wow, what did she fall into?" said Karra Kestian, an old friend. She had been a nobody in high school, a regular mouse, and now she was out there playing tennis with Kenny Rogers and attending the Grammy Awards!

The young couple, armed with only their marriage license, Kitty's college degree, and Jose's dreams, left Illinois for the bright lights of New York, where she got a job as a schoolteacher. Jose scrubbed dishes at the swank 21 Club for extra money and transferred his academic studies to Queens College, City University of New York, in Flushing. Even this early in their relationship, the dynamic Kitty's dreams of being an actress or working in broadcasting began to fade. She shelved her plan to obtain a master's degree, and Jose made it clear that she was to support his career. They would reach the stars together faster that way, he said.

They both wanted kids, but agreed that children would have to wait until they could escape the not-so-genteel poverty in which they were living, while Jose studied to become an accountant, just like his success-ful father. They were so poor that once when Jose was faced with a three-dollar school charge, he had to persuade his instructor to wait until the next payday.

His thirst for excellence never dimmed during those hard years, however, and a teacher would later recall that Jose would approach after class and bombard him with questions on how he could get a better grade. Teachers found him to be an excellent student in an age when young people were getting turned on by marijuana, protests, and a new singing group called the Beatles. Kitty and Jose may have listened to *I Wanna Hold Your Hand,* but they simply had no time to become hippies. The British mop-tops may have changed the hair fashion for kids, but Jose Menendez knew he was headed for a Brooks Brothers world, and the vivacious Kitty looked forward to the country club set. They would continually bolster each other's cour-age during those early years, knowing that hard work now would pay off later. Certainly, being an account-ant was not a glamorous sort of career, but if he played his game correctly, Jose felt he could make financial magic from those credits and debits.

He was right, of course, because he was always right. Straight out of college in 1967 with the treasured

CPA degree in his pocket, the talented Cuban refugee was recruited and hired by one of New York's top accounting firms, Coopers & Lybrand. At the time, he and Kitty lived in the village of Monsey, in Rockland County, just north of New York. Jose, the poor student who had shared dinners of peanut butter and ham sandwiches with his wife, had become Mr. Menendez, a hotshot young accountant with a good job, and each business day he would join the throngs of commuters taking the train to New York.

A short time after taking the job, he was dispatched to Chicago to run an audit for Lyon's Container Service, a shipping concern, where he politely peppered company officers with suggestions and ideas on how to improve their balance sheet.

The corporate officers liked what they saw in the young number cruncher visiting from New York. He was well dressed, knowledgeable, polite, charming, extremely smart, and spending extraordinary amounts of time on the audit. Clearly, this young fellow had leadership potential.

So the client made him an offer he could not financially refuse, and at the tender age of twenty-three, Jose Menendez became the comptroller of Lyon's Container, a position that would be only one of many corporate stepping-stones. Three years later, only ten years after having left Cuba to sleep in an attic and scrub dishes for the smarmy crowd in Manhattan, Jose was named president, earning a salary of seventy-five thousand dollars a year.

A look backward could indicate that perhaps he was *too* successful in Chicago, and as the age of mergers and takeovers began to gather steam in the United States, a larger company swooped in and purchased Lyon's right out from under the feet of its youthful president. The new owners wanted to put their own man at the controls, and Jose Menendez suddenly didn't have a job.

He was not concerned, because he had a belief of almost religious intensity in himself and his ability, partially because of a small book that was published in 1968. It was only 108 pages in length, but it was a kick to the head for thousands of hard-charging executives who read it because it reinforced the basic message that they were doing things right. Written by Og Mandino, *The Greatest Salesman in the World* became a bible to the success-oriented, particularly someone like Jose, who was only beginning his professional career and could find in Mandino's precepts the signs he needed to follow to achieve the American dream.

Menendez became so taken with the small volume that he memorized huge chunks of it and would recite them aloud. And although the book was little more than blue-sky philosophy of the self-help genre that would swamp bookstores in the coming years, Menendez took it to heart and eventually would force his sons to learn its passages. They, too, would be able to recite Og Mandino and put his precepts to work in their own lives.

The Greatest Salesman in the World tells the supposedly two-thousand-year-old legend of a fictional camel herder named Hafid, who went off to sell a robe, but could not, and instead used it as a blanket for the baby Jesus. As a reward, he received a kiss on the cheek from the Virgin Mary and was guided back to his encampment by a bright star in the heavens. His master was so impressed that he gave Hafid a set of ten leather scrolls, each of which held a secret that, when combined and followed, would turn the camel boy into a multimillionaire supersalesman.

The biblical-style analogy and the allusion to the

Ten Commandments immediately appealed to Jose, and he followed the book's instructions to read each "scroll" three times a day for thirty days. The messages were powerful and positive, just the thing for an up-and-coming young businessman whose primary possession at that point in his career was his willingness to outwork everyone around him. Persistence and tenacity became his lodestar, and he would guide his future by Mandino's words:

> I was not delivered unto this world in defeat, nor does failure course in my veins. I am not a sheep waiting to be prodded by my shepherd. I am a lion, and I refuse to talk, to walk, to sleep with the sheep. I will hear not those who weep and complain, for their disease is contagious. Let them join the sheep. The slaughterhouse of failure is not my destiny. I will persist until I succeed.

Because he had such confidence, along with contacts and a reputation as a successful executive, Jose was not out of work for long after the takeover at Lyon's. In 1972, another company that he had done some auditing work for while at Coopers & Lybrand had an opening for just such a bright young man, and Menendez went into the rental car business, as an employee of Hertz. Actually, he was more than an employee. Jose Menendez was not out at the rental counter filling out forms and worrying about getting a customer into a Chevrolet. He signed on as an executive in the car-leasing division, but within a year, with his usual combination of flash, concentration, a swift financial mind, and long hours at the desk, he made a huge career leap to become Hertz's chief financial officer, an executive vice-president at age thirty-five, and then the company's general manager.

After Jose's death, his former boss, Bob Stone, told *People* magazine that "I never knew anyone who worked harder, or worked toward more goals. If I had stayed at Hertz, he would have become president of the company."

But at that level of play, careers go in different directions. Hertz's corporate parent was the gigantic RCA Corporation, which was always on the lookout for new leaders. It was decided that Jose Menendez had potential, but needed to work off some of the rough edges and learn how to move in the realms where real money could be made.

In 1980, the company made a shrewd gamble, under the assumption that a successful executive can run anything. The company that had as its most famous logo a curious dog staring into the flared horn of an old gramophone decided to try Menendez in its record division, RCA/Ariola. This was akin to throwing Brer Rabbit into the briar patch, because Menendez, always ready to feed his ego, immediately felt at home in the glamorous world of entertainment and show business. The fact that his salary jumped to five hundred thousand dollars a year did not diminish the attractiveness of the new position.

Cuban by birth and strongly attracted to the musical sounds coming from south of the border, Menendez began to travel, and travel, and travel some more. Mexico, the countries of Central America and Puerto Rico were frequently on his passport, and he almost wore a groove into the air between New York and Miami. South Florida was where a new sound was being made, and Menendez knew that it had crossover potential, and that soulful, toe-tapping Latin music did not have to be confined to mariachi wedding songs.

He signed mainstream stars, of course, such as teen heartthrob Rick Springfield, but was never reluctant to renegotiate a contract with musicians that would tilt favorably toward the company. He shopped abroad for talent, too, landing Duran Duran, Princess Di's favorite rock group, and the Eurhythmics out of Great Britain to an RCA contract. But his real stars were down south, and as Jose convinced the company to open an office in Miami, he successfully brought in such stars as Jose Feliciano, Menudo, and Emanuel. Jose's passion for Latin music paid off in big bucks for his new company.

It was not all gloss and stars, however, for detractors claimed that, while he might be good at selling new talent on the company, Menendez lacked the cautious, insightful kind of managerial skills that were needed to keep corporate RCA happy. He was seen by some to be a cowboy, always off on an adventure but not particularly careful with the details.

Several were critical of the way the always aggressive Menendez would ship out a huge number of new recordings, which made the up-front sales, paper profits, and the supersalesman look terrific. But long months later, the cascade of returned merchandise would negatively impact the balance sheet, wiping out millions of dollars. The RCA corporate bosses felt that a sharp, trained accountant should not be making such errors.

He also caught criticism for pushing his employees too hard, expecting them to possess the same demonic drive for excellence that he had. Most people did not, which kept Jose in a frenzy. He was trying to be a superstar every waking minute of the day, but was having to pick up the imagined slack where he thought his people were failing him. The way he treated people, not his success at signing recording artists, would stamp his fate at RCA.

Again, there was a corporate buyout, and giant RCA was gobbled up by a bigger giant, General Electric, in 1986. There was a new president, one who didn't like

the way the abrasive Menendez dealt with people or
the fast-and-loose way Jose handled the music business.

Jose had expected that the GE takeover would bring
him even more money, power, and prestige. He expected the success he had brought to the record division would earn him, once again, the posh position of
executive vice-president, this time of RCA itself. He
misjudged the opposition badly, for he had stepped on
too many toes, and it was payback time. During a
tense confrontation behind closed doors, Menendez
was officially stripped of his rank and told he could
stick around and run a smaller part of the company.

Or, he could leave, which is what he did.

4

The Boys

The oversized tennis racket swung in a downward arc and, just past its zenith, caught the rising furry ball smack in the heart of the taut strings. With a muffled, thump, accompanied by a grunt of effort, the ball sailed toward the net, hit the tape across the top edge and fell to the court floor, bounced twice, and died like a bird.

Lyle Menendez bit his tongue in anger, wincing, not so much at his poor serve as in anticipation of the criticism sure to come from the man standing nearby. As he expected, his father lit into him as if Lyle had made some world-bending error that had brought shame onto the family. Jose Menendez would not tolerate failure, and being unable to hit a decent tennis serve, to not even get the damned ball across the *net*, for God's sake, was about as miserable a failure as could be envisioned. The boy, his white shirt and shorts soaked with perspiration, stood there and fiddled with the racket as his father barked about having to try your hardest, all the time, and never quit, never stop wanting to be the best, to be able to beat everyone else. Lyle glanced at the court, which was littered with tennis balls on both sides of the net, and thought about how tired he was. He had been smacking practice

serves for almost an hour, his arm felt as if it were
about to fall off, and his dad was acting as if some
cardinal sin had been committed. Jose Menendez finally stopped talking, tossed another ball to Lyle, and
watched with pride as the boy flipped it into the air,
went to a forward-leaning tiptoe, and smashed a serve
into the opponent's court. Not bad, Jose thought to
himself with a surge of pride, not bad at all, for Lyle
was only twelve years old.

The tidy world of Jose and Kitty Menendez had
changed dramatically by 1968, five years after they
were married, with the birth of Lyle. And when Erik
came along three years later, in 1971, they suddenly
had a family, a complete unit. Kitty, who grew up with
an absentee father, and Jose, who had been separated
from his family as a teenager, were determined that
their own children would enjoy a special world of
privilege, insulated by a tight-knit family. To comple-
ment the proud surname of Menendez, Jose gave them
completely Americanized, suburban first and middle
names, almost Nordic in their whiteness. Joseph Lyle.
Erik Galen.

With Jose's burgeoning salary and position at Hertz
and RCA, the family jumped up several rungs in the
social ladder, moving to a two-story Tudor-style house
at 69 West Shore Drive in the township of Hopewell,
in the rolling countryside adjacent to Princeton, New
Jersey, an hour from Manhattan by commuter train. It
was an important choice for Jose because of the
historic significance of the area. The Continental Con-
gress had met in Princeton in 1783, George Washington had crossed the Delaware River and fought a
pivotal battle of the American Revolution there, and
U.S. presidents James Madison, Woodrow Wilson,
and Grover Cleveland had called it home. Jose har-
bored a secret desire to someday enter politics himself
and was inspired by the Gothic elegance of Princeton

University, only a few miles from his front door. Someday, he swore, my boys will be students there.

Their new home sat next to a man-made body of water called Honey Lake. Surrounded by trees, the house was yellow, with brown trim. Significantly, their back lawn was taken up by a tennis court. It wasn't much more than a tract home, not as well maintained as its neighbors, but the tranquil location in Mercer County, with sixty square miles of forest and farmland, made it an attractive address. Another reason for moving to New Jersey was that Menendez family members were nearby. Jose's sister Terry and her husband, Carlos Baralt, were living in the nearby township of West Windsor, and his mother, Maria, was in Belleville, about forty-five miles to the north.

This would be home for Jose, Kitty, and the boys for most of the sixteen years they would spend in the Princeton area. They would move to a much larger home and a much more prestigious address inside Princeton proper less than a year before the family had to make another major move—to California.

If kids needed space to grow, then they should grow well in the lush roominess around Hopewell.

As babies, the boys were perfect specimens, both mentally and physically, as if Jose and Kitty had ordered them from a menu. The proud father was certain that, with his guidance, they would never have to wash dishes to survive. The world would be at their doorstep and all they had to do was scoop up the best things life had to offer. And to work hard. Nothing would stop the Menendez boys! Jose decided that he would be the best father ever and imbue his children with his own innate drive for excellence. How well he succeeded was measured by Erik's comment following the murders that, "We are prototypes of my father. He wanted us to be exactly like him."

* * *

The brothers had few playmates because Jose did not want his kids to associate with children who might not possess the same inner steel and drive for success. He would ply them early and often with the sayings of Hafid the camel boy, particularly the rule about not hanging around mediocre people. His own motto was, "If you're weak, you lose."

Spared nothing financially, and with no chores to do around the house, the boys were free to concentrate on the one truly fun thing in their lives—sports. But even while swimming in the pool, kicking around a soccer ball, or out on the tennis court, they could not stray from their father's blueprint for their lives. He would watch from a picture window in the living room as his sons played outside, and he steered them into competitive activities. Even splashing in a swimming pool became a job, a task, a goal, so eventually, even sports ceased to be much fun.

Inside the house, at night, Jose the executive, perhaps fresh from a boardroom meeting, would sternly preside over dinner, peppering the youngsters with questions, a grilling that grew tougher as they grew older. Miss a question and he would brusquely order them from the table to a dictionary or an encyclopedia to find the answer before returning to their food. Jose had a thirst for knowledge, and, damn it all, so would his sons! The one thing they learned early was that Daddy insisted on perfection. Nothing was easy, and second best just would not do.

But Jose was wise enough to know his boys could not do everything perfectly, so when Lyle was twelve and Erik nine, he had a long talk with them. Choices, he said, had to be made. Sacrifices. They could pick their sport, and he would furnish them with the best professional coaches and materials needed for them to become stars. He didn't want just success, he wanted national championships!

To his delight, and with not-so-gentle suggestions, the boys both picked tennis as their game, leaving soccer behind. It was an important point, because on a soccer *team,* one person is part of a unit and strives for the success of all, helping teammates to excel so all may win. Working in a collaborative effort was not Jose's style. Tennis, now, was a one-person game. You did it or you didn't. You owned your mistakes, you owned your victories, and you slaughtered your opponents, *mano a mano.* Jose thrived on this kind of competition when he was a swimmer, just as his mother had achieved great success of her own in the pool.

The boys could still swim at the Bedens Brook Country Club, but tennis would be their pathway to stardom. While Daddy was out killing the business world, Lyle and Erik would be expected to do the same on the tennis courts.

That did not mean, he clearly told them, that work could be neglected at Princeton Day School, a private, preppy academy located in the hilly countryside along The Great Road. No public school education for Jose's boys.

A wide driveway leads through an expanse of perfectly green lawns to the beautiful PDS campus, laced with trees sixty feet in height. The approximately eight hundred students are tended by almost one hundred teachers, and the average class size is only thirteen students. Almost all students go on to college, and Jose considered the education that his boys would receive there to be well worth the stiff tuition of about ten thousand dollars per boy, per year.

Such a school, followed by a solid Ivy League university, would give Lyle and Erik an edge in the outside world, and Jose always sought an edge. He told them that if you wanted to succeed hard enough, you could do it all, which meant Lyle and Erik had to

hit the books as hard as they slapped tennis balls. "It
was difficult because you had to be a great tennis
player and be great in school," Erik remembered.

Jose also had a hidden agenda. He knew that tennis
was a sport for the upper class and that success on the
courts would open many a future door for his boys.
He allowed himself to dream of Wimbledon, the international tennis circuit, and the Menendez brothers
holding silver cups aloft in victory. Quick to take
offense at any slight that hinted of racism, Jose believed that tennis was going to be the great equalizer
for his sons. While some friends might Anglicize his
name to "Joe," he waved his heritage like a flag. He
was Jose! But never would the boys be looked down
upon as less than white bread kids with all the advan-
tages of WASPs.

So tennis practice would start at 6:30 A.M., when
Jose would haul them out to the court and smack balls
toward the sleepy kids. Rain was no excuse for not
practicing. Weekends and holidays, even Christmas,
were not an excuse to put down the rackets. Let the
others, the mediocre, the losers, the sheep, take the
time off. A champion would not pass up the opportunity to practice. For uncounted hours of their boy-
hoods, Lyle and Erik batted balls back and forth
across the net, thinking that they were doing something important, something like making their father
proud of them.

A coach once asked the teenaged Lyle why he
played only with adults instead of with some rather
good players who were his own age. The boy said that
if he practiced with such kids, they might grow used
to him and he could not properly intimidate them
during a match.

And it paid off, just as their father predicted.

At Princeton Day School, where tennis was equivalent in popularity to football at a public high school, Lyle Menendez was the school's top-ranked tennis player and was given the adulation due a star quarterback.

During his middle school years at Princeton Day, before that fateful choice that forced him to equate tennis with life and self-worth, Lyle was a quiet, but not an unpleasant, boy. Wearing a black leather jacket and speaking with his jaw clamped tight, he would try to make other kids believe he was a tough guy just in from the ghetto, a street-smart punk with a lot of dough. He was always ready to loan a fellow student a few bucks, and earned the sobriquet of "Lyle the Loan Shark." He was trying to conquer a nervous stutter, for which his father mocked him, wanting perfect speech, like everything else. Therefore, Lyle would speak while keeping his mouth in a tight line, fighting for control of every word. For a bake sale in the eighth grade, Lyle became an overnight school legend by dishing out his homemade chocolate-covered dog biscuits to admiring adults. On a more serious food note, it was about that time he fell in love with the taste of chicken wings that were produced at a little hole-in-the-wall café a block from Princeton University. One day, years in the future, he would buy the place.

Tennis changed young Lyle. He started to play and started to win, bringing home first-place trophies for the family to admire. Kitty went to every match, and if he could not attend, Jose insisted on a blow-by-blow description of the game by telephone. Once, calling from an airplane, Jose hung up, only to be chastised by a seatmate for being too hard on the boy. But the Menendezes weren't interested in second-place hardware, so only the cups denoting a championship were displayed on the family's trophy shelf. Eventually there would be more than sixty such trophies amassed to glitter uselessly, tiny memorials to meaningless achievements.

Off-court, Lyle became straitlaced and rather boring. But put a tennis racket in his hand, and the boy became obsessed. He was *on* the school's team, actually its anchor, but he could have cared less about the squad. He knew why he was there, and it wasn't to please some stupid school coach! It was to please Jose, who had a higher standard. Winning the French Open someday might be enough, but Lyle knew better than to drop a match in prep play.

He would viciously berate his opponents, who were astonished that the otherwise mild-mannered Lyle Menendez was even more critical of himself than he was of them. A ball into the net was cause for a string of curses, and a single misplayed shot might cause him to erupt in a terrible temper and smash a tennis ball as hard as he could, sailing it over the fence and into the parking lot, or break a racket in his fit of fury. It was better, many tennis players decided, just to leave Lyle alone. Even Jose noticed the fiery explosions and hired a coach to work with Lyle on court etiquette, hoping to tame his actions before he became a screamer like John McEnroe.

That kind of outburst was only for the courts. At home, he obeyed his father without question. Act like a kid, run through the house, and Lyle might be grabbed by his father, taken into a back room, and punched in the stomach. Such lessons were learned quickly. Screwing around with some linesman was one thing. Crossing Dad was something else.

Lyle joined no other school organizations; he didn't hang out with the guys; he didn't do drugs or get drunk. Schoolwork was secondary to tennis, and it was not unusual for Kitty or Jose to do a homework assignment for him to submit to his Princeton Day School instructors. Spanish teacher Alice Hercz received beautifully composed homework assignments, but then Lyle would flunk basic Spanish grammar tests in class. It was obvious who was writing the assignments. Erik was caught cheating in Janet Stolzfus's religion class and broke down in tears when he was scolded. But the teachers were afraid to confront the powerful pair of Jose and Kitty Menendez, known to the faculty as the "parents from hell."

In his final years at PDS, Lyle's image completely changed. There simply was no room, no time for hardly anything other than tennis. Gone was the pleasant dude who cooked up the chocolate doggie treats. In his place was a swaggering, surly young man who made sure his fellow students knew he was rolling in money, driving the hot red Alfa Romeo convertible that his parents gave him in his senior year. Instead of jeans and casual shirts, he dressed in designer outfits and, with his dark good looks and intensity, *knew* that he was one overpowering son-of-a-bitch.

He constantly collected tickets for speeding, and his license was suspended so frequently that neighbors became used to the sight of a limo pulling up to the Menendez house to take Lyle to a tournament because he had been grounded again. Finally, the cops took away his license altogether and when he was again nailed for speeding, his mother hired a lawyer to handle the case rather than let her scofflaw son take the heat. The lawyer convinced the court that overhead power lines had interfered with the police radar gun. The lesson was not that Lyle should quit speeding, but that money could take care of a problem.

Jose Menendez could finally relax a bit at night, knowing that his elder son was becoming just as big a turd as he was. What he didn't know was that the cocky, self-assured tennis bum, when the lights were out, in the privacy of his own bedroom, surrounded himself with stuffed animals and went to sleep in a cuddly, furry nest of bunny rabbits and teddy bears that demanded absolutely nothing from him.

He played tennis with menace in his heart, not joy, attacking the game as if it were a blood sport, ranging all over the court with his killer shots. Success did not come cheap, but it did come. The Middle States Tennis Association listed Lyle as the top player in its eighteen-and-under division, and by the time he graduated from high school, he was nationally ranked as thirty-sixth among all junior players. Lest he ease up, his father reminded him that being ranked thirty-sixth was not the same as being ranked number one.

But there was one other thing worthwile in the life of Lyle Menendez. He had a girlfriend, and around her he softened like warm dough. The senior yearbook named the tennis star and Stacy Feldman as the "most married" couple at Princeton Day. Around Stacy, Lyle found a comfort zone, a place where Jose could not reach him. According to friends, he was totally devoted to her.

So when Stacy finally realized that the teenage romance that had spanned several years was not working out to her satisfaction, and told Lyle that it was over, he was devastated. He loved her so much he had even given her one of his special teddy bears! Only he knew how much that stuffed animal meant. To try to get her back, Lyle decided on a more conventional approach, and offered her a fur coat. When Stacy still said no, he launched an avalanche of flowers in her direction. Eventually he got the message, however, and his puppy love relationship sank before his eyes.

Naturally, his 1986 senior yearbook at PDS carried a photograph of Lyle playing tennis. He chose a couple of inspirational, take-no-prisoners Og Mandino quotes to be his yearbook legacy, and student editors, giving all seniors a bit of a roasting, filled in mock answers to some questions, stating that no one could imagine Lyle Menendez "doing manual labor," that the thing that most intrigued him was "money," that he could be found "in trouble," and his bête noire was "speeding tickets."

Meanwhile, Kitty Menendez thrived in New Jersey. She did volunteer work with the Princeton Community Tennis Association and almost every day would drive her Mercedes up Rolling Hills Drive, through the dogwood and forsythia, for a few hours at the Bedens Brook Country Club. While the boys played on the clay tennis courts or swam in the pool, Kitty would play bridge, Monopoly, or paddle tennis inside. Occasionally, her partners would discover her cheating. Kitty would deny doing anything improper, of course, then turn around and do it again.

She was considered quick and efficient in her work, but quick to take offense if someone other than she was assigned to drive a big-name tennis pro around town. A typical tournament might see one of the boys charging around the court, yelling insults at an opponent, while Jose telegraphed silent signals like some wild third-base coach in baseball and Kitty braced an official about a controversial call. "The whole family was obsessively competitive," said one family friend of the win-at-all-costs attitude that was the Menendez trademark.

Another friend remembers Kitty as a monotoned talker who constantly jabbered about how much she owned, how well her husband was doing, about her sons' athletic victories and famous celebrities they knew. Oddly, that was only around the Princeton crowd. When she returned to high school reunions at Oak Lawn, she tried to blend with her former friends, never bragging about her money or position. Perhaps she no longer saw any of that group as competition.

* * *

In 1985, as Jose was pulling in big bucks at RCA and his future looked unlimited, he moved the family to 57 Mountain Avenue in Princeton Township, an estate of six acres surrounded by tall trees and overlooking the Mountain Lakes Nature Preserve.

There was nothing small about the new home, which was almost a parody of wealth, chosen to advertise that the kid from Cuba had finally made it, Jose Menendez had *ARRIVED!* A half-mile asphalt drive-way, bordered by towering trees and lush shrubs, led to the isolated two-story colonial house. From the sweeping back lawn they could hear the sound of water falling over rocks, spilling from one lake to another. There was a swimming pool, and a tennis court was immediately added. Except for the small boathouse, once a caretaker's cottage, there were no other houses in sight. Thick woods stood around them like leafy castle walls, and they were only a mile from PDS, five miles from the country club, and a short drive to Princeton Junction, where Jose could join the hundreds of other area residents on the hour-long train ride into Manhattan's Penn Station.

This was a very important move for Jose, for it was Princeton proper, the home of wealth, privilege, and old-line distinction. He wanted a slice of that respectability, and he wanted his boys to carve even bigger slices. For that, he had mapped out his educational plans for them. Frequently, he drove his Jaguar past the centerpiece of the town, Princeton University, with its old-world charm and Gothic spires beside Carnegie Lake. He felt warm and fuzzy inside thinking about Lyle and Erik putting on their blue blazers and strutting around that gorgeous campus. He just loved the idea of them having résumés that might include the American Whig-Cliosophic Society, the oldest college political and debating society in the nation, founded by James Madison and Aaron Burr.

It irritated Jose that he'd had to settle for that chintzy little college in queens, so his sons would redeem him. They would by Ivy. The Menendez boys would make their mark at Princeton, even if the family had to cheat now and then to make it possible. He knew that a place like Princeton didn't want losers.

Erik grew up in a world of giants. It seemed as if he were a puny twig surrounded by mighty redwoods. His father was God, and his brother had left big shoes for a pair of tiny feet to fill. His mom might not have been a redwood, but she at least was a sturdy oak that could weather the blows of adversity. As the smallest fish in the Menendez gene pool, it was natural that Erik turned inward.

In one important way, Erik received direct benefits from having Lyle as his older brother. No one messed with him at Princeton Day School. The brothers bore the only Hispanic names among the several hundred students at PDS, but he would endure no taunts of a racist nature, for to mess with Erik meant you were also fucking with Lyle's little bro, and that was not a very wise thing to do.

The boys, who alone knew the regimen under which they had to live, stuck together when away from home. Their mother, on many days, would drop them off at the country club at 10:00 A.M. and not pick them up again until the club closed at 7:00 P.M., when the boys would be sitting on the gray slate steps of the little clubhouse. Members complained that she used the elite club as a day-care center.

Neither boy really fit in with the happier cliques at PDS, where they were considered to be somewhat mysterious loners, who giggled at their own private jokes. Since losers were to be excluded from their world, the only true winners they knew were each other, and they had no close friends.

And while Lyle had acted as a sort of bulldozer, clearing a path for Erik in school, he also built up the confidence of the quiet, moody boy, calling him by a private, comic book–style nickname. Erik became "the E-Man" and a boy's imagination could impart all sorts of powers to such a fictitious character.

Watching Lyle soar into the tennis rankings spurred Erik on to do the same. He, too, went through private coaches as if they were potato chips. Coaches were fired by Jose at a whim if he thought the boys were not advancing quickly enough in their mastery of the game. He also drove the boys to distraction not only during practice sessions, but during tournaments, too. Jose, ignoring the rule that a player cannot be assisted during play, would flash hand signals, a private code, to his sons on the court.

Erik's one consistent coach, the one he trusted the most, was his brother, Lyle. Ironically, Erik was proving to be the better athlete, for where Lyle had a chunky, solid build, Erik was growing into a beanpole with long arms and legs. Where Lyle had to run, Erik could easily lope. Even though he was three years younger, he learned to hold his own with his brother, the star of the PDS team. When he was eighteen, he was ranked as the number seven eighteen-and-under player in Southern California, and fourty-fourth in the nation.

He was also good in the water. Not of the championship caliber of his grandmother, or the collegiate competitive level of his dad, but Erik's lanky build allowed him some aquatic talent. That was a mixed blessing. While he developed into the country club's best breast stroker in his age group, people recall Jose marching alongside the pool during races, yelling at Erik. When the race was over, the boy would be pulled dripping wet from the water by Jose, who would shake him hard and criticize him loudly. Competitors were receiving congratulations, but the E-Man was having the riot act read to him by his father. Only then would he be eligible for a hug. Having his spirit crushed on a regular basis dimmed his interest in swimming, and although he continued to compete, he never poured his heart into it. Having to excel in tennis was hard enough.

He had been bred for success, toughened from the cradle to achieve more than anyone could reasonably expect. When he was only eighteen months old, his father would make him hang by his skinny arms from a pole far above the ground. If he screamed in agony, Jose would only call him a sissy. Jose didn't want wimps for sons. When he discovered young Erik was afraid of cemeteries, he would drop him off in one and leave him standing there, terrified, among the tombstones. "Everyone can compete. Only one can win," his father would pound into him. You had to be tough.

His schoolwork, like Lyle's, was somewhat lackluster, probably because Mom and Dad did much of the homework. He rarely smiled, but within himself, the sad and withdrawn boy developed the soul of a poet. In later years he would begin to write things, making up poems, stories, and even a screenplay.

On the tennis court, he endured the same tough regimen that his brother had—the endless practices, the demands for perfection by his father, the expectations to succeed at all costs. Luckily, Jose had already decided that Lyle would become the leader of the family in future years, so Lyle had to carry the brunt of the horrible load. Erik learned that the best way to survive was to keep his eyes and ears open and be as quiet as possible. Psychologists would say such behavior indicated that he was only stuffing his true feelings deep inside, internalizing them, and making himself

not so much into a championship tennis player—which
he would become—as a ticking time bomb.

When Erik Menendez was alone, and looked into a
mirror, he saw a boy with zero self-confidence, and
knew from long experience that nothing he did would
ever be good enough for his father.

One of the many tennis coaches that labored with
the boys in New Jersey would later recall that the
family seemed as if they had stepped from a photograph. Jose was handsome, fit, and, although very
stern, always ready to temper his criticism of the boys
with a hug or a kiss. Kitty was sweet and caring,
ferrying her sons to their assigned tennis matches.
Lyle and Erik were strong and athletic, determined to
play a hell of a game of tennis, and never got into
trouble.

The coach had no idea who these people really
were.

5

Moving On

The year 1986 would be a turning point for the Menendez family, a dramatic shift in personal plate tectonics that would put them all on a course that would lead to an inevitable collision.

The first priority was for Jose to find another job after being dumped rather unceremoniously from his lofty position at RCA/Ariola in August of 1986. At his career level, he could not take just any position, for he had a gilt-edged life-style to maintain and his pride and ambition certainly would not allow him to step backward professionally. From scrubbing pots and pans at "21," he had risen to frequently dining in the ritzy restaurant. He knew the difference between rich and poor was that rich was better.

By now, his reputation as a hard worker and a man who could pull money in for a corporation was well known, and Jose was certainly well plugged in to the entertainment business. His track record was impressive, having started as an accountant, then running a shipping business, from there jumping to the nation's largest vehicle rental agency, and then leapfrogging into the world of show business and music with RCA/Ariola. The possibility that he might have to enter a new field did not phase Jose. In fact, after fourteen years with RCA, he felt ready for a new challenge, and after banking the one million dollars that RCA had coughed up to buy him out, Jose had the luxury of being able to shop around for a new position. It was just a matter of mining those contacts he had made over the years. Surely, somebody out there had room for an aggressive, go-getter, bottom-line kind of guy. This was the 1980s, after all, and people were getting *rich* making deals, and Jose Menendez could make deals with the best of them.

Opportunity soon came knocking, exactly as he knew it would.

America was discovering that their television sets had a new and exciting use. Videotape was a hot market and excecutives with their eyes on the future could easily discern that, in years to come, a nation of couch potatoes would be plugging into their VCRs for everything from exercise videos to motion pictures. Slicing off a part of such an expanding market was not a gamble, but a license to print money.

An innovative California independent movie production company, Carolco, saw just such a business opportunity and jumped at it, acquiring a video-distribution and -duplication firm that was losing money but had a lot of upside potential. Carolco was rolling in cash, having hit the celluloid jackpot with Sylvester Stallone's hugely popular *Rambo* movies, along with some of the action-packed films of Arnold Schwarzenegger. Wanting to expand its markets, Carolco bought a large percentage of International Video Entertainment, known as IVE, with headquarters in plush offices in Woodland Hills, a Los Angeles suburb.

The company held the possibility of becoming a gold mine, but only true believers could see that. It was difficult to look past the approximately twenty million dollars that IVE posted as a loss in 1986. Financial analysts said the company was teetering on the verge of bankruptcy, when Carolco came along and took advantage of the depressed earnings to hammer out a low purchase price. Once that was done, Carolco needed somebody to lead the turnaround project, somebody with a lot of talent, a winning record, optimism, and drive. The new chief would have to be an unusual person, with a thick skin and a big enough ego to survive the Hollywood jungle.

Peter Hoffman, Carolco's president and chief executive officer, found just the man he wanted in a good-looking hustler who had recently lost out in a power play over at RCA. He offered the job to Jose Menendez, who was happy to see the brighter side of a corporate takeover for a change.

Not only sunny California, but the movie business itself! Jose was certain that his destiny was calling. The hard work he had plowed into corporate America was about to pay off. For a man who needed his ego steadily stroked, Hollywood was the best place to be, where his motto of "a deal a day" could be improved to a deal every hour. When Carolco made its offer, Jose jumped at the chance.

He had lived in the East ever since coming to America in 1960, but felt he had no real roots there, nothing to hold him back. True, other members of his family had gravitated to the same area, and family dinners and Saturday cookouts were pleasant, but Jose felt that with air travel what it was, he would never be more than a jet plane away from New Jersey. He was ready to take his Horatio Alger dream one step further, and Go West to prove the Gatlin brothers had been wrong when they sang that "All the gold in California is in a bank in the middle of Beverly Hills, in somebody else's name." With the same confidence and single-minded work ethic he applied to everything else, Jose had no doubt that he could become what is known in Hollywood jargon as a *player*. Some of that California gold would end up in his own bank account.

To test his theory, he told Carolco he would take the job, for a salary and bonus of one million plus per year. Sure, they replied. No prob. Come on out and let's do lunch, baby. Well, he thought, this would be somewhat different. Maybe he should have asked for more. He promised to never again make the mistake of underestimating his own worth.

The major problem, which Jose saw as no problem at all, was moving the family. Kitty Menendez saw it much differently.

While Jose had been jetting around the world, scoring large on the business success scoreboard, she had settled into her upscale New Jersey life-style. Years of seeing him gone for weeks at a time had forced her to reach out for companionship; Kitty had woven a network of close friends and was heartbroken at the idea of having to walk away from her comfortable life in New Jersey.

Their conversations about the new job were not pleasant, but she knew it was a losing battle. In their relationship, she had long ago realized that Jose was king. She knew that he loved her, and she certainly loved him, at times calling him twice an hour while he was at work just to hear his voice and talk over major decisions, like what kind of pizza to order for dinner.

The new house in Princeton was her castle. During the sixteen years they spent in Princeton, Kitty Menendez had become somebody. She did not know what would become of her in Los Angeles. From what she knew of L.A., such a move would be a frightening experience. She lived within a protected circle of people who cared about her. In Los Angeles, she would have to start all over again.

There was more to it, of course, and they both knew it.

Kitty was no longer the perfect little beauty queen whom Jose had plucked out of Middle American suburbia like a trophy. In 1986 she turned forty-five, and the parade of passing years had left its marks. She tried the diets and the exercise but was a victim of what doctors call "the natural aging process." She was still a very attractive woman, but gravity and time had taken a toll.

Life, of course, was awfully unfair, for her husband, a few years younger than herself, seemed to look more distinguished as he aged. She was accumulating a bit of pudge, and struggled with wrinkles and graying hair that she dyed to a light blond. He had that full head of jet black hair, the dark eyes and olive skin that had first attracted her to him, and he had stayed slim through playing tennis with the boys. And he had money, and power, and position. Which, she knew, also meant that he had girlfriends.

Kitty tried to cope with Jose's string of affairs in a number of countries, and rarely confronted him. There were ways she could mask the pain, such as pills and liquor, but it still hurt. The very idea of letting him go to California, to lunch with all of those starlets at Spago or attend parties surrounded by models and actresses, was enough to make her grab her pill bottles and down a few bliss-giving tranquilizers. She knew that Jose considered her his anchor, that he could always come home to her and the kids after his latest fling in Rio or Paris or Miami. She still worried that someday he might seek a divorce, that he might get so turned on by a new woman, someone *younger*, that he would cast Kitty aside. It was one of the penalties for being the older woman married to such a dynamo. In an article in *Playboy* after her murder, Kitty was quoted as telling a friend, "If I wanted to have a marriage at all, if I wanted to save my marriage, I had to make the move and give it all I had."

She was unaware that Jose made no secret during his flings with the young and the beautiful that he would never leave his family to marry them. The mistress might believe she could replace the current spouse, but there was no doubt that Jose would ever trade away his two sons. It was better, the girls knew, to take the money and the fun and, when the glow dimmed, say goodbye and let Jose go home to his family and off to the next girlfriend.

Jose, trying to find a way to make everybody happy with the California deal, proposed that Kitty remain behind in New Jersey. Lyle was graduating from prep school and applying to Princeton University. The two of them could remain on the East Coast while Jose and Erik set up shop in Los Angeles and flew back to Princeton for the weekends.

Dumb idea, Kitty said. Forget it. We will go to California together, as a family.

Oh no we won't, said Lyle, I'm staying here. Erik had two years of high school left and would therefore accompany his parents to the Golden State. Lyle, however, had other plans. He had been turned down by Princeton in his first attempt to get into the Ivy League university for the fall semester of 1986, and he wanted to stay close to await another chance at getting in. When the moving vans pulled away from the mansion at 57 Mountain Avenue, he remained behind to live in the boathouse until the university could come to its senses and let him enroll.

While bumming around on the tennis circuit later that year, he met Jamie Pisarcik, a beautiful, slightly older woman who would become his girlfriend, almost become his wife, and remain steadfastly in his corner during the trying years to come. Unlike Lyle, who was between high school and college, Jamie Pisarcik was already done with the classroom. Now she was trying to establish herself on the women's professional tennis tour. Pisarcik had no idea that when she met the dashing Lyle Menendez, a killer tennis partner five years younger than herself, her life was in for such a dramatic change.

Jose found his family a place to live in the western Los Angeles suburb of Calabasas, just inland from Malibu. At first they stayed in a rented house, because the eight-thousand-square-foot cream-colored palace that he and Kitty had purchased as their permanent home, with its spectacular mountain scenery, wasn't up to her standards and needed to be completely remodeled. Kitty, having left her friends behind, poured thousands of dollars into the project, expanding it by three thousand square feet, as she toiled to make the place, which occupied fourteen prime acres of rolling hillside, into a showplace. Kitty Menendez was a dream come true for California contractors; she spent money like there was no recession on the horizon. She even cajoled her husband into writing the checks needed to nudge the swimming pool over a couple of feet to clear space for an entertainment area.

Fine, said Jose. Erik checked into Calabasas High School, became an average student, but was an immediate star on the tennis team. He happily shed the drudgery of the East for the open, laid-back styles of the West. California, he determined immediately, was his kind of place. Cool dudes, great chicks, plenty of sun, and freeways that were made for hot wheels.

Jose plunged headlong into his new job, in which he actually sat on the Carolco board of directors, alongside Sly Stallone, Rambo himself. He called singers such as Kenny Rogers his friends. There were Hollywood parties galore, and beautiful women, and money to burn. Best of all, the brass left him alone to run his shop the way he saw fit.

"He was by far the brightest, toughest businessman I have ever worked with. He was always ahead of his competition," Ralph King, one of Jose's executives, told the *Wall Street Journal*. An article in *Vanity Fair* quoted a Menendez crony as saying, "He was the perfect corporate executive. . . . He was focused, specific about what he wanted from the business, very much in control. He believed that whatever had to be done should be done—with no heart, if necessary."

As Jose came on board, IVE bought an interest in Lieberman Enterprises out of Minneapolis and changed its name to LIVE Entertainment. The video and the software products would be something for him to tackle down the road, but Jose, with his accountant's nose, knew he had some throat cutting to do at headquarters first if he was to put the money-losing company back on track. Bam. He shut down the plush Woodland Hills offices. Bam. He fired people by the dozen, slashing the payroll from 550 workers to 167. Bam. In a single year of his leadership, LIVE Entertainment went from an almost twenty-million-dollar loss to a solid position in the black, posting earnings of more than two million dollars. The Carolco people were quite pleased.

They were so happy reading the balance sheet that they didn't notice that Menendez was still struggling with some leftover business. When Carolco had started buying into the game—before Jose arrived—IVE was owned by Noel C. Bloom, who was known to law enforcement officials as one of the state's largest distributors of raunchy, X-rated movies. The California attorney general's office also said that Bloom once was linked to organized crime. Bloom claimed Carolco had not lived up to its bargain and owed him a few hundred thousand dollars. Carolco, wanting to move its new video business a large number of notches above the X-rated movie audience, handed the problem, with its murky link to organized crime, over to its new president, Jose Menendez.

6

Calabasas

Calabasas is on the western edge, the Good Side, of
Los Angeles County, less than a mile beyond the city
limits, out where money buys prestige, comfort, style,
and security. Living there, you could be near the city
but not have to endure the plagues that bothered
people about that troubled metropolis—things like
dirt, crime, and danger. Distance and walls and landscaping were the answers, and Calabasas offered all of
that and more. Los Angeles was not secure little
Princeton, New Jersey, and having read all about
drive-by shootings on the freeway, having seen thousands of television shows depicting crime in Los
Angeles, Jose felt that moving his family into the
Calabasas enclave would be money well spent. They
would all be safe there.

Calabasas is not really much of a town, although it
has a couple of small shopping centers and a tiny old
village area anchored by a Farmer's Market, the Sage-
brush Cantina, and a "coffee oasis" called Savannah.
The biggest business in town is the Motion Picture and
Television Hospital and Health Center. Calabasans
make their money elsewhere, then bring it up the
Ventura Freeway, hang a left at the grandly named
Parkway Calabasas, four wide lanes of perfect road

divided by a grassy median. On both sides, for the length of the parkway, access roads point off like spokes to provide access to hillsides filled with pale-walled stucco homes capped by roofs of red Spanish tile. A series of gently rolling hills have been mowed as flat as a marine's haircut and houses stand along their dulled crests.

Lush landscaping of bright ground cover, leafy ficus trees, towering eucalyptus, bashful willows, and splashes of purple bougainvillea is fed by reclaimed water that has turned the native wild brown scrub into a gorgeous garden of color. The difference between Calabasas and hundreds of other such developments around Southern California is the size and design of the homes. A rather ordinary house of thirty-two hundred square feet goes for a half-million dollars, even in a depressed real estate market. Despite the damaged economy, there are few homes for sale in Calabasas and even more are being built, sold out almost before the paint dries on the stucco. Where Parkway Calabasas suddenly comes to a dead end at a cyclone fence, one development company has posted a sign promising that the road will soon stab even deeper into the hilly wilderness to provide a new pack of half-acre "ranch estate homes."

The Menendezes would live in that kind of midlevel splendor while Kitty spent two years overseeing the remodeling of their $950,000, five-bedroom home in the more spacious and desired locale along Mulholland Drive.

Perfectly polished BMWs, Porsche convertibles, Mercedes-Benz and Rolls-Royce motor vehicles, too expensive to be called cars and most of them wearing personalized license plates, ghost along the secluded roads and converge upon the Calabasas Golf and Country Club, an emerald expanse that follows the

valley floor. Signs remind members to maintain deco-
rum by not changing clothes in the parking lot.

Around the country club are the neighborhoods of
expensive homes, protected by fences and gates and
guards and placards warning that RESIDENTS ONLY are
permitted inside. So the breadearners, with their elite
wheels, can play golf on the weekend and, Monday
through Friday, head into L.A. for work.

From Calabasas, out where the Ventura Freeway,
old U.S. 101, knifes between the Santa Monica Moun-
tains and the Simi Hills, the commuter's car pops onto
the Ventura, heading east, sun in the driver's eyes,
and joins the throng of traffic moving at a parking-lot
pace, skirting around Tarzana, Encino, and Van Nuys.
Where the highway bends south, the Calabasas executives can reach Studio City, Hollywood, and Beverly
Hills as well as downtown L.A.

And by living on the west side of the county, they
escape the worst of L.A.'s urban sprawl but are still
close enough to reach the power center of the entertainment industry without much delay, driving through
the morning smog bank that hangs like milky haze just
above the palm trees.

It is not unlike being on an isolated island, far from
Los Angeles. There is a dark twist to places like
Calabasas, however, for it is also a prison of privilege,
where the walls that block out the outside world also
lock the residents inside.

While the movers and shakers like Jose scoot downtown, they leave their wives and kids in the village.
The wives fight boredom by spending money. The kids
hop into their own cars and head for shopping malls
elsewhere. The fathers have plenty of excitement at
the office, but the spouses and offspring have to create
their own. Jose had a precise grasp on his business
world, but he was ignorant of what was festering in his
own backyard.

* * *

Jose had enough to keep him busy in his Van Nuys office, into which he had shifted the LIVE operation. In 1987, he found himself in the midst of a nasty legal fight with Bloom, whom he detested as a moral degenerate for the man's porno background. Skin had nothing to do with the final showdown, however, as Bloom tried to purchase from a toymaker, Hasbro, the rights to make a film based on one of their best-selling dolls. *G.I. Joe: The Movie* never got off the ground, but in Los Angeles Superior Court it took on the importance of a *Gone with the Wind*.

Bloom, in a breach of contract suit, charged that Carolco and Menendez had illegally blocked his access to those rights. Naturally, Jose displayed all the charm of a great white shark when he was called in to testify before a referee trying to decide the case. There was a poisonous odor of hatred in the air by the time the legal wrangling was done. The aloof, arrogant Menendez irritated just about everyone in the courtroom and was totally surprised when, in September 1988, the referee ruled against Carolco, saying he thought that Jose had tried to pull an unethical squeeze play to force Bloom from the picture. The company appealed, and in a settlement that was finally made a short time after Jose and Kitty Menendez were murdered, Carolco was directed to pay Bloom a half-million dollars.

Jose did not spend much time worrying about the problem, for he considered it just temporary, and such bumps had to be anticipated in business. Anyway, he knew that no matter what was happening in his corporate surroundings, things were better on the home front. He was wrong.

Lyle had done several things over the months since high school graduation that had outraged Jose, starting with his failure to be admitted to Princeton. It was the

dream of the Cuban immigrant turned millionaire that
his boys be seen, not only as tennis champions, but as
scholars of the first rank. He would not consider letting
them go to some state-supported university, for only
the prestige of the Ivy League was good enough for
his offspring. Bragging rights were involved, too, and
Jose would in future years proudly boast that Lyle was
at Princeton, which was almost the truth.

Lyle had failed, *failed!*, to get into the school on his
first try, but a year later, in the fall of 1987, he was
accepted and finally was able to walk the campus of
his father's dream. Princeton knew a good deal when
they saw him, too, for although Lyle's high school
grades were not outstanding, he did have a couple of
special things going for him. First, he was a tennis-
playing fiend who would help the university squad.
Second, since the university received federal funding,
it had to meet guidelines on accepting minority students, and Lyle Menendez might also fall neatly into
the Hispanic category. Lyle became a Princeton freshman.

Big deal, thought Lyle. He was there because the
Old Man wanted him there and it was better than
having to work. At least Princeton had a tennis team,
a consolation so minor that he all but ignored it. Jose
was destined to grind his teeth on that, too, for his
hotshot tennis-playing son made the team, all right,
but was only good enough to be the number six player
on a six-man squad! That meant he was *last!* The
thousands of dollars, the hundreds of hours, the private coaches, sweat, the travel, the tournaments, and
the dreams all boiled down to the fact that Lyle simply
was not dominating the university's thirty-seven
courts. He might not be strong enough to carry out
the Menendez destiny.

The disaster was partially cushioned by the fact that
Jose was still able to crow in the boardrooms of Los

Angeles that his oldest boy was at Princeton. His listeners didn't have to know more than that, and until Lyle turned his act around and became the successful young Renaissance man he had been groomed to be, Jose did not plan to tell anyone that the kid seemed to be a bit of a jerk.

Then Lyle dropped the other shoe—or more aptly, a block of concrete—on his father's head. Princeton had this funny thing called an honor system, in place since 1893. "It has been successful because generations of undergraduates have respected it, and by common agreement have given it highest place among their obligations as Princeton students," states the university's catalog. In fact, final admission to the university is contingent upon the new freshman signing a letter promising to obey the honor code. Big deal, thought Lyle, who had been trained carefully since childhood to lie and cheat to get ahead.

In his first semester, Lyle had to do a laboratory paper for Psychology 101, a rather simple entry-level course. The newspaper in Princeton would later write that the instructor realized that Lyle's report looked amazingly similar to a report handed in earlier by another student. He was accused of plagiarism.

Lyle was called before the disciplinary committee for a hearing that lasted four hours, and during which he read a short treatise on ethics that was written by his father specifically for the meeting. The committee was not impressed and handed him the minimum one-year suspension. He had just managed to get into Princeton, a year after graduating from high school, and already he was history.

Jose Menendez dashed across the country to rescue his son and arranged a private conference with the president of the university. He rolled out the charm, the reason, the sales pitch, but this was not Hollywood or some Miami sound studio. This was a part of the

Ivy League that Jose had not expected to encounter. The school had rules against things like cheating, and the administrators refused to make exceptions for violators of the century-old honor code. Lyle was only one of their freshmen. Their students were all bright, and many came from wealthy homes. Jose was told that Princeton had gotten along without Lyle Menendez since it was founded in 1746, and could probably survive without him for still another year. Thank you for coming by to express your concerns, Mr. Menendez, and goodbye.

First the school had shown Lyle the door, and now Princeton had kicked Jose out, too! His failure—the word he hated with so much passion—to bend the university to his will altered his priorities, and instead of blaming his son for cheating, Jose focused his fury upon the university. By this time, Lyle was hardly a factor at all, because the plagiarism had grown into a standoff between Jose and Princeton, and Princeton had won.

At least he was able to salvage something. Before flying back to the West Coast, Jose told Lyle that, while he was out of school for another year, he should continue to live near the university. That way when he got back to California, Jose was still able to say, with a bit of truth, that his son was at Princeton. But Lyle had to find new accommodations, because he could neither stay in the school nor live in the boathouse any longer. In the fall of 1987, the Princeton estate had gone on the market, and such was its beauty that the buyer was not another homeowner, but Princeton Township itself, which wrote Jose a check for $1.5 million.

Lyle eventually came out to California to while away the time until he could restart his nonexistent academic career. He tried working for his father, but his heart obviously was not in it. Spoiled, and the boss's kid to boot, he quickly made enemies among the people who worked for a living at LIVE by showing up late and unapologetic, ignoring orders, barely paying attention, and junking work entirely on sunny afternoons in favor of whacking tennis balls. "Nasty, arrogant, and self-centered," was the way some co-workers described him.

He tried other things to burn up the days, too, but felt that it was all too far beneath him. Really, delivering pizzas in the family Mercedes, the car's lush leather interior becoming aromatic with the smell of pepperoni and onions, was too ridiculous for words. Once, when he picked up a forty-dollar paycheck for some small job, Lyle observed that he could have come up with that much money just by shaking out his dirty clothes. He did not like the real world, for he was destined for greater things, because everybody said so.

Jose wondered what the hell was wrong with Lyle. Suddenly, he started to wish that his rambunctious elder son could be more like his mild-mannered, polite, and well-behaved younger son. He did not realize that Lyle, the jock, and Erik, the poet, were already more alike than he knew. That lesson was just over the horizon and building momentum like a storm.

7

Friends

For Erik, the transfer to Calabasas High School was nothing short of a passage from shy young boy to cocky young man. He was finally out from beneath the deep shadow cast by his big brother, for no one in California had ever even heard of Lyle Menendez. Back in Princeton, Lyle may have been a big frog in a small pond, but out here he would be just another rich kid. Erik no longer had to measure up to his brother, as he had always sought to do back at Princeton Day.

That did not for a moment mean that his father had lowered his expectations for his younger son, but at least Erik was accepted by his peers for who *he* was, and not measured by his brother's accomplishments and shortcomings. As a result, Erik made new friends, chums with whom he could explore the vaunted California life-style. Things were much freer and more interesting in Los Angeles than back in staid New Jersey. Out here, Erik could put on his sunglasses and cruise the wealthy playground of nearby Malibu, or wind through the isolated and quirky Topanga Canyon, or over to the anything-goes life-style of Venice Beach, or just watch a golden sunset over the Pacific Ocean, and return to his luxurious home knowing that tomorrow would offer as many adventures as he had experienced that day. Being good-looking and rich in Los Angeles was not a half-bad way to spend your last years in high school. Just living in Calabasas indicated that his family had money, and being newly rich certainly was not considered gauche in this new neighborhood. Most people had plenty of cash and Jose Menendez was just another millionaire. He wasn't looked down upon for not being able to trace his family tree back to colonial days.

By early 1988, Erik had already made his mark in Calabasas High, also a place where old-family ties meant little because California was made up of transplanted people. Everybody was from somewhere else. With his father traveling so much on business and Lyle back at Princeton, Erik grew closer to his mother while hanging out with new friends. He had his own private telephone answering machine that regularly received calls from admiring girls, who liked the way the lanky Erik Menendez, with his California tan, looked in those tennis shorts.

A particular chum was Craig Cignarelli, the equally handsome and confident captain of the Calabasas High tennis team, on which Erik was the top-seeded star. As well as competing on the court, the two spent many a balmy evening together, without girls, driving through the canyons at night, parking up on one of the hilltops overlooking the Pacific, and spending hours in bullshit sessions. The two felt that they could be honest with each other, something they found very hard with other, ordinary teenagers. Cignarelli's father was an executive at a major studio, just as Jose was a bigwig in the video business. The boys had money, they were sophisticated, had good looks, they played tennis, and they knew how to order waiters around. And they consoled each other that it was not their fault they were smarter than everyone else they knew, particularly other students, who were just *kids*. Craig

called Erik "the Shepherd," and Erik's nickname for
his closest buddy was "the King." Cignarelli would
later say that "People really looked up to us. We had
an aura of superiority." Such were the fantasies of a
couple of rich teenaged boys who had never really
ventured into the outside world.

They were on the courts one day, punishing tennis
balls in a mean practice session, when the friendship
was violently solidified and they got a taste of the
downside of L.A. life. A couple of students from the
rival El Camino High School, not as cushily upscale
as Calabasas, taunted the tennis players and spit at
them. The King and the Shepherd, confident in their
superiority, were not about to let such an insult from
Untermenschen pass unchallenged. This was a mistake, for the El Camino boys had a bunch of friends
cruising by, who happily jumped out of their cars to
help beat the hell out of the rich Calabasas kids. Erik
suffered a broken jaw, Craig had some cracked ribs,
and they now had a friendship that was bonded in
shared blood and pain. Since they had been outnum-
bered on the field of battle, they lost no honor by
being beaten, and their fight only enhanced their popularity at school.

Back up on the scruffy hilltops one night, they
continued their long, rambling discussions about life
in general and themselves in particular. Erik was discovering his passion for writing, and Craig considered
himself to be just as talented in that field as in all
others. The nickel finally dropped for them. This is
Hollywood, right? Our parents are in show biz, right?
Let's write a screenplay! How hard can it be to write
a script that would be better than anything the studios
are turning out these days?

So the Shepherd and the King retired to a Kern
County mountain cabin owned by Cignarelli's family,
for they knew that to be creative, you had to be alone.

Over several such retreats, they produced a couple of screenplays, one of which would later catch police attention. They spent three whole days putting that idea on paper. A mere mortal might take a year or so to do a screenplay, wasting time with research and polishing dialogue and individual scenes; but then, the King the the Shepherd were not mere mortals. Three days seemed to be plenty. Anyway, they were getting bored. When they came down from the mountain, like a couple of smart-alecky young Moseses come to save Hollywood, they had written a sixty-plus-page screenplay that they entitled *Friends*. Their mothers proudly helped them type the story into proper form and told them how good, how original the story was. The studios were not interested; almost everybody in Los Angeles has a screenplay in his purse or pocket, most of them bad, like *Friends*. About the only audience the sophomoric effort ever attracted would be police investigators, who would wonder how the hell Kitty Menendez could have typed up such a damned thing without an alarm bell or two starting to clang.

The sons of two wealthy families had written a story about the son of a wealthy family who one day reads his parents' will and learns that, upon their deaths, he will inherit a cool $157 million. The main character, Hamilton Cromwell, is described in the screenplay as smiling sadistically as he makes that discovery.

The heart of the story bears a remarkable, if not amazing, resemblance to something that would soon happen for real in Beverly Hills.

"A gloved hand is seen gripping the doorknob and turning it gently. The door opens, exposing the luxurious suite of Mr. and Mrs. Cromwell lying in bed. Their faces are of questioning horror as Hamilton closes the door behind gently, saying . . .

" 'Good evening, Mother. Good evening, Father.'

(His voice is of attempted compassion, but the hatred completely overwhelms it). All light is extinguished, and the camera slides down the stairs as screams are heard behind."

Hamilton, naturally, is a pretty smart cookie and had planned The Perfect Crime. He is off to kill other people, too, and does in a girlfriend by strangling her with a rope. The bodies are stored in the basement freezer of his home. Hamilton is eventually undone and faces the punishment of a society that he had looked down upon from his lofty perch of superiority.

At one point in the story, the bloodthirsty star says of his father (and we do not have to hazard much of a guess to figure out who wrote these lines during the few days the young authors spent in that mountain cabin): "Sometimes he would tell me that I was not worthy to be his son. When he did that, it would make me strive harder. . . . Just so I could hear the words, 'I love you, son.' . . . And I never heard those words."

What a wonderful story, Kitty Menendez thought, as she typed her son's creation. What a blueprint, police thought, as they read it months later.

Things were going well for Jose down at the salt mines, too. LIVE Entertainment was turning the corner financially, after his slash-and-burn management technique finally stopped the dollar hemorrhage. The company had actually ended 1987 in the black and for 1988, if projections were accurate, LIVE Entertainment looked as if it would have earnings knocking on twenty million dollars, a fantastic turnaround that was primarily due to the tireless efforts of Jose Menendez.

Carolco knew it had to protect its investment or watch some other company in the glitzy but predatory world of corporate Hollywood snatch away their moneymaking manager at LIVE. What Jose did for them, he could do for others.

So Carolco and LIVE made some financial arrangements to reward Jose and keep him happy and loyal. First, there was a deferred compensation scheme that would allow Jose to stash away a bunch of cash now but not pay taxes on it until it was actually delivered to his bank account. The high salary, the perks, the annual bonuses were all jacked up to keep him happy, and he was given a contract that extended through December 31, 1991.

To protect themselves, however, should some outlandish and unthinkable disaster befall Jose—say his corporate jet ran out of gas someday at thirty thousand feet—they bought what is known in the business world as a "key-man" life insurance policy that would guarantee the company would not be left penniless, like some little widow, should the breadmaker suddenly keel over. The policy, a good measure of what Jose's leadership actually meant to LIVE, was for fifteen million dollars.

As a final gesture, the company sweetened the deal a little bit more by lining up a five-million-dollar personal policy for Jose, with the beneficiary to be named by him. As soon as Jose took a routine physical examination, it was anticipated he would name Kitty as his sole beneficiary, normal under California community property laws, with his two sons to inherit the estate when she passed away. According to a will that Jose had drafted in 1980, when his career was nowhere near the successful level he was currently enjoying, Kitty would receive the entire estate upon his death, with the boys receiving equal shares upon her death.

For Jose, after having to endure the humiliation of Princeton screwing over Lyle for that little cheating incident last fall, the summer of 1988 was shaping up as something more enjoyable. Business was great, Kitty was happy with the new house-remodeling project, and Erik was adjusting nicely to his new school.

Lyle, however, was still causing problems. He had
fallen in love with Jamie Pisarcik, and in the summer
of 1987 they had announced that they were engaged to
be married. Jose was infuriated, saying his son was
only nineteen years old, much too young to take a
wife, particularly a woman who was older than Lyle.
In his fulminations, Jose seemed to lose track of the
fact that he also had rebelled against his own father to
get married when he was nineteen, to a woman older
than himself.

But Jose had won the battle against his son, or so he
thought. Lyle and Jamie did not get married, but Lyle
had asked for money so he could accompany her when
she played the summer European tennis circuit. No,
Jose ordered. Lyle must attend summer school to
prepare for his reentry to Princeton. Right, Dad, said
Lyle, and headed back to New Jersey just long enough
to set up a dodge that would funnel Jose's support
checks into a special bank account that he could draw
on from abroad. Then he took off with Jamie, going
with her on the tennis tour of a dozen cities in Europe
for three months. Jose would not find out about the lie
until much later, and when he did, he was not a happy
camper. He thanked his lucky stars that Erik was
doing better than Lyle.

But Erik was bored and restless, too. Riding the
canyons, scoping out the beaches, hitting the malls
with his father's credit cards, listening to thumping
rock music, playing tennis and hanging out with his
pals, and watching the sun go down beyond the waves
had lost that sheen of early attractiveness and had
become routine. One thing that any teenager does not
suffer well is routine, which they equate with dullness.
It wasn't only him, for when school let out for the
summer of 1988, everybody else was bored, too.

What could they do for excitement? They were

surrounded by the pale stucco of the Calabasas land-scape, where all the houses basically looked the same. Got to break out, man. Got to *do something*. Lyle had come back from Europe, faced his father's wrath with the same equanimity with which he was facing the dreaded sentence of returning to Princeton, and he agreed. As the Valleyspeakers around them would say, nodding wisely, they were, like, totally bummed out.

Out riding at night, in the balmy Southern California air, they could look in the lighted windows and see people watching television. Couch potatoes, glued to the flickering sets, living vicariously as the years passed them by. That was not for the Menendez boys or the guys surrounding them. Let the others be living room veggies; these dudes wanted to walk on the wild side. Not, of course, down the southeast L.A., where the Crips and Bloods would have been happy to see a carload of swaggering rich white boys pull up and try talking some jive on ghetto turf. But out in the quiet-ness of the 'burbs, eyeing those sleepy TV watchers gave the boys some ideas on how to put a little action in their lives.

Why not wait until some of them went to sleep and break into their homes, do a so-called hot prowl bur-glary while the residents were still asleep in their beds a few rooms away? *That* should be enough to get the old adrenaline pumping.

So they did. As the summer nights spread over Calabasas, Erik, the powerful E-Man, started breaking into those innocent upscale homes and stealing. Since he was not exactly shoplifting at Kmart, he was pleas-antly surprised to count a night's take in the hundreds, the thousands of dollars. Great way to get spending money without having to ask his father and put up with the lectures on hard work. There was a sense of danger when he crept into a darkened house, some-thing that he thoroughly enjoyed.

He and his accomplices stole cash. They stole jewelry. They even helped steal a hundred-pound safe, burglarizing the home of a friend whose parents were on vacation. Calabasas was having a summertime mini-crime wave and the cops suspected the culprits were not the professional sort who would hit an area and leave. Had the little hell-raising gang made it through the summer, the crimes probably would have fallen off sharply when classes and sports resumed at Calabasas High.

The police did not take the thievery lightly, feeling that a dark house being burgled was a bit more serious than a kid having a few beers too many. Popping open a car trunk one day, the cops found a stack of stolen material and evidence that pointed straight at the Menendez boys. Among the items the young thieves had lifted was a hundred thousand dollars' worth of jewelry and cash, good enough to be classified as a felony-sized offense called grand theft burglary.

Suddenly, Jose Menendez found his little world of success turned on its head again. Until now, it had only been Lyle who screwed up. Now Erik was in a mess up to his bushy black eyebrows, and the cops did not seem too impressed that the storky-looking boy could play a mean baseline tennis game. When they looked at the kid, they saw only a crook.

Furious at what had happened, Jose attacked this problem with the same zeal he applied at LIVE Entertainment. Determined that his son would not have to spend time in jail, he hired a top-notch defense lawyer, Gerald Chaleff, to represent Erik.

Soon afterward, Jose drove with Chaleff to the Malibu sheriff's station, where the tight-lipped, angry father had to do the menial labor of unloading boxes filled with Erik's illegal haul while detectives checked it against an inventory of stolen goods. He also wrote out a check for eleven thousand dollars to cover the things that had vanished since his boy had stolen them.

A deal was worked out with the prosecutors that would wipe away any mention of Lyle's participation in the crimes if Erik took the fall for the whole thing. As a minor with no previous trouble with the law, he appeared contrite enough in court for a judge to tap him on the wrist. He was sentenced to community service with the homeless, and an order was entered that both brothers undergo some professional psychological counseling. It was hardly the same sentence that would have been dealt to a black ghetto youth with a public defender as a lawyer, but after all, this was the civilized side of Los Angeles, and boys sometimes make mistakes, don't they? Why ruin their lives just because they stole stuff that was worth more money than most of the population would earn in a year?

There was one thing left, however. The case had made big news in Calabasas, and neighbors were rather uncomfortable that the little thief, as uncontrite as ever, was still out there. Just as he had blamed Princeton for Lyle's problem of cheating, Jose blamed the crowd that Erik ran with, and not his son, for the trouble. It seemed he was always ready to place blame everywhere but on the two boys he had raised to be exactly like himself. He could yell at them, but damned if he would allow anyone else to do so.

Around the office, Jose began to complain about the thugs who had beaten Erik. His own tires were being slashed, he said, and the expensive cars were being spray-painted. The family hated to pick up the telephone because of anonymous threats from people on the other end. No doubt about it, Calabasas was going to hell in a handbasket, and the cops obviously couldn't control the crime. He told associates he was going to move out of there and find somewhere safe for his family.

So, in the inimitable words of the *Beverly Hillbillies* theme song, they loaded up the trucks and they moved to Beverly . . . Hills, that is. Swimming pools. Movie stars.

8

Murder

Yellow crime scene tape was strung between the elm trees at the front of the big house, giving it the look of a white cake wrapped with a bright ribbon, and flashing emergency lights of patrol cars and other official vehicles brushed the fronts of the surrounding mansions with a twirling rainbow of red, yellow, and blue.

Beverly Hills police officers swarmed to the scene within minutes of the 911 call from Lyle Menendez, and the first officers found Erik curled on the curb in a fetal position, screaming, incoherent, and crying. Lyle was nearby, having been told by the 911 operator to get out of the house, not only for his own safety, but so the cops would be able to immediately spot them upon arrival.

When the police went inside, they knew that two dead people were probably in there, but they wanted to be damned sure nobody else was, so they approached carefully. There was a chance that whoever had done the killing might still be around, clutching the powerful weaponry that had blown away Kitty and Jose Menendez. While the investigation started inside the house, cops, some with guns drawn, crouched behind car fenders and edged carefully through the manicured shrubs of nearby houses, looking for possible intruders. They issued stern warnings to residents awakened by the commotion to stay indoors, and as a helicopter noisily stirred the night sky and danced its searchlight over the area, neighbors peeked from behind heavy drapes in darkened bedrooms as the unusual drama unfolded. Residents were shocked into stony fear. The frightening appearance of the squad cars, their sirens wailing, the intrusive clatter of the helicopter were not familiar sounds in this posh enclave of wealth.

With the boys isolated behind the fence in the spacious driveway, police carefully edged into the wide hallway, their black shoes squeaking lightly on the white marble floor. An overhead skylight was dark, and the large, green-carpeted staircase that swept up the right wall to the second floor was empty. Looking into a huge drawing room on one side of the hallway, they saw a black baby grand piano that seemed small in the forty-foot-long room, but no signs of movement. They checked a small sitting room and dining room on the opposite side of the hall and found nothing there, either. They knew the bodies were allegedly in a rear room of the first floor, but a primary lesson in police work was to proceed slowly and methodically. You never knew if someone might be lurking in a dark corner, waiting in ambush.

The doors to the television room at the far end of the front hallway were open, and upon entering, veteran officers almost gagged at the sight. It was nothing less than a massacre. Such scenes might be everyday occurrences in far-off places like Bosnia or South-Central Los Angeles, but this was Beverly Hills, which averaged only two murders a year! "Things like this don't happen here," a neighbor would observe later.

It was difficult to recognize the remains of the shattered corpses of Kitty and Jose Menendez as even human. The oriental rug beneath Kitty and the sofa on which Jose was sprawled were soaked in dark blood, almost as if cans of maroon paint had been dumped on them. Blood and strings of human tissue smeared the parquet floor and were plastered on the walls, the big built-in bookcase along the rear wall, and even on some of the sixty first-place tennis trophies that had been won by the Menendez brothers. It was a violent scene of unheard-of proportion in that serene little village, and the Beverly Hills chief of police, Marvin Iannone, would observe, "I have heard of very few murders that were more savage."

A published report would later quote retired detective Dan Stewart, whom the family hired as an investigator, as saying, "I've seen a lot of homicides, but nothing quite that brutal. It would be hard to describe, especially Jose, as resembling a human that you would recognize."

Jose was in shorts and a sweatshirt, and what was left of his head was misshapen and the skull was hollowed. According to the autopsy, that was due to the "explosive decapitation with evisceration of the brain." Somebody had literally blown his brains out. Kitty, lying near his feet and wearing sneakers, sweatshirt, and jogging pants, had likewise been pulverized, with massive damage to the chest, right arm, left hip, and left leg, as well as the "multiple lacerations" of her brain caused by one contact shot that had reduced her face to fleshy pulp.

No one was unhappy when the bodies were finally covered with tan blankets, strapped to gurneys, and hauled away by ambulances for autopsies. Some cops felt autopsies were not needed, for what kind of doubt could there be of how the Menendez couple had died? This wasn't something sneaky, like poison, or some wound that would be hard to detect, like a knife inserted between the ribs. Somebody, probably more than one person, had simply stormed into the big house and shot the shit out of those two people.

Once it was determined that no gunmen were still skulking about the place, and the bodies had been removed, the investigation could begin in earnest, although there was little that would be learned that night.

Police determined that the six-bedroom house with a red tiled roof, itself, had an interesting history. Built in 1927, it was the only one of its style on the block, and a 1974 remodeling had left it with a courtyard, a swimming pool, a tennis court, and a two-story guest-house in the rear that had its own sitting room, bedroom, and a full bath above a two-car garage. The sand-colored metal gate that gave the garage access to the alley was locked. The spread was no doubt the home of a high roller, for Elton John had lived there in 1987, and other such entertainment luminaries as director Hal Prince and the singers Prince and Michael Jackson also had once called it home. When a member of the huge Saudi royal family leased it for a while, he had paid thirty-five thousand dollars a month. The current owner, Jose Menendez, now deceased, had purchased it for a cool four million bucks.

Neighbors, police found, were of little help. One said he had been watching a James Bond movie on television and didn't think anything was unusual when he heard some popping sounds, like firecrackers going off, about ten o'clock. Gunfire in Beverly Hills is not an every-night experience, nor are firecrackers, but no one reported the unmistakable roars of shotguns being fired.

Investigators pieced together that the couple, who had lived there for less than a year, had been alone in the house Sunday night, for the maid had the night off and their two sons had gone out to a movie. The boys were distraught, as could be expected of a couple of kids who had come home from a night out to find their parents butchered in their home.

They seemed like good kids. Neat and athletic looking. Lyle, the older one, said he was a student at Princeton University. Impressive. Erik, the younger boy, had just graduated from Beverly Hills High School and was headed for UCLA. Also impressive.

Trying to be helpful, the boys said they had gone out that night to see a James Bond flick, *Licence to Kill,* over at Century City, only to discover long lines waiting to get into the theater. Changing their plans, they said, they went back to see *Batman* again. A detective asked if they still had the ticket stubs in their pockets but was told the stubs had been thrown away.

After watching the film, in which the main character's parents are killed in front of him by an organized crime thug, the brothers cruised over to the Santa Monica Civic Auditorium to chow down at the "Taste of L.A." food festival. While there, they telephoned a friend, hoping he could meet them for a beer at the popular Cheesecake Factory, a favored hangout of the Beverly Hills young, rich, and restless.

They sheepishly admitted to police that, since Erik was too young to drink legally, they had driven home to pick up a phony identification card, and in doing so had missed linking up with their pal.

When they drove up to the mansion, they told police, they noticed the gate was open, a rather unusual event. They parked in the courtyard and found the front door unlocked, too. The alarm system was not on, but that was not unusual, since their father was always complaining that they set it off by accident all too frequently. But when they saw the television room doors wide open, they felt a surge of fear, and when they looked inside, they discovered their murdered parents. Erik told a detective that there was an

eerie cloud of thick gray smoke still lingering in the
room.

A normal procedure for murder investigators is to test
for the presence of gunshot residue on the hands and
clothing of potential suspects. Microscopic particles
of powder and other trace elements normally flash
back onto the shooters and will cling to them for up to
six hours after they've pulled the trigger. But the
particles are not indelibly present and can be removed
by simply washing the hands, or even by putting hands
in pockets. Eventually, those important particles will
vanish, so the testing must be conducted as swiftly as
possible.

Crime scene kits usually contain cotton-tipped ap-
plicators with one end cut away, a solution of 5 percent
nitric acid to be sprayed onto the hands or the swabs,
and a series of plastic test tubes. Then the investigators will dab the palm and back of each hand and seal
the swab in a test tube for laboratory analysis. In one
variation, a small aluminum roller of sticky cellophane
tape is rolled over the webbed portion of a person's
hands. Either way, the tests can conclusively prove
whether a person has been handling a firearm.

Although the cororner's office would test to determine whether Kitty or Jose had fired a gun that evening, investigators did not perform any such test on
either Lyle or Erik. Compassion apparently replaced
common police sense after the boys had been steadily
interrogated for hours.

Another basic step in such an investigation is to photograph and sketch out the crime scene for later analysis. Even that would prove of little help in this case,
because so many shots had been fired and the resulting
blasts had erased any sense of logic from the scene.
Then there was the curious fact that no shotgun shells

were discovered. Whoever had committed the slaughter had carefully picked up each and every one of the numerous casings and taken them away.

A normal crime scene analysis would show the location of all such shells and all of the shot patterns. This helps to reconstruct the crime by deducing the positions of the assailants and victims and the direction from which the shots came. If a shot passes through some fixed object, such as a piece of furniture, then the path of that shot can be ascertained.

But at 722 North Elm Drive, there was a vast amount of damage to the room as well as to the victims. Trying to separate each of the individual shots and determine the sequence was impossible. When a buckshot cartridge is fired from a shotgun, the shot, like small ball bearings, will stay close together at first, then spread as they cover more distance. The result of a contact shot, with the gun barrel against the victim, is a devastating, explosive impact powerful enough to decapitate a human head. Even up to eight inches from the barrel, the wound inflicted would be almost circular, as if a single huge bullet had struck. Such gaping wounds are sometimes referred to as "rat holes" by cops. But by ten feet, there is usually a central opening wound surrounded by single small holes from the scattering shot. By ten yards, the scattering shows a pattern that may spread over an area of sixteen inches or more.

The bodies and the surrounding furniture and walls bore a wide spectrum of damage. The room looked more like an explosion in a meat market than a precise murder scene.

Another peculiar thing the detectives noticed was that there was no indication at all of a struggle by the victims. Dishes of ice cream and berries were still on the coffee table. Jose had obviously been sitting there with his feet propped up, watching television. He had to have heard something before all hell broke loose, but neither he nor his wife seemed to have been trying to take evasive action. Robbery didn't seem to be a motive, for the house had not been ransacked. The deaths, although horribly bloody, had obviously been planned. Whoever had come through those French doors behind the sofa had nothing but murder on their minds.

The investigation continued throughout the following day, Monday, and at the conclusion, police had found no weapons, picked up no fingerprints, discovered no shotgun shells, and had not even been able to determine a motive for the slayings.

There was no doubt that this was going to be a widely publicized test of the 128-person Beverly Hills Police Department. The department had already suffered enough indignity in the Eddie Murphy comedies about Beverly Hills cops, and now a real double murder that was bound to capture the attention of the media had been handed to the men and women who wore the badges in one of America's wealthiest enclaves. There was no doubt about this one. It was starting at ground zero, but it had to be successfully concluded. The department's image was at stake, and being a relatively small unit compared with the Los Angeles metropolitan police force, their every action would be examined in the microscope of public opinion. When the superrich people whom they protected started getting blown away by shotguns, other superrich people with powerful political connections tended to get nervous. No one knew this more than Detective Les Zoeller, who would become the lead investigator, about as uncomfortable a spot as could be imagined, as August 20, 1989, came to a close.

* * *

Everyone knew, of course, that just because a family has money does not mean that they are safe from the vagaries of violent life. Every once in a while around the well-heeled neighborhoods of Los Angeles, some unhappy rich kid snuffs his parents, and there is damned little the police can do other than sweep up afterward.

There was, for instance, the clubbing death of Marguerite Miller, the wife of President Reagan's attorney, Roy Miller, back in 1983. The murderer was none other than their twenty-one-year-old son, Michael, who was found guilty of first-degree murder in a shushed-up trial from which the media was barred. The young murderer was adjudged insane and shipped off to a mental hospital rather than a hard-time prison.

That same year, another twenty-one-year-old, Ricky Kyle, killed his father, Henry Harrison Kyle, the president of a motion picture production company, Four Star International. The prosecutors said Ricky had killed out of greed, while the defense said the father was abusive. Although his mother believed he should not go to jail at all, Ricky Kyle was sentenced to a mere five years.

So naturally the police were going to be suspicious of the grief-stricken Menendez boys. Tears might buy them a little time, but they would not wash away police curiosity. Their stories would be thoroughly checked as part of the ongoing investigation.

But there was something that was even more disturbing as the investigators began to unravel the career of Jose Menendez. There was the situation with Noel Bloom, who had been suspected of being involved with organized crime, and the cops had also begun to analyze an event from the previous January.

Jose Menendez had decided that, with the new financial strength he had brought to LIVE Entertainment, the time had come to stop slashing costs and to start building, by purchasing profitable smaller companies with similar business interests. He began to delve into the world of corporate takeovers, which had buffeted his own career so many times. One of the first acquisitions, in January 1989, was a chain of music stores, and in the process he again bumped into allegations that organized crime had penetrated the music field.

His target was Strawberries, an eighty-five-store retail chain based in New England and owned by Morris Levy, and the price tag of about $40.5 million was in the proper range.

There was one major hitch. Levy had been convicted only a few months earlier on a charge of conspiring to extort money from a record wholesaler. LIVE knew the price for Strawberries was a bargain, apparently reflecting the stress that Levy was under, since he had been sentenced to pay a two-hundred-thousand-dollar fine and spend ten years in prison.

Authorities said Levy had been considered a business associate of Vincent "the Chin" Gigante, reputed to head a crime family in New York. And, according to the *Los Angeles Times,* the FBI had a wiretap recording indicating that organized crime figures held a 25 percent stake in Strawberries. Levy denied all such accusations.

However, no prospective buyer would be interested in the company should such connections to the mob turn out to be true. It was a question that LIVE had to, and did, clear up before writing a check, for no ethical executive in his right mind would want to be in bed with the Mafia. While Jose did not directly participate in the negotiations, he did go on personal visits to some of the stores and hired a law firm in Boston to conduct an intensive background search for any improper dealings. When the lawyers gave Strawberries a clean bill, LIVE went ahead with the purchase.

Nevertheless, the stench of organized crime would haunt the investigators trying to figure out who had blown Jose and Kitty Menendez into hamburger.

There seemed to be no problem with Jose's complicated business history. Indeed, the company he headed, LIVE Entertainment, had just posted a second-quarter profit of $1.5 million, almost triple the figure for the comparable period of the previous year, with much of the revenue attributed to Jose's coup with the Strawberries acquisition.

Officials at LIVE quickly put out a press release that said the "whole company is in shock" over the slayings. "The loss of Mr. Menendez's services could materially adversely affect the business of LIVE, although management believes that LIVE and its subsidiaries possess sufficient management depth to operate successfully." The LIVE executive committee met swiftly to appoint Carolco president Peter M. Hoffman to be acting chairman of the LIVE money machine, while LIVE senior vice-president Roger R. Smith was promoted to acting CEO.

Jose was dead, but business had to go on.

Jose's sister, Marta Menendez Cano of West Palm Beach, Florida, told the Associated Press she was certain Jose's death had something to do with the fact that he had refused to do business with the mob. But the police had some problems with that scenario. For starters, the killings did not *look* smooth enough to have been carried out by professional contract killers. The disarray in that television room smacked of amateurism, not of someone who wanted to get in, kill Jose, and get out with the least amount of problems. Maybe if Jose had been found handcuffed, a strip of duct tape over his mouth, and two neat bullet holes at the base of his skull, then the investigators would be more apt to believe the mob did it. Normally, a mob hit would not include the wife, and certainly a professional killer never would have spent an inordinate amount of time picking up the spent shotgun shells.

It just didn't add up. But since the police had no clues and no hot suspects, they had to spend a lot of time at first proving that the mob was not responsible, for they could not discard the possibility that Menendez, with his Hispanic surname, might have run afoul of some crazy South American drug scheme. Only when these questions were resolved could the police focus their efforts elsewhere.

Particularly on the victims' sons, Lyle and Erik.

9

Memorials

VIDEO EXECUTIVE, WIFE SLAIN IN BEVERLY HILLS MANSION. BOTH SHOT REPEATEDLY, POLICE SAY

With that page-one headline on the morning of Monday, August 21, 1989, the *Los Angeles Times* launched what would eventually become a media circus that would spread the Menendez affair to almost everyone in America. It was heaven-sent headline material because it had everything—macabre shotgun murders, wealthy victims, Beverly Hills, tennis-playing children of the elite, and hints of a bloody organized crime rubout smack in the middle of Tinsel Town.

But that firestorm of publicity was still a few months down the road. The local media in Los Angeles ran the early stories, and the wire services picked them up and spread them across the country for readers interested in the latest Hollywood scandal. But the story did not make the big jump to the network news shows, nor to the weekly newsmagazines. After the first splash of "Oh my God, did you hear what happened out in L.A.?" coverage, the Menendez murder story faded quickly.

The first order of business for the shocked Menendez family was to bury their dead.

The bodies were released following the autopsies performed by the Los Angeles County Coroner's Office on Wednesday, August 23, the results of which were kept sealed by police. Other than saying Kitty and Jose were shot to death, officials remained silent as the investigation continued.

On Friday, August 25, under the baton of a public relations wizard hired by LIVE, a somber memorial service for the slain couple was held in the screening room of the Directors Guild of America headquarters. The location for the service had been carefully chosen to portray Jose Menendez, who probably had never been inside the building in his lifetime, as a full-fledged member of the world of entertainment, for who else could rate such a prestigious location to have nice things said about him?

Some two hundred people gathered on that late-summer day to honor Kitty and Jose, and a pair of executives from LIVE Entertainment, a corporate name that seemed odd under the circumstances, delivered moving eulogies about the departed CEO. It was apparently hoped that the service would distance the company from the ugly rumors floating around that Jose and his wife had been bumped off by the mob. If unchallenged, that could be bad for business.

Brian Andersen had flown in from Illinois and spoke in quiet, loving terms about his sister, Kitty, who had almost been forgotten in all the excitement about the murder of her important husband. She was as absent in death as she was in life, but finally, buried, she would be his equal in every respect.

Then came the touching comments delivered by the shaken sons—Lyle and Erik—who remembered their parents in fond, sometimes tearful, words. Gone were the thoughts of a father who drove them without mercy and a mother who stood by and let it happen. Gone were the rebellious boys who defied their authoritarian parents while keeping their palms out for money. Present for the service were a pair of sad-eyed young men, clad in suits of mourning as black as their hair, who could only remember an idealized father and mother that had tenderly raised them amid unbounded love and warmth.

They were a study in contrast. Erik was an emotional and whimpering boy who needed constant comforting during the service, while Lyle kept his spine stiff and his face neutral. He knew that Jose had not cried at the death of his own father in 1987, and he would not break down in front of all these people today. Lyle, who wore his emotions so openly that he would blow up when he didn't hit a tennis ball straight, showed nothing on the death of his parents. He was dignified, no doubt, but he was also portraying a puzzling picture for someone who should have been stricken by grief.

On Monday, August 28, a clear and warm end-of-summer day, the memorial ceremonies were moved to Princeton. In death, Jose Menendez would accomplish one thing that he never did in life: receive a tribute from the Ivy League university that had been so much a part of his dreams.

First, however, there was a bit of a family spat that needed to be settled. Jose had been a Roman Catholic and Kitty a Protestant, so a deal was reached in which three services would be conducted! That would pacify both religions.

At 9:00 A.M. on Monday, Father Brendan Scott held a funeral mass at St. Paul's Catholic Church on Nassau Street, and about sixty people attended the one-and-one-half hour memorial. Father Scott was impressed at how Lyle wove an almost magical spell with a well-thought-out eulogy. For thirty minutes, the boy spoke of his father's drive for success and how Jose had always emphasized the importance of his sons' becoming good men. The crowd of old friends and acquaintances was impressed.

From the church, the mourners drove and walked the few blocks to the Mather Hodge Funeral Home, where funeral director Peter Hodge held a brief prayer service before the pair of white steel caskets, and a few mourners spoke.

The marathon memorial troupe, caskets and all, then went down the street to the Princeton University Chapel for the main service. Normally, the university only allows a chapel burial for faculty or students who have died while attached to the university. Somehow, the families got around that detail. Just like the Directors Guild setting in Los Angeles, the chapel was mainly window dressing for Jose's last rites.

The chapel is a magnificent place and one of the largest college chapels in the world. Inside the old-world Gothic edifice, the mourners passed over mammoth stone blocks worn smooth with the years. Arches towered overhead toward a peak three stories above them, and an eight-thousand-pipe organ played hymns. They took their seats in the nave, on oaken pews made from wood intended for Civil War gun carriages. Huge amber glass lights hung from the ceiling on heavy iron chains, and large stained-glass triptychs filled the side windows.

Although more mourners joined the group for the final service, the crowd was still swallowed by the vast church. Dr. Joseph Williamson, Princeton's dean of religion, performed the half-hour rites. Then the group was on its way again, winding its way through ancient Princeton Cemetery two blocks away as the university clock tower began tolling its noon chimes.

The mourners followed the caskets down gravel lanes, past Norway maple, cherry, oak, and elm trees, some of which were three hundred years old. The distinctive fifty-foot-high ginkgo trees had not yet dropped their foul-smelling fruit, which in season forces mourners to forsake the pathways and walk on the graves of the long-ago buried. In the furthest corner of its twenty-one acres, surrounded by a fence covered with junipers, was the plot designated as the final resting place for Kitty and Jose. It was a considerable distance from all other graves, as if they were to be as isolated in death as they were in life. After four separate services, plus final graveside rites performed by Dr. Williamson, Jose and Kitty were finally allowed to rest as the university chimes concluded their fifteen-minute concert.

Established in 1757, the cemetery is the final resting place for most presidents of Princeton University, as well as President Grover Cleveland and Aaron Burr, a man who was his country's vice-president and also its most famous traitor. Like the long-dead Burr, the sons of Jose Menendez were not all that they seemed.

The mourners looked up as they departed, and saw a flock of ugly vultures circling overhead, their wings blocking the sun in awful symbolism. The carrion-seeking birds frequent the area, fed by a nearby farmer.

Two simple markers were placed on the pair of graves, later to be replaced by a black granite head-stone two feet high.

The irony was overwhelming. Defeated in his personal showdown with Princeton over Lyle's cheating, Jose Menendez would now be able to haunt the hallowed halls that had rejected both him and his older son.

Meanwhile, in Beverly Hills, police were still puzzling their way through the crime. They had been deluged with suggestions of who had done it, ranging from drug lords in Colombia to thugs out of Fidel Castro's Cuba, or even right-wing Cuban exiles; some said it was the mob trying to get revenge for Jose's business deals. Or was it just burglary, general mayhem, or something even more sinister, such as a family disagreement? "We are looking into many aspects in this case. Whether it's robbery or revenge or business related, we don't know. There are many possibilities," Robert Curtis, a police spokesman, said with great understatement.

They checked out a white hatchback car that was seen in the area because it was similar to a vehicle spotted in Northridge, the scene of an earlier murder when a producer of X-rated videos had been killed. They wanted to talk to the directors of Carolco, including Sylvester Stallone, in their effort to find out what the hell was going on with Jose Menendez. About the only thing they knew for sure was that the motive wasn't robbery. Lyle had told them nothing was missing from the big house.

Police, not knowing which way to turn, had to look at everything. That included the business connections, particularly that huge insurance policy of fifteen million dollars being paid off by the American General Life Insurance Company of Houston. LIVE had named two of its financing institutions as beneficiaries: the Bankers Trust Company of New York picked up ten million, while the remaining five went to Credit Lyonnais Bank Nederland. The cops were quickly satisfied that there was nothing unusual, but the jittery LIVE leadership hired a New York law firm to conduct a private inquiry of its own. It was the same firm that had once represented Morris Levy in his problems with the extortion charge, but the lawyers said that Levy was no longer a client, so there was no conflict of interest.

To help the investigation, the Menendez family and business associates posted a twenty-five-thousand-dollar reward for information that would lead to the capture and conviction of the murderers.

10

Spree

"At one point, I expect that we were suspects, absolutely, for a while," Lyle Menendez told the *Los Angeles Times* in an interview, adding that the police had eliminated Erik and him from their inquiries.

Actually, the police were concentrating more and more on the possibility that the sons had committed parricide, the murder of their parents. All other leads had been thoroughly checked and no other explanation seemed half as likely. The question was simple: Who would benefit the most by the death of Jose and Kitty Menendez? The answer was Lyle and Erik Menendez, the grieving sons.

The boys had become almost mawkishly sentimental since the deaths of their parents, sitting still for interviews with reporters, confiding to family, friends, and lawyers, cooperating with the police, and, in general, acting totally out of character for a couple of young men who had been traumatized by the slaughter of their parents.

They were both presenting new sides of their personalities. Before, they hardly ever talked of Cuba, and neither of them spoke Spanish, but now they chatted on and on about how their dad had wanted to be the first U.S. senator born in Cuba, how they might consider high political office themselves to lead the fight to overthrow Fidel Castro, free their father's homeland of communism, and legally tie Cuba to the United States as a territory.

"My brother wants to become president of the United States," Erik declared in an October interview. "I want to be senator and be with the people of Cuba. I'm not going to live my life for my father, but I think his dreams are what I want to achieve. I feel he's in me, pushing me." Brave words indeed for a guy who just graduated from a high school known more for the designer clothes and free spending of its students than for its academic achievement.

The brothers spoke as if destiny beckoned. But their comments, for the most part, were grandiose flights of fancy about what *they* were going to do with their newly minted freedom. It is not abnormal for the relatives of murder victims to practically perch on the desk of a police detective in order to stay current with the latest developments. But it seemed as if the Menendez boys could have cared less about how the police were faring in tracking down the mysterious figures who had murdered Jose and Kitty. This was most unusual, police thought. Most unusual indeed.

Lyle, who had shown little interest in anything other than himself, was suddenly talking about running a commercial empire, of buckling down and taking care of business, almost as if he had assumed the leadership mantle dropped by his father. Erik was getting over the heartbreak he displayed at the funeral very nicely, telling people he planned to stop fooling around now and work night and day on his tennis game so he could become a professional player.

The crushing loss of their parents had been tempered by the immediate dispersal of a $650,000 insurance policy on Jose's life. When the will, which had been written in 1980, was filed with the Santa Monica

Superior Court, it was learned the boys would also inherit an estate valued at about $14 million—primarily the Beverly Hills house that was assessed at $5.5 million, and the Calabasas home at $3.5 million, both of which they planned to sell. Then there was about $5 million in LIVE stock and other assets. Lyle and Erik were also informed that LIVE had taken out a $5 million life insurance policy for Jose's family at the same time the company did its key-man insurance deal, and the boys would get that money, too.

Lyle, in his new role as the frugal and serious man who had forsaken the playboy image, told the *Times* that the new wealth would be carefully invested and wisely spent. "It would be revolting to just take a large sum of money and just either blow it or live just comfortably. I want this generation to do so much more than the last one," he said.

For anyone familiar with the history of Jose Menendez's rise from washing dishes to the apex of the entertainment business, the pronouncement that Lyle, who had never gotten his fingernails dirty anywhere other than on a tennis court, planned to surpass the accomplishments of his father seemed somewhat farfetched, to say the least.

To police, it seemed that Lyle and Erik had fourteen million good reasons—all of them dollar bills bearing George Washington's picture—for murder, and as they watched the boys' antics over the next few months, their suspicions began to solidify.

One development in particular bothered the investigators.

In one of the second-floor bedrooms on North Elm, officers found mention of a new will on a computer disk, but their hackers were unable to retrieve the information. When they learned that two weeks after the murder Lyle had talked to a computer expert about how information could be erased from a disk, eye-

brows were raised. The information on the disk was
never recovered. They could only speculate as to
whether Jose had been updating the will written in
1980, before he had acquired as much wealth as he
had amassed in California. If he had rewritten some
portions, then might he have written out or reduced
the shares going to his heirs? At that stage of the
investigation, with so few clues, anything was possible.

Erik and Lyle had obviously rethought their career
goals, and college no longer figured in the plans of
either. Lyle told a reporter that he considered the
academic system to be flawed, particularly since people trained in such an environment might not be willing
to consider new ideas once they graduated at the age
of twenty-five. It didn't occur to him that most students graduate several years before that because they
get into college on the first try and don't lose an
additional year by getting thrown out for cheating.

After getting nailed for burglary, Erik had moved with
his family and enrolled in Beverly Hills High School.
If Calabasas High had been a little slice of heaven for
him, then Beverly Hills High, dripping with snob appeal, was like reaching the top of Mount Everest.
From there, in his senior year, he could see the world
far below his feet. He stepped up a few notches in the
social world, played tennis for the school, carried a B
average, and never wanted it to end. But his high
school years were done, and he had graduated in the
spring of 1989. His grades were good enough to get
him into an upper-tier college, but Erik hadn't wanted
to dismount the social merry-go-round of the rich and
listless young people with whom he hung around. He
wanted UCLA. But with the death of his parents, Erik
now became satisfied with his high school diploma

and, convinced he was smart enough already, dumped the plans to go to college at all.

Lyle, likewise, figured he had spent enough time, a full semester, in the classrooms at Princeton. He had resumed his Ivy League student life in the spring of 1989 and was not impressed with the place, particularly having to live in Gauss Hall like he was some *kid*. He left the water running until sinks overflowed and damaged dorm rooms below. He repainted his room, against university rules. He threw out the gear of another student because he refused to share a room. He just didn't give a shit.

Luckily, he still had Jamie. They had broken off the engagement, but that was seemingly unimportant, because just as he had followed her to Europe, she came to Princeton to be with him. Jamie had an apartment off campus, which she shared platonically with a male roommate named Donovan Goodreau, who was a waiter at the restaurant where she found a job. Goodreau, a personable guy, struck up an immediate friendship with Lyle, and when Jamie finally threw him out of the apartment, Goodreau moved into Lyle's dorm room, another rules violation that they both ignored.

Donovan Goodreau became a close friend of Lyle Menendez, but that didn't mean he could not be used. While they shared that little room and raised hell at Princeton, Lyle stole his pal's identification card, a move that would have disastrous consequences.

So Lyle had returned to Princeton once again, to be near the places he knew and among people with whom he felt comfortable. So what if he had an abysmal record as a student! Princeton was as much his home as Beverly Hills, and he delivered a moving eulogy as he helped bury his parents.

Then, once Mom and Dad were in the ground, it was party time.

*   *   *

What came next would leave a bitter taste in the mouths of the investigators and would shock observers for years to come. The brothers went on a spending tear that would have brought envy to the dewy eyes of a Valley Girl on Rodeo Drive.

First, they just could not bear to stay in the spacious mansion on North Elm Drive, returning to it only when they absolutely had to. People took their reluctance to go in the front door, and particularly the way they avoided the damaged television room, as normal. The boys stayed there some of the time, but intended to sell as soon as the estate cleared probate. In the meantime, they just had to make do with what life had dealt them.

So they began bouncing between luxury hotels and apartments in the fashionable sections of Los Angeles, finally renting adjoining bachelor apartments in chic Marina City Club Towers in Marina del Ray for $2,500 a month. They liked a penthouse that seemed like a bargain, only $990,000, and put in a down payment, only to back out of the deal later.

Lyle and Erik explained that the fast, footloose moving from one swanky hotel room to another was needed because they feared that the same mobsters who had done in their parents were going to get them, too. They told friends that during one trip out, some unidentified men had sidled up and said that they were next on the hit list. Lyle hired a set of burly body-guards to accompany him everywhere he went, even on a test ride of a new Porsche. His new employees, knowing what had happened to the kid's parents, started wearing bulletproof vests. Lyle had told them his parents had been murdered by "either the cartel or the mob."

New wheels were definitely needed, because renting stretch limos all the time was such a bother. The flaming red Alfa Romeo, which Lyle had never really liked anyway, had to go. The expensive sports car that he derided as "a piece of shit" soon was replaced by a gunmetal gray Porsche 911 Carrera, with a price tag of sixty-four thousand. Brother Erik chose to trade in his own Ford Mustang 5.0 in favor of a sexy little ragtop, a tan Jeep Wrangler.

The bodyguards noticed some pretty strange happenings, particularly when Lyle jumped out of the limo while it was still moving to run into a shop and spend money. The limo and a trailing car containing more guards would pull over and wait. And spend he did. Eventually, the muscle men stopped raising their eyebrows when the stocky kid, who looked like a miniature version of writer Stephen King, would shell out fifteen grand for a gold Rolex wristwatch, or buy twenty-four thousand dollars in sound gear from a single store, or an armful of silk shirts at ninety bucks a pop.

Lyle was spending wild and free but wanted desperately to present a serious mein, to become responsible and respected as his father had been. To him, the answer lay back in Princeton.

While running up a ninety-thousand-dollar tab on the American Express card of his dead father, he took the luxury cross-country MGM Grand Air shuttles between California and New Jersey, where he was busily establishing Menendez Investment Enterprises. When the estate was finally settled, he planned to plop a good deal of cash into that corporate front and launch his business career as a brilliant entrepreneur. There would be real estate investments, show business productions, shopping centers, stocks and bonds! Lyle Menendez was going to pick up where his father had left off and conquer some financial dragons.

He chose to start with a fast-food joint that sold chicken wings to students.

In January 1990, using the unsettled multimillion-dollar estate as collateral and talking a good game, Lyle walked away with a bank loan of three hundred thousand, which he used as a down payment for Chuck's Spring Street Café, where he had first tasted chicken wings as an eighth-grader. The little eatery, so small that it was claustrophobic, with half of the total footage taken up by the food preparation area, was in a tony neighborhood only a block from the Princeton campus. It had a total price of four hundred thousand.

"It was one of my mother's delights that I pursue a small restaurant chain and serve healthy food with friendly service," the pious young entrepreneur said to a reporter from the *Princeton Packet*. He gave thanks to his mom for providing him with "energy and creativity." When he stood at the door of his new business, he was only one block away from the cemetery where he had only recently buried his parents. "This place will always be special," he noted. "It's only a few hundred yards from where my mother is buried."

He had to be close to the business, so he spent another $130,000 for a light gray condominium on Canal Pointe Boulevard, across from a shopping center and fronted by tennis courts. But he had little time for tennis now. Strangely, the young man actually seemed to be turning over a new leaf. He rose early to attend to business, flew to New York to talk with lawyers and accountants about his long-range business plans, and would return to the restaurant kitchen at night, surprising workers by pitching in to do whatever was needed to please the customers out front, sometimes even stirring sauce while wearing an expensive cashmere sport coat.

Lyle's grand plan included changing the name of his restaurant to Mr. Buffalo's, altering the motif to a western look of wagon wheels and wooden floors, and serving customers with a smile. When the restaurant that would be the linchpin of his future fortune was a success, he would branch out and open a whole herd of Mr. Buffalo's, from coast to coast. He already had his eye on a second piece of property at the Quaker Bridge Mall on Route 1, and planned to expand quickly to sites at UCLA and Rutgers, then open a new Mr. Buffalo's every two months.

In reflection, the people who worked with and knew Lyle Menendez said later that he seemed almost possessed. Those who had known the go-for-the-throat business acumen of Jose Menendez could nod in agreement when discussing Lyle's sudden thirst for business success. "Obsessive" was a good word to describe what was going on, they said. In another phrase, Lyle was actually *becoming* Jose.

Erik Menendez was not exactly sitting still while all of this was going on. He, too, had a bad case of the spends, but he learned that perhaps he was somewhat over his head when he anted up forty grand to sponsor a rock concert at the Palladium in Los Angeles, only to wake up one morning and find his new partner, and the money, long gone. It was not an auspicious start for the kid who was going to free Cuba.

He sought solace in something that he knew more about: tennis. Erik had decided that the professional tour was summoning his talent, and to polish his game to those exacting standards, he hired a fifty-grand-a-year private coach. They began to travel extensively, staying in plush surroundings and spending whatever Erik thought was needed to hone him to a competitive edge.

Noticing that he usually lost in the first round, observers felt that not only was the kid not yet ready, he wasn't ever going to be able to play in the big leagues. Being a star in high school didn't mean you could hold your own against the best players in the world.

Relatives played down the spending sprees of the brothers, saying they were just trying to buy their way out of grief, noting that a severe emotional jolt can often lead to compulsive behavior, such as spending a ton of money. As one put it when asked about the $650,000 insurance payout that Erik and Lyle had worked their way through so quickly, the family didn't think it was "that much" money.

Police watching the money hemorrhage came to an entirely different conclusion. The Menendez couple had been slain on August 20 and by the end of the year, their sons had gone through a million dollars.

But the cops, no matter how they held the crystal ball, still saw only fuzzy images. They clearly suspected Lyle and Erik by now, but months were passing and the investigators still had nothing to tie it all together. Worse, nothing seemed on the horizon that might help them, nothing but time.

11

Therapy

As part of the legal deal that was cut to settle The Great Calabasas Burglary Caper, the judge had ordered up psychological counseling for the Menendez boys. That was not a severe sentencing measure in the monied arena of Los Angeles, because almost everyone there is talking to some shrink or another anyway. In a place so taken with New Age get-well-now imagery, it was akin to being ordered to remember to brush your teeth. Kitty Menendez was already seeing her own therapist, Dr. Les Sommerfield, and she asked him to refer her to someone who could see Erik.

Sommerfield recommended L. Jerome Oziel, Ph.D., and by doing so, launched a series of events that would carry the most serious of consequences while simultaneously providing some soap opera–style comic relief, as if Abbott and Costello had merged with Perry Mason.

Oziel was a dapper and handsome forty-three-year-old practitioner who shared a suite of Beverly Hills offices at 435 North Bedford Drive with several other therapists, including Laurel Oziel, his wife of twenty-one years, who was also a marriage and family counselor and a licensed clinical social worker. With their two young daughters, the Oziels lived in a large home in fashionable Sherman Oaks.

As with most things in the tangled Menendez case, Oziel had many facets.

While he was considered a first-rate psychotherapist, he also had been placed on probation for five years by the state board of psychology in 1986 after being found guilty of unethical conduct for having bartered with a patient unable to pay a bill. The man was to work off the outstanding debt by performing work around the Oziel home, such as installing a hot tub.

While he was a thorough professional in so many ways, he also had a flair for publicity and was always ready to give a news reporter a nifty quote or two on whatever the psychological crisis of the day happened to be around Los Angeles. He was a member of the attending faculty at the School of Psychiatry and Behavior at the University of Southern California. And while he was a loving husband and father, he also was carrying on a wild and woolly affair with an attractive woman six years younger than himself, by the name of Judalon Rose Smyth.

The amount to which Erik actually opened up his inner feelings to Dr. Oziel during those sessions is questionable, however, because the youth signed a waiver that gave the therapist permission to share Erik's comments with Jose and Kitty Menendez. With such a breach of confidentiality built into the relationship, it would be doubtful that a young man would confide anything bordering on darkness about his parents. Even so, Erik grew to trust Oziel and would remember him warmly, a friend to whom he could confide something that was eating him alive.

It was the afternoon of Halloween, October 31, 1989, when Oziel received a telephone call from Erik Menendez, who wanted to come in and talk. His voice seemed tight, his manner tense, and Oziel immediately gave him permission to come to the office.

Erik pulled up to the Bedford Drive address in his new Jeep Wrangler at 4:00 P.M. and went inside, then rode the elevator up. In the small waiting room, he pushed a button that illuminated a light inside Oziel's office and the doctor came out to escort Erik down the narrow, twenty-foot-long inner hallway. The boy was clearly nervous about something, his eyes darting back and forth, and he told Oziel that he didn't want to talk in the office. The therapist knew no one else was around and that, in any event, the door would have been locked throughout the session. Such promises of secrecy made no difference to Erik. He wanted to be out in the open air, away from the confining walls that made him feel claustrophobic, as if he were locked up in a jail cell.

The two of them went back downstairs, strolled around for a bit chatting, used the rest room at a nearby restaurant, sat on a park bench for a while, and finally headed back to the office. Erik had been cagey in his conversation at first, not touching on whatever may have signaled the need for an emergency visit, but Oziel stayed with him, letting him talk. Of course, the more serious matters soon came out. The boy was openly agitated and spoke of being depressed, even entertaining thoughts of suicide.

Oziel had no doubt that Erik's depression was directly connected to the recent horrible deaths of his parents, and his patient confirmed as much, saying he was haunted by vivid images of his dead mother and father, and that he was suffering from the most awful nightmares. Softly encouraging him to continue speaking, Oziel soon had Erik talking of how great a man his father had been, of how much he missed his mother. Oziel steered their path back toward the office.

But as they crossed the sidewalk, the lanky youth stopped and leaned against a parking meter. Two dark eyes, heavy with sadness, pierced Oziel, then glanced away, and Erik spoke the words that would drop a bomb on everyone connected to the case.

"We did it," he told Oziel. "We killed our parents."

It was as if the cork had been pulled from the bottle. When they were back upstairs in the privacy of his office, Erik unleashed a flood of detail about the murders of Jose and Kitty Menendez, while the astonished Oziel, bound tightly by the confidential nature of the patient-therapist relationship, sat there dazed as he listened to a horrifying murder story.

It began, Erik related, the week before the slayings, as he sat in the television room himself, watching a made-for-television movie entitled *The Billionaire Boys' Club,* about a group of affluent young men from Beverly Hills who became swept up in greed and murder. Erik was fascinated, and called his brother Lyle into the room to watch it with him. As the movie rolled along, the boys could not help but notice the strange similarities between what they were seeing on the screen and their own lives. Of particular interest was a segment in which a son who wants to get his family's fortune puts out a contract to have his father kidnapped, tortured, and killed.

Erik told Oziel that both he and Lyle believed that Jose was going to disinherit them by drafting a new will, and that they hated Jose for making them toe the line in such a dominating way throughout their lives. Since they felt it was impossible to continue living beneath his unforgiving yoke, and spurred by the movie, they decided to kill him.

As for Kitty, Erik said the boys did not really want

to kill her, too, but could not think of any way to do away with their father without murdering her. Anyway, they rationalized, she was a terribly unhappy woman and, although she did not deserve their death penalty, at least they would be putting her out of her misery. Investigators would later put a different spin on that, pointing out that if Kitty was not dead, she would have been the beneficiary of Jose's will. For Lyle and Erik to get the money, she had to die.

Oziel interrupted the spiel and suggested that Erik call Lyle and get him down to the office immediately. In only ten minutes, a worried Lyle stormed through the door to join them. Meanwhile, Erik had continued his story, telling the therapist of driving down to San Diego to purchase the shotguns, and described how, on the night of the murders, he and Lyle had carefully retrieved the spent shell casings, changed the clothes that were soiled by their parents' blood, hid the clothes in a Dumpster, and stashed the weapons deep in a canyon off of Mulholland Drive. Erik said he fired the first shot.

Lyle erupted in anger when he learned that his younger brother had spilled the beans. Everything had been going so well! Wasn't it the perfect murder? And Erik went and told Dr. Oziel everything! While he calmed down outwardly, he still seethed on the inside. In answer to a question, Lyle said he felt his father would have been proud of him for such an effective murder.

During one part of the session, Oziel carefully explained that there was a difference between a crime that took place in a moment of heated passion, such as an argument, and a crime committed to reach a specific conclusion. In the latter case, it was called sociopathic behavior, the therapist explained. He would later testify that at that point the brothers "looked at each other and said, 'We're sociopaths.' "

The fury was boiling in Lyle, and at one point he openly threatened to kill Oziel, too, if the psychologist told anyone about the confession. Lyle was blazing mad at Erik for compromising them but still enough in control of his own actions to know that he had to make Oziel stay quiet.

When they finished telling their shocking tale, and the evening shadows gathered for Halloween, when ghosts and goblins appear, the boys sat in Erik's Jeep outside the office to talk over what had happened and what they should do next.

"How do we kill Dr. Oziel?" Lyle asked calmly, as if he were looking for a piece of a puzzle. Erik, still shaken by the four-hour session, the equivalent for him of an emotional earthquake, replied that he just wasn't up to killing anyone else.

They met Oziel again two days later, on November 2, and related that they had indeed considered killing him to keep their secret. But Lyle said it was decided that it probably would not look too good for them if, shortly after the deaths of their parents, their therapist also turned up dead.

Oziel would testify later that he had received their message loud and clear. "I was of the firm belief that Erik and Lyle were planning to murder me," he said.

Jose and Kitty Menendez had been killed on August 20, and by November 2, Jerome Oziel knew all about it. By picking up the telephone and calling the police, he would have brought two murderers to justice. But because of patient-therapist confidentiality, and fearing for the safety of his family and himself, not to mention his lover, Judalon Smyth, he chose to keep quiet.

Almost. He would confide his notes and thoughts, and some future sessions with the Menendez brothers, to tape recordings.

Under normal circumstances, whatever a patient

tells a therapist is confidential, but the Menendez boys crossed a significant line when they threatened Oziel. It was a mistake that would jump up and bite them time and again in coming years, for while they might scare him into being quiet, they had erased the barrier of guaranteed confidentiality.

The brothers became aware of that fact in an ensuing legal battle to determine whether Oziel's library of autiotapes should be turned over to state prosecutors. In a talk with a buddy, Lyle Menendez confided, "If the police get their hands on those tapes, I'm fucked."

How right he was.

Actually, without even being aware of the existence of Oziel and his tapes, investigators were drawing closer to finding out the truth of what had happened at 722 North Elm Drive.

On November 17, they interviewed Erik's screen-writing buddy, Craig Cignarelli, who related that, while visiting the Beverly Hills house not long after the murders, Erik had hinted, in oblique but detailed references, that he and Lyle had pulled the triggers. It was just like the theme of their screenplay, *Friends*—rich boys killing their parents.

Detectives had another talk with Cignarelli twelve days later and convinced him to set up a dinner meeting with Erik, during which Cignarelli would wear a recording device beneath his shirt in hopes of catching a replay of the confession. When they met at Gladstone's, a popular beach-area fish restaurant, Cignarelli wore a body wire and placed on the table a second recorder disguised to look like a pocket calculator. In a reversal, instead of embroidering the statements he allegedly had made earlier to his best friend, Erik changed the story entirely. He now told Craig that he had been lying, that he and Lyle had nothing at all to do with the deaths.

So as the year drew to an end, and the police work continued to plod slowly along, the brothers' ability to keep the secret of how Jose and Kitty Menendez had been executed was slowly breaking down.

It was if they were standing dangerously close to the edge of a cliff, whistling in the wind as the sun went down. In a few months, Judalon Smyth was going to push them right over the edge.

12

Arrests

Judalon Smyth and Jerome Oziel met through a telephone call she made in June of 1989, while she was trying to track down the author of a self-help audiotape entitled *Through the Briar Patch*. She was in the business, she told him, of duplicating and producing such tapes herself, and encouraged him to think of nationwide distribution of audio- and videocassettes.

It was not long before Oziel, the nice-looking psychotherapist, and the pretty, thirty-seven-year-old Smyth began seeing each other, forming a strange relationship that would become staggeringly difficult. In later years, lawsuits would bloom over this peculiar affair, with Smyth and Oziel each portraying it from extraordinarily different viewpoints. But at the beginning, all seemed sweetness and light.

She was a petite woman, with a wide-ranging interest in things somewhat off the beaten path. Her audiocassettes included titles such as *Insights into the Sensuality and Sexuality of the Aquarius Woman*, she published a newsletter for collectors of dolls, and she peddled sparkling crystals and rocks of New Age trendiness. Those were her occupations. Her personal life was likewise off tempo, and when she came into

Oziel's sphere, Smyth had a track record for love that could have leaped straight from a Hollywood script.

Her claims of being born in Yokohama to an abusive mother who once dangled her over a balcony contrasted with exuberant remembrances of being a teenaged star of daytime television dramas in Japan. Her first marriage ended abruptly when a plane crash killed her husband and left her with a monthly stipend of $475.

By 1974, Smyth claimed, she was living with Wall Street wizard Kenneth Moss, who made a mint in stocks and bonds and retired to live a party life at the age of twenty-six. He went to jail after a pal, Robbie McIntosh, of the rock group Average White Band, overdosed on drugs at a Moss party where the host-supplied cocaine had turned out to be heroin. Next stop for the peripatetic Smyth's love train was Mark Roy, who ran a well-known, upscale massage parlor called Circus Maximus in Los Angeles. To prove her love, she made a sexy videotape for her new husband, in which she wore little or no clothing and masturbated for the camera. They divorced three years later when Roy discovered that his wife was taking full advantage of their agreement to have an open marriage. In a pique, she tried to enlist some of Roy's other former wives and lovers to squeal on his financial habits to the Internal Revenue Service.

It was clear that strange things happened to the men who had relationships with the auburn-haired beauty. Dr. Oziel would not be an exception.

Her meetings with Oziel soon turned into something more than chats between a dashing shrink and a bubbly beauty who collected Barbie dolls. By the end of 1989, according to Smyth, they were embroiled in "timeless love," while Oziel conceded only that a social relationship had turned into an "emotional entanglement." Sliding down love's long hill once again, she resorted to a suicide attempt in October, and in December, hospital emergency room physicians diagnosed her latest collapse as due to depression.

On December 11, Oziel received another telephone call from Smyth, who convinced him that she was desperately lonely and scared. The doctor and his wife agreed to let her move into the guest quarters of their Sherman Oaks home on a temporary basis. It was a decision that Jerome and Laurel Oziel would soon come to regret.

When 1990 arrived, Judalon was still in the house, and had wheedled five thousand dollars from the doctor in January. She says it was a gift; he says it was a loan, backed by a signed promissory note to repay. She says she was drugged when she signed it. February saw Smyth rearrange the living room furniture while the Oziels were at work, and in March she allegedly started having secret talks with the ten-year-old Oziel daughter about how Smyth might replace her mother. There was much, much more in the stormy relationship and it all would become cannon fodder for the media and the lawyers before long.

The critical moment came in March, after Oziel reportedly learned that Smyth was sharing confidences with his little girl. Finally, the psychologist ordered the woman, troubled or not, to leave his home.

True to form, she would have a surprise or two up her sleeve for her former friend and lover. Judalon Smyth dropped by the Beverly Hills police headquarters to talk with the detectives investigating the Menendez murder case.

The emperor Napoleon once conceded that one of his generals had all of the necessary attributes to be an excellent field commander, but he wanted to know, "Is he lucky?" For in many fields of endeavor, from fighting a battle to conducting a police investigation, when all is said and done, the outcome sometimes hinges on things totally beyond the control of the generals and detectives. The element of luck cannot be underrated, particularly when there is a woman scorned.

On March 6, 1990, the irate Smyth met with investigators for six hours, telling them that she had been present in Oziel's outer office in October and November when he had met with the Menendez boys, and through the thin office walls she had overheard them admit killing their parents and then threatening to kill Oziel if he turned them in.

The woman obviously knew some inside information, for she was able to flesh out the details as she went along. The shotguns had been bought somewhere between Los Angeles and San Diego, she said, and the doctor had tape recordings of his sessions with the brothers that would confirm her statements.

As a witness, she wasn't all that police wanted on the credibility front, but a lead was a lead, and her story was enough for them to obtain a search warrant. They realized that her personal knowledge of the information would be ruled invalid in court because it was hearsay at best. If she had been listening through walls, she was not a direct participant in any conversation, and could not really say exactly who had said anything.

But those tapes! If the police could find the tapes, Smyth became almost irrelevant because the recordings might possibly contain the exact words of Oziel, Erik, and Lyle and who knew what else? From the tapes, it would be a simple jump to put Oziel on the stand and have him, not Smyth, as the key prosecution witness. With a witness who could say the boys had told him directly that they'd committed murder, the prosecution would have a slam-dunk confession with which to impress a jury.

The cops were exuberant. From out of nowhere, a golden apple had fallen into their laps. Judalon Smyth had appeared without warning and handed over the strongest lead yet in the perplexing and aggravating investigation.

The next morning, Thursday, March 8, Beverly Hills detectives, a swarm of officers, and a court representative called a "special master" showed up at Oziel's home carrying a search warrant. Their unexpected appearance astonished his wife, Laurel, who answered the door still wearing a bathrobe after climbing out of the shower.

They announced that her husband was possibly in possession of evidence related to the commission of a felony and demanded the key to a safe-deposit box. By the time Oziel could protest the searches of his home, bank, and office, asserting the privilege of confidentiality on behalf of his clients, as he was required to do by the ethics of his profession, the police had located the safe-deposit vault and grabbed seventeen cassette tapes, diaries, and notes.

Then they took an odd investigative step. Instead of putting the material directly into evidence containers and sealing it up, they actually listened to a couple of the tapes, allegedly to make certain they had the right ones. They liked what they heard.

Finally, after almost seven long, grueling months for the police, it was time to go pick up the bad guys.

Less than two hours later, around 1:00 P.M. on a cool Thursday afternoon, a convoy of heavily armed Beverly Hills police officers zoomed up to 722 North Elm Drive just as Lyle, at the wheel of Erik's Jeep Wrangler, was pulling out of the secluded driveway. He had stayed up late the night before playing chess with a friend, and was heading out with a couple of Princeton pals for a late lunch.

One police car swung to a stop in front of the Jeep, and Lyle hit the brakes, knowing this was nothing but bad news. He jammed the gears into reverse, but a police van skidded to a stop behind him and he smacked into it while trying to move backward. In an instant, the street was alive with cops waving pistols and riot guns and shouting the loud, no-nonsense yells they use to instill fear and control a situation. "Get the fuck out of the car and lay down," one officer bellowed.

In a blink, three Ivy Leaguers were sprawled on the pavement like common criminals in a drug bust, gun barrels against their heads and cold steel manacles being clamped on their wrists. It happened so fast that most of the neighbors missed it all.

His two shaken friends from Princeton were interviewed and released, but Lyle was hustled down to the Los Angeles County Men's Central Jail and was booked on two counts of suspicion of murder. His world was collapsing, but he kept cool and maintained his innocence, even when the steel door clanging shut behind him. Only then, in the silence of a jail cell, did he start to reflect on what possibly could have gone wrong. Erik wasn't even in the country, so he could not have told anyone. Lyle was also convinced that they had scared the therapist into silence. So what had gone wrong? He knew nothing about Judalon Smyth.

One down, one to go. Lyle was in the can, but where was the younger Menendez kid, Erik?

Following his dream, Erik had been in Israel for the past two weeks, playing, and losing early, in a professional tennis tournament. Naturally, he had taken along his full-time coach, Mark Heffernan, and they were bunking with old Princeton tennis friends who lived just outside of Tel Aviv.

Erik had finished dinner, bunked down with a thick objectivist Ayn Rand novel, and was sound asleep when his brother was arrested. About 7:30 A.M., his host received a call from an excited secretary at the tennis center that had hosted the tournament; the girl said something was wrong, that Erik's brother was in trouble in the States.

Erik started working the transatlantic telephones, dialing his luxury condominium in Marina Del Ray to talk with his female roommate, whom he had met when they were on the tennis team at Beverly Hills High School only a year before. "I hope you're sitting down. Lyle was just arrested," she said.

In Israel, clasping the telephone to his ear, Erik Menendez felt as if he had been punched in the stomach and broke down, sobbing uncontrollably. He made some other calls, to talk to relatives and a lawyer, as the enormity of what had happened slowly seeped in.

The last thing he wanted was to be arrested at all, but he knew far worse than simply being arrested was to be flung into a jail in the Middle East, where the nice protections of America's constitutional system did not apply. He knew he had to get out of Israel fast, before the Beverly Hills cops requested that the tough Israeli police pick him up. Those guys were accustomed to dealing with dangerous terrorists and would not waste much energy pampering a rich American kid who was to be accused of killing his parents.

Without his telling Heffernan the whole story, they packed hurriedly and dashed to Ben-Gurian Airport to catch a flight to London. They got out of the country just in time. Shortly after Erik's plane lifted off from Tel Aviv, cops from Interpol came knocking at the home where he had been staying.

From London, a puzzled Heffernan flew directly

back to Los Angeles, alone. He had spent every day for a month with Erik, who had shown little distress about the deaths of his parents as he had concentrated solely on improving his tennis game. Now the kid seemed to be falling apart. It wasn't until he arrived back in California that he realized what was really wrong with his young friend and client.

The nineteen-year-old Erik, alone in the London airport, decided he didn't have life's answers after all, and flew to Miami for a conference with relatives. Their advice was direct and simple. He had to give himself up.

Erik let the Beverly Hills police know he was coming in, then boarded a commercial flight out of Florida. When the aircraft taxied to a halt at the Los Angeles International Airport at 1:10 in the morning on Sunday, March 11, 1990, four detectives were waiting for the dark-haired, serious-looking young man who stepped into the terminal.

Having escaped from Israel, it would have been simple enough for someone with a lot of money and connections to fly to another country, change his name, and start life anew. Instead, Erik Menendez had flown back from half a world away to surrender to the cops, and a family lawyer said the boy wanted to be able to give himself up with dignity. Another of his lawyers said it showed Erik possessed tremendous character and strength. The police were appreciative enough not to wrestle him to the ground at the airport, but nonetheless quickly clamped on the handcuffs. After all, he was suspected of using a shotgun to kill his parents, so he had to be considered dangerous, no matter how gentle he might look. They stuffed Erik into a cell near his twenty-two-year-old brother. Same charge. Suspicion of murder.

On its staid business pages, the *New York Times* reported the next day that the stock of LIVE Entertainment, which had fallen from its $25-a-share perch with the murder of Jose Menendez, had recovered nicely with the news that the Menendez boys were under arrest. With the bugaboo of organized crime finally dispelled, Wall Street responded promptly, and LIVE posted a $1.50 gain to close at $17.50 per share. Its parent company, Carolco, rose fifty cents a share to end the day at $11.50.

There was more than a surge of confidence at company headquarters. From the horrible moment of Jose's death, when trading in LIVE stock had been temporarily halted, the company had operated beneath the shadow of the insidious comments about mob involvement. Now that was over. And there was a bonus, too—an unexpected one, worth several million dollars.

The company had taken out that key-man policy on Jose, but it also had given him a five-million-dollar personal life insurance policy. Long before the arrests, the Menendez brothers, accompanied by a lawyer, had dropped by to see about that and were stunned to learn that it was invalid; Jose had never taken the time to undergo the required physical examination that would have put it in force. Still, there was something wrong with the company collecting so much and giving nothing to the family, plus there was the possibility of a lawsuit, so the leadership had begun considering a generous payout to settle the issue. On a day in early March, when the subject was on the table, an officer broke into the meeting and announced that the boys had been arrested and charged with the murders. The policy issue was immediately shelved, saving the company hundreds of thousands, if not a few million, dollars.

13

The Media

The story exploded into the headlines.

Variety, the bible of the entertainment business, blared: SONS CHARGED IN DEATHS OF LIVE TOPPER MENENDEZ, WIFE.

The *Los Angeles Times* geared up for the major story suddenly blooming in its own backyard with SONS NAMED IN DOUBLE SLAYING IN BEVERLY HILLS.

Throughout the nation, Hollywood-watchers were kept abreast of the shocking developments, as newspapers big and small ran stories on the murders of Jose and Kitty Menendez, while television tabloid producers had happy heart attacks, overjoyed with a juicy double murder with glitzy overtones.

Hollywood had been awash with plans for action-packed Menendez-murders scripts almost before the bodies were removed from the scene of the crime back in August of 1989. Stories were the lifeblood of Los Angeles. After all, hadn't Erik even coauthored the rather peculiar screenplay *Friends,* about a rich kid who murdered his parents for the money?

And that was *before* the arrests of Lyle and Erik!

Craig Cignarelli, in the role of real-life best friend, had confided to a reporter that he had plans for a big-money script based on his inside knowledge, although his lawyer said Craig was definitely not peddling his screen rights "at this time." Cignarelli's father was an executive at MGM/UA.

New World Television and CBS were able to announce in March of 1990, the same month the boys were arrested, that agreement had been reached on what show business types call a "development." Their contact was actress Karen Lamm, who had known Kitty Menendez for a year. Under Hollywood rules, this qualified the slender blond as a total confidante of the murdered woman. Lamm, who also happened to be an aspiring producer, knew a good thing when she saw it, and explained to the *Los Angeles Times* that she had begun her push the previous December to scare away potential competitors. "It's piranhas coming at each other, and they're all ready to bite. The point in announcing it as quickly as we did is that we were on this months ago, and this is a done deal, and it's important to let people know that," she said. At that point, it was still three years before the case would go to trial.

Movie maker Carolco, taking the moral high road, eventually said it was not interested in producing any "docudrama" on the unfortunate slayings of its former executive, Jose Menendez, and his wife. The company further said it would oppose any such project's being made. Their decision came only after the *Times* reported that a producer linked to Carolco had already been working the phones to Cignarelli and others, trying to line up their rights on the story.

A slight cool front had settled over Los Angeles by Monday, March 26, 1990, as Hollywood got ready for its biggest party of the year—the Academy Awards. There would be only seven degrees of difference between the high and low temperatures for the day, 61 and 54, so the actresses planning to attend the extravaganza had to consider whether to wear a wrap over their fine, off-the-shoulder gowns. Jessica Tandy would walk away with the Best Actress award for *Driving Miss Daisy,* and Daniel Day Lewis would be chosen best actor for his riveting performance in *My Left Foot.*

If Oscars had been given out for the worst performance in a court of law that day, Lyle and Erik Menendez would have been the unanimous winners for their surly and arrogant appearance in the Beverly Hills courthouse.

At 1:00 P.M., just as a cable television channel began running back-to-back episodes of *Father Knows Best,* the doors swung open to the municipal court of Judge Judith O. Stein and a smaller version of the media circus that would enfold the movie stars that evening surged forward to grab the few available seats. Hollywood and its fictionalized stories would have to wait a while, because, for the moment, the representatives from such august publications as the *Wall Street Journal* and the *Los Angeles Times* sat elbow to elbow with reporters from famed alternative journals like *Rolling Stone* and *Playboy* and the titillating shouters of the television tabloids, such as *Hard Copy.* All were clamoring after a piece of the Menendez action, a true drama of life.

And death. For what was happening in that second-floor courtroom that Monday afternoon was the start of a long legal process that eventually would either vindicate the accused brothers, imprison them, or even place them in the gas chamber at San Quentin. The two young men were on trial for their lives.

But when the boys entered the hearing, it was as if they either did not know about the possibility of a death sentence, or weren't worried about it, or just didn't care. What transpired over the next few minutes shocked thousands of people who would eventually watch it via television reports.

When an inner courtroom door was opened, Lyle and Erik were ushered in by a group of muscular deputy sheriffs. The brothers had been in jail for two weeks, but neither looked nor acted as if anything were amiss. Normally, a prisoner is contrite and worried and simply overwhelmed by the process. But being cowed by their surroundings simply was not in their Menendez blood, for they had grown up to be winners, not losers. They wore their arrogance that day on the sleeves of their dark, tailored sport coats, and sauntered into the court as if they were thinking of buying the place.

As they joined their lawyers, Gerald Chaleff and Leslie Abramson, at a table, the boys scanned the audience that was spread in the theater-style seats behind the bar. In the front row were two extraordinarily beautiful and California cool young women. Lyle smiled at Jamie Pisarcik, stylish in a dark green dress, with her golden hair cut short. Erik flashed a grin at Noelle Terelsky, whose hair cascaded to her shoulders. Seated beside them was the tanned tennis coach, Mark Heffernan, who had been with Erik in Israel.

Also in the front row was Maria Menendez, the seventy-five-year-old matriarch of the ill-starred clan, who held an unshakable belief in the innocence of her grandsons. She anchored a large delegation of family members that fanned out behind her, and the two defendants nodded and smiled and gave little waves to them, too. So far, there was little to indicate that Lyle and Erik were up before the judge for anything more serious than a traffic ticket. It seemed that they expected the defense lawyers to quickly clear up the misunderstanding so the brothers could take their rooting section out for a long, late, liquid lunch.

Then Judge Stein, a little woman sitting up on her high bench and wearing a black robe, had the audacity to violate the upbeat mood.

She clearly was not impressed by the tanned and trim young men who slouched casually in their chairs, legs crossed and comfortable, trading glibness and wisecracks with their lawyers, turning now and then to wink and smile at their girlfriends, family, and friends. Fear wasn't in the courtroom. Lyle looked as if he were chairing a board meeting of his one-store chicken wing empire, and Erik, with his jug ears sticking out, seemed to be sitting through a rather boring lecture. They totally ignored the deputy who stood just behind them, with a pistol on his hip. Veteran reporters who had attended trials throughout their professional careers were amazed at the sophomoric behavior. *Didn't these guys know what was going on here?*

Stein peered at the brothers over a pair of glasses that sat low on her nose and, in a nasal voice the boys apparently found hilarious, ordered them to stand up. They did, barely able to keep from giggling in her face.

"You have been charged with multiple murder for financial gain, while laying in wait, with a loaded firearm, for which, if convicted, you could receive the death penalty," the judge read from the charge sheet, then glanced down at them. "How do you plead?"

They averted their eyes, realizing it would be impolite to break up in laughter at the judge's twangy tone.

"Not guilty, Your Honor," replied Erik, almost with a smirk.

"Not guilty," echoed Lyle.

When it was done, the well-dressed, cocky young men were returned to their bleak existence in jail after the momentary burst of brightness. They had proven they were cool and had held up nicely before their supporters, but when they left the room, each had been charged with two counts of murder in the first degree. The charges carried what was known as a "special circumstance," which meant they could be executed if found guilty.

Perhaps their attitudes were adjusted the next week when they read *Time* magazine's long piece on April 2 about California's getting ready to implement the death penalty for the first time in twenty-three years.

Among the 247 people on death row in the state, and 2,200 nationwide, was Robert Alton Harris, a cold-blooded killer who was running out of time. Harris had been sentenced to die for the brutal murders of a pair of San Diego teenaged boys only six months after he had finished a prison term for beating a man to death. After killing the boys, he had calmly eaten their hamburgers. His case had become a national battle between a society that was bone weary of violent criminals getting off with mild punishment and the forces that insisted capital punishment was barbaric and not effective. Harris's appeals would drag on for another two years, but he finally was put to death by cyanide gas on April 21, 1992.

What might have truly caught the attention of the Menendez brothers in that article was that San Quentin's execution chamber contains not one, but two, chairs—A and B—side by side.

The media pounced on the Menendez arrests and the subsequent hearing. *People* magazine got into the coverage race early and would revisit the story periodically with picture spreads on the photogenic brothers. The March 26, 1990, issue of *Newsweek* chipped in with "Where There's a Will, There's Murder." *Time* magazine caught up in October 1990 with a page on "The Hottest Show in Hollywood."

Esquire dispatched columnist Pete Hamill to do a job on the freewheeling life of the rich in Los Angeles, and in June 1990 ran "Murder on Mulholland." Even the hard-as-nails Hamill got sucked into the Hollywood vernacular. From the viewpoint of a writer, particularly one from something as easternly snobbish as *Esquire,* it was simply too good to pass up. His conclusion was that the slayings of Jose and Kitty were "one of those American stories that combined the pious certainties of Horatio Alger with the shadowy world of film noir."

New York editors and publishers began to spend lunch hours talking about the mess out on the Left Coast, and saying tsk-tsk, isn't that just like California? If the story did nothing else, from a New Yorker's viewpoint it might draw the media spotlight to Los Angeles and away from the Big Apple's own bizarre brand of violence. Hollywood was offering death styles of the rich and famous.

The murders happened on the turf of the *Los Angeles Times,* one of the best newspapers in the United States, and its competition, the *Los Angeles Daily News.* The *Times* has a slight inferiority complex, because in the power centers of the East Coast, it seldom ranks alongside the *New York Times* and the *Washington Post.* That is not because of content. It is simply a bias born of geography. So *Times* reporters go out of their way to be thorough, as if they have something to prove. The result in the Menendez story would be excellent continuing coverage of the strange twists and turns, and presenting the case without the bells and whistles of sensationalism. Of course, in this murder case, there would be no need to embroider. The facts alone spoke volumes.

With its own ponderous reporting, the *New York Times* periodically mentioned the story, and even the *Wall Street Journal* covered it, under the guise of reporting on how the entertainment world, in which Jose was involved, fared amid the turmoil. Magazines and periodicals on subjects as diverse as the law, psychiatry, and the entertainment business also would get into the act. In fact, if you lived in California, it became difficult *not* to know something about the Menendez case.

The major media break in the case, however, came not from daily journalists, nor even in a newsmagazine or from a hotshot television reporter with gazillions of dollars to spend on a story. Of all places, the story vaulted to national attention in the perfumed pages of *Vanity Fair*. In the October issue of 1990, which devoted its cover and lead story to actress Debra Winger, sandwiched between the advertisements for fashions, cosmetics, jewelry, and exotic travel was a story headlined RICH KIDS, DEAD PARENTS, authored by Dominick Dunne. If the Menendez case did not have enough coverage already, a real writer had latched on to the story and would tenaciously stick to it until it was finished. Dunne, who openly loves high-society crime stories, stamped the case with his own celebrity image, thus finally qualifying it in the eyes of Those-In-The-Know as something more than just mere murder.

Not only did Dunne profile the case thoroughly, but he gave the first overview of the tangled relationship between Dr. Oziel and Judalon Smyth. Oziel would file a lawsuit over the story.

Six months later, *Playboy* magazine hit the newsstands in March 1991 with an exhaustively researched piece by journalist Robert Rand, entitled "The Killing of Jose Menendez" and illustrated with a full-page drawing of a pair of fired shotgun shells bordered by five drops of gelatinous blood. The magazine also contained some inadvertent irony, because its special pictorial for the month featured a bevy of young Cuban women, some of them almost wearing clothes, under the title of "Cuba Libre." And one of the Playboy Party Jokes was, "Parents at Beverly Hills High

School were delighted to hear that the administration
had added a shop class to the curriculum—until they
found out that it was a field trip to Rodeo Drive.''

Although *Vanity Fair* gave the bizarre details of the
crime to a mostly female audience, and *Playboy* clued
in its male readers, the Menendez story lost steam
after the fiery surge of publicity. Almost all media
interest drifted elsewhere as the case coasted into the
long and boring months that were to proceed the trial.
After all, there was something brewing on the far side
of the globe, as *Newsweek* pointed out with a story
about Iraqi dictator Saddam Hussein, who the magazine said was "Public Enemy No. 1." Within a few
months, the Desert Storm war would begin, and with
Americans fighting overseas, few publications or television outlets would waste time on something like the
Menendez mess.

Meanwhile, the sideshow between Smyth and Oziel
increased in pace and volume, almost as if it were
designed to keep people from forgetting what was
happening in Los Angeles.

On May 31, 1990, Smyth filed a lawsuit in Santa
Monica Superior Court that charged Oziel with just
about everything but the Great Train Robbery. The
civil suit alleged that she was his patient, and that the
doctor had beat her, raped her, threatened her, hyp-
notized her without permission, choked her, drugged
her, forced her to sign a promissory note for the
disputed five thousand dollars, and made her listen in
on his session with the Menendez brothers. She said
she had been told to call the police if the session with
the brothers turned violent. Anyway, she claimed,
Oziel fell short in the love department. Her lawyer
simultaneously filed complaints against Oziel with the
California Board of Medical Quality. Smyth soon
would tell her story on ABC-TV.

Oziel responded, calling a news conference on September 14 at the posh Beverly Hills Hotel to refute all of Smyth's "totally false, bizarre and defamatory allegations." With his wife, Laurel, at his side, Oziel read a formal statement in which he claimed he had never asked Smyth to eavesdrop on anyone during a therapy session. He denied any assaults took place, and said she really did owe him that five grand. Just as ABC had profiled Smyth's story, they would later put Oziel on the tube.

Oziel sidestepped the issue of whether Smyth was his lover, but Laurel Oziel said she was aware of a "social relationship" that existed between her husband and Smyth. She said the woman had pursued Jerome without letup in a failed campaign to steal him away and, in effect, had held the family hostage in their own house.

As *Time* observed, "the key witnesses are behaving like fruitcakes before the trial even begins."

None of this was welcomed by the police and the prosecutors trying to cobble together a case against the brothers Menendez, who were due for a preliminary hearing on October 22. Realizing the feud between the two important witnesses was bound to slop over into the investigation, officials swore that they had enough evidence to put Lyle and Erik away without either Oziel or Smyth playing a further role. That was smoke, for the prosecution would desperately need Oziel's testimony about the confession before a jury.

Some things were coming together nicely on the investigative front, however, particularly the combing of gun shops in San Diego, where they eventually found that a couple of Mossberg 12-gauge shotguns had been purchased for $199 each a few days before

the murders by someone who was thought to be Erik
Menendez.

To meet standards of the U.S. Bureau of Alcohol,
Tobacco, and Firearms, legitimate weapons dealers
require that a 4473 form be filled out, giving the name,
address, and other information on the purchaser. The
person who had bought the shotguns used a fake photo
identification card, one that in reality belonged to Lyle
Menendez's former good buddy Donovan Goodreau.
The person who bought the weapons sort of matched
Goodreau's physical description given on the license.
It was Erik Menendez. Police went to court to try to
obtain handwriting samples from the jailed brothers
for comparison.

Elsewhere, a report popped up that an expended
shotgun shell had fallen from one of Lyle's jackets
back at Princeton. But the source would turn out to be
very peculiar, and eventually took off for the South
Seas, not to be heard from again.

Nevertheless, police said they were comfortable
with the hard evidence that was being built in the case,
and never had really thought the mob was involved
with the murders. Russ Olson, the chief of detectives
for the Beverly Hills force, confirmed that the cops
had been looking at the brothers almost from the start
of their investigation. "From the very outset, we had
suspicions of the boys' involvement. As more evidence developed, it pointed in only one direction."
Beverly Hills Police Chief Marvin Iannone said attention had focused on the boys very early, and he openly
speculated that the motive for the murders was simple
greed.

As District Attorney Ira Reiner put it during a news
conference, "We are alleging as a motive financial
gain. I don't know what your experience is," he told
reporters, "but it's been our experience in the district

attorney's office that fourteen million dollars provides ample motive for someone to kill somebody.''

Relatives disagreed. According to them, the police hadn't been able to come up with anything worthwhile and so had decided to stick the rap on the brothers. Backed by the eventual proceeds from the multimillion-dollar estate, they went in search of the best criminal defense lawyers money could buy. "The police don't know these kids like I do," Carlos Baralt, an uncle, had told media members. "We don't think in the least circumstance that they are guilty of what they have been accused. We are behind the boys one hundred percent.''

Then the prosecution team suddenly fell on its face, which the defense team loved but had nothing to do with creating. District Attorney Reiner, no stranger to catching lightning bolts of disturbing publicity, removed Deputy District Attorney Elliott Alhadeff from his position as lead prosecutor in the Menendez case in September, without giving a reason. Alhadeff, with twenty-four years in the office of the D.A., had been such a high-profile attack dog that he had only recently been named Prosecutor of the Year by the Association of Deputy District Attorneys.

Alhadeff played down the change as possibly a clash of personalities, but the association, which represents all of the prosecutors in Los Angeles County, took the unprecedented step of announcing it did not have confidence in the judgment of the district attorney.

So the Menendez bag was dropped on the desk of Deputy District Attorney Pamela Ferraro, who had been one of the prosecutors in the famed McMartin Pre-School trials, with their highly publicized allegations of child molestation.

With the prosecution in disarray, witnesses feuding, investigators trying to figure out why so many people were lying to them, the brothers being held without

bail, relatives not knowing what or whom to believe,
and the defense's legal team just forming, the whole
pack headed into one of the most important segments
of the case.

A ruling was needed on whether the all-important
audiotapes made by Oziel could be used in court. It
was a battle that neither side could afford to lose.

14

Tapes

Investigators opened a Pandora's box of questions when they seized Dr. Oziel's cache of cassette tape recordings of his sessions with Lyle and Erik. Their discovery not only would affect the case they were examining but would require them to settle important legal and ethical points.

Not only did the seizure itself, and what may have been learned from it, come into some question, but the content of the tapes threw the whole case onto new legal ground. Before the Menendez prosecution could go an inch further, lawyers and judges had to hammer out the crucial point of confidentiality, or privilege, between a psychotherapist and a patient. Like everything else in the bizarre case, the issue took on a life of its own, leaving attorneys arguing vague points, psychologists wringing their hands, observers wondering just what was really going on, and the brothers sitting in jail.

In California, it is never unusual for a murder trial to drag on for what seems like infinity. In the Menendez case, it would take three years of legal wrangling before the matter of the tapes was decided firmly enough to allow the trial to start. Then it would erupt anew at a crucial moment of those proceedings.

The issue of limits of confidentiality was not exactly new in the state. Years earlier at a university, a patient had told his psychotherapist that he planned to murder a woman acquaintance. The therapist alerted campus police, who briefly detained the patient, but no one warned the woman the man had named as his potential target. The patient, once released by the police, killed her.

The civil case that followed, known as *Tarasoff v. Regents of the University of California,* created new law when the California Supreme Court decided that unlimited protection of a patient's threats of such violence was not a good thing.

"We conclude that the public policy favoring protection of the confidential character of patient-psychotherapist communications must yield to the extent to which disclosure is essential to avert danger to others," the court ruled in its majority decision. "The protective privilege ends where the public peril begins."

Therapists agreed that potential victims should be notified, but they still insisted upon wearing the cloak of privileged communications on everything else they heard from their patients, claiming their link was just as strong as the bond between lawyer and client or between priest and parishioner. If the state's highest court had used plain logic in its ruling, the therapists could be equally levelheaded in proclaiming that if they were not shielded by law from having to give up their secrets, nobody would talk to them in the first place, including mentally ill people who might be prone to violence.

The California Supreme Court ruling has since been worked into the laws of other states, creating an exception to the privileged conversations when a therapist reasonably believes that disclosure of information to authorities is needed to prevent a threat from becoming reality. Almost every state now requires that therapists disclose pertinent information if it appears that the patient represents a real threat to physically harm someone. Only in Ohio does the therapist have absolute protection of patient sessions, and even there, confidentiality may be violated without legal risk if the therapist believes he must act to prevent violence.

Just because the Beverly Hills police had the Oziel tapes did not automatically mean the recordings would find their way to a jury. Until the lawyers cleared away the confidentiality question, the tapes were merely a handful of cassettes that might as well contain country-western music. With the tapes, the prosecution was strong. Without them, anything could happen.

A few days after the arrests, District Attorney Reiner told a news conference that the seized tapes were crucial to the prosecution case and that because the brothers had threatened the therapist the cassettes could be used in court. Gerald Chaleff, one of the defense lawyers, protested that the material remained privileged, primarily because it consisted of admitting to a crime in the past and did not present a future danger to anyone. Oziel might have felt there was the potential for future dangers—to himself; nonetheless, Chaleff argued that the tapes should not be used at all. The views were staked out far apart and neither side was about to make a deal.

The first major legal step came on March 22, when Superior Court Judge James Albracht held a private session on the tapes, a subject that was so complicated that the judge said he did not even know what to call the question at hand, which was Oziel's attorney asking that the tapes be returned.

A central question was the performance of the "special master" who had accompanied the police raiding party. The master, in normal cases, guides the search and if police find anything, the master seals it until a judge can decide the admissibility of the potential evidence. In the Menendez case, the special master allowed the police to listen to some tapes *before* sealing them, and Lyle was arrested a few hours later.

While that issue was being considered, Albracht also had to rule on a number of other points, ranging from whether the forms filled out by the purchaser of the 12-gauge shotguns should be made public, to whether a videotape of the search of Oziel's office could be released to the media. With the case only a few months old, the court was deluged with motions. It was a legal storm that would not abate for years.

The court got its first taste of the Oziel-Smyth show in June, during an all-day hearing behind closed doors. Through her attorney, Smyth said that an "informal therapeutic relationship" had existed between herself and the therapist, and that it eventually became personal. Through his attorney, Oziel said she was never a patient, just a tape duplication service peddler who had developed a "romantic fixation" on him. The court had to listen to them, in private, for days, as Albracht tried to decide what to do about the Oziel recordings. The long sessions took place in a courtroom that had cardboard taped across its windows and an armed guard at the door to prevent snooping cameras and reporters from looking inside.

Also locked out were the prosecution lawyers. Since they had not yet heard the tapes, and could not until the judge ruled on the secrecy issue, all the state's attorneys could do was file written legal briefs and, like everyone else, wait.

* * *

In one significant change from the usual script, the arrested Menendez brothers came into court one day shackled and wearing V-necked blue prison garb instead of their usual spiffy, Italian-cut suits. Five burly guards came in with them. A few days earlier, a deputy had found that the chain that linked Lyle to Erik had been neatly sawed, almost to the point where a good stomp on the metal would have broken it. The deputies searched the brothers, searched their cells, and, although nothing of importance was found, word was leaked that a possible escape attempt might have been planned. But the next week, a spokesman for the jail said there was no evidence that the boys had cut through the metal links. Already facing two counts of murder each, with special circumstances that could earn them the death penalty, Lyle and Erik were not accused of planning an escape.

The next major move forward in the case came on August 6, when Albracht issued a sweeping decision that would permit the prosecution to use all of the confiscated tapes as evidence in the murder trial.

"I have ruled that none of the communications are privileged. I have found, by a preponderance of the evidence, that Dr. Oziel has reasonable cause to believe that the brothers constituted a threat and that it was necessary to disclose those communications to prevent the threatened danger."

This was the equivalent of a legal earthquake, powerful enough to send every psychiatrist and psychologist in California into therapy. Albracht was saying that if a therapist discloses *anything* from a confidential session, then the entire record is opened for review, not just the part in question.

"If the judge's ruling is upheld, it brings a virtual end to the psychotherapist-patient privilege," protested defense lawyer Leslie Abramson, who promised an immediate appeal. She said the ruling reduced the vaunted confidentiality issue to "secret-keeping" that could be violated by a gossipy therapist.

Chaleff agreed with Abramson that "this is very dangerous to the psychotherapist-patient privilege. If the patient said one thing wrong to the therapist, everything told to him would no longer be privileged. I cannot imagine this is what was intended." Still another of Erik's lawyers, Howard W. Gillingham, put forward a more succinct view, calling Albracht's ruling "malarkey."

The prosecution stayed low to the ground, delighted with its substantial victory.

Albracht, continuing to be as vague as possible in his public utterances, said only that the tapes "concern the brothers' emotional and psychological state after the murder of their parents." But developments had indicated the exact tapes under discussion covered a six-week period in the fall of 1989 and included conversations, Oziel's recollections, and a taping of one psychotherapy session.

The California Supreme Court had verified such a can-opener approach to confidentiality with its decision in *People v. Clark*, when they wrote that "the reason for the privilege—protecting the patient's right to privacy and promoting the therapeutic relationship—and thus the privilege itself, disappear once the communication is no longer confidential."

Albracht said Oziel had noted that the Menendez boys had made threats against him during their sessions, and the judge said the threats met the requirement for providing an exception to the rule of privilege. But Albracht knew that an appeal was bound to be filed, so the judge sealed his written opinion until then.

By confiding to his wife and mistress that the Menendez patients had indeed considered killing him, Oziel had irrevocably crossed the boundary by letting the two women peek beneath the veil of privilege. Oziel "had reasonable cause to believe the brothers constituted a treat," Albracht said.

Next stop was the Second District Court of Appeals in Los Angeles, which overturned Albracht's thoughtful decision a week after he issued it and handed victory to the defense team. The three judges on the appeals panel said the prosecutors could file an appeal if they wished. They did so wish, and more paperwork flooded into the system.

Meanwhile, Erik refused to turn over a handwriting sample the cops wanted to compare with the signature on the gun shop documents. His lawyer, Leslie Abramson, claimed that the police had no right to expect him to give a sample when everyone knew they were "going to misuse it." Authorities said that Erik's refusal could be viewed as evidence against him. No big deal, claimed Abramson.

As expected, the matter of *Menendez v. Superior Court,* Case No. S017206, soon vaulted up to Sacramento for a ruling by the California Supreme Court. In September, the high bench agreed with the lower appeals court to stay Albracht's ruling. But it also instructed the Second District Court of Appeals to conduct a detailed examination of the issues. The lower courts had misunderstood the Supreme Court's *People v. Clark* decision and had gone too far in implementing those misunderstandings, the Supreme Court declared. The view that privilege "disappears once the communication is no longer confidential" was much too sweeping.

Since this was all happening in Sacramento about the same time that Judalon Smyth was on national television describing how she had eavesdropped in Oziel's office and heard the brothers confess, it seemed that the secrecy issue was really a moot point. It did not take a rocket scientist to figure out what was on the tapes that the courts were guarding so zealously. The lawyers only hoped that enough potential jurors could be found who had not watched television or read a newspaper in the past few months, because the intense media coverage was threatening to overturn the fair trial boat.

In March of 1991, the Court of Appeals changed its mind, too, and now agreed with Albracht, saying the confidentiality link between patient and therapist had been severed. The court ruled that the seized tapes were not protected because of the threat made to Oziel. Victory went back to the prosecution. To no one's surprise, defense lawyers said they would appeal to the state Supreme Court.

By now, the original seventeen cassettes had been pared down to four of direct influence on the case, and for the first time, details of their contents were released by the appeals court.

Three of the cassettes contained verbal notes that Oziel had dictated following sessions with the Menendez brothers on October 31, November 2, and November 28, 1989. The other tape was the conversation between the boys and the therapist on December 11 of that year. According to court documents, Oziel noted that during a walk in a park, "Erik revealed in detail the planning and execution of the crime, including [the] fabricated alibi defense."

The November 2 tape mentioned that both Lyle and Erik had discussed why they pulled the triggers. The court papers quoted Oziel as saying, "They didn't kill their parents for money, but rather out of hatred and out of a desire to be free from their father's domination, messages of inadequacy and impossible standards."

The documents spelled out more material that, if presented in evidence at the trial, could have a damning effect. Specifically, it described how Lyle erupted in anger when he learned that Erik had spilled the beans to Oziel.

"I can't believe you did this! I can't believe you told him! I don't even have a brother now! I could get rid of you for this! Now I hope you know what we are going to do. We've got to kill him and anyone associated to him." This astounding comment came from the previously secret testimony of Judalon Smyth. The court papers tactfully settled the romantic issue between them, declaring her to be the therapist's "paramour."

"I can't stop you from what you have to do, but . . . I can't kill anymore," the papers said Erik replied.

The court revealed Oziel had testified that Lyle told him, "It wouldn't look too good if I [Oziel] disappeared too soon. It would start to become obvious that it wasn't too healthy to be associated with the Menendez boys since people who did seemed to die a lot and always with shotgun shells around."

Then, the documents said, Lyle Menendez peered at the doctor as if he were a cobra and Oziel were a cornered mouse, and asked if he was afraid. When Oziel replied he did not choose to live in fear, he said Lyle coldly responded, "Neither did my father."

The Menendezes' threat was loud and clear, and was underlined by Oziel's follow-up decisions to tell his wife and Smyth, buy some shotguns himself, and check out his home security system. The man, the court decided, had been afraid for his life, and that met the exclusion rule.

"Where a psychotherapist has reasonable cause to believe that his patient poses a threat to himself or

others, the psychotherapist may disclose otherwise
confidential communications to prevent the threatened
danger,'' the appellate court ruled.

The courts had placed an obvious stick of legal
dynamite in the hands of the prosecutors, all because
Lyle had opened his big mouth and played tough guy
with his shrink.

Trying, and failing, to clarify the issue, the state Supreme Court eventually confirmed anew, two years
later, that the privilege between patient and therapist
did indeed vanish because of the Menendezes' threats
against Oziel. But the court ruled that two additional
tapes Oziel had made from sessions with the brothers
would remain sealed and secret because they did not
contain enough evidence of threats to meet the standard for breaking confidentiality.

All said and done, a single tape—containing the
notes from the vital October 31, November 2, and
December 11 sessions—was left to be the linchpin for
the prosecution case.

The matter now went back to the trial court of Judge
Stanley Weisberg, who held a final series of closed-
door sessions and eventually ruled that the cassette
had been taken legally and that Oziel would testify
about its contents.

After three years of legal wrangling, the prosecution
got its wish—they had breached the wall of confidentiality between therapist and patient and could tell the
jury that the killers had not only confessed, but had
threatened to kill again.

That seemed to be it. All of the challenges, the back
and forth, the uncertainty had been decided.

But the issue of the tapes was like some mythical
thing that refused to die. It would still be wiggling as
the trial itself reached its climactic moment, when the
prosecution would finally lay its sputtering stick of
dynamite at the feet of the defendants.

15

Abuse

On an afternoon in early June of 1993, after the Menendez brothers had spent more than three years in jail, things began to change rapidly. Throughout the long years of legal arguments about the psychotherapy tapes, the defense team had not budged from the pleas of not guilty that the two had entered during their extraordinary arraignment before Judge Stein.

It was looking likely, however, that the tapes would be allowed as evidence, which would blow the not guilty plea right out of the water. It would be difficult indeed for the Menendez brothers to cling to the claim of innocence if they could be heard on tape admitting to the murders.

So an alternative defense was needed, and word had been circulating among court-watchers for some time that the high-ticket defense lawyers had a terrific new tactic.

"We will present evidence that our clients believed themselves to be in danger of death, imminent peril, or great bodily injury when their parents were shot," Leslie Abramson declared in a hearing before Judge Stanley Weisberg. Translated from lawyerese, that meant that although the last things Kitty and Jose Menendez saw on that bloody night in 1989 were the blasting shotguns fired by their sons, Lyle and Erik only pulled the triggers because they were "in danger of death themselves." Since the nearest thing to weapons found in the victims' possession were the bowls of ice cream and berries, this was almost an impossible reach of logical thinking.

The defense team was not starting from square one, because much of the spadework had been done seven years earlier in the case of Arnel Salvatierra, a seventeen-year-old boy who was charged with first-degree murder for the assassination-style slaying of his father, newspaper executive Oscar Salvatierra. The father had been killed while he lay asleep in bed, and his death had worn a temporary disguise. Just as police had to investigate whether Jose Menendez was killed by organized crime, the Salvatierra case investigators had to examine whether the victim, who was with the *Philippine News* and was based in Los Angeles, had been slain because of his strident opposition to the powerful Filipino president Ferdinand Marcos. That link had been established because of a death threat he had received in the mail. Later, the boy confessed both to writing the letter and to shooting his father.

But, the defense said, he had little choice in the matter, because the elder Salvatierra had incessantly abused his son, both psychologically and physically. It took some doing, some fancy courtroom footwork, some extraordinary pleadings before the jury, but when the trial was over, Arnel Salvatierra walked out convicted of nothing more than voluntary manslaughter, sentenced to nothing more than probation. His lawyer was the same Leslie Abramson who had been meeting weekly for the past three years, ever since the family came up with her huge fee, with Lyle and Erik Menendez. What she had done for Salvatierra, she planned to do for the Menendez boys.

The guts of their defense was going to be that Erik

and Lyle were forced to storm into the television room and slaughter their parents with multiple shotgun blasts because they had been the true victims, and that Jose and Kitty were the villains in this story. The Menendez boys, those athletic and rich sons of privilege, so strong that each had considered becoming a professional athlete, were to be displayed to the jurors as the quaking victims of child abuse. Of course, there were some obstacles, such as the boys' never having said anything to their psychologist about the abuse and there being no medical evidence, no photographs of bruises, but that wasn't enough to derail the defense.

"This is a family violence case," Abramson had declared in a mid-May hearing, confirming hints that had appeared in court papers. She intended to move it from parricide to abuse.

The first recorded case of an abused child in the United States was not documented until 1874, almost a century after the American Revolution. That did not mean there were no abuse cases prior to that, but this particular incident finally imprinted itself on the national consciousness. In New York City, authorities searching a dirty tenement found a young girl chained to her bed, starving. The bureaucracy was thrown into a furor as the aggressive "yellow press" newspapers of the city jumped on the news of little Mary Ellen, forcing officials to do something to rescue the child. The problem was that New York was totally unequipped to do anything, for the city had not a single office to deal with incidents of child abuse. So the authorities literally treated her like a dog. Among the laws that did exist were some dealing with safeguarding beasts, and Mary Ellen was plucked from the apartment by the Society for the Prevention of Cruelty to Animals. A short time later, New York established its Society for the Prevention of Cruelty to Children.

In Fall River, Massachusetts, eighteen years later, a young lady named Lizzy Borden forever linked the subjects of abuse and parricide, and her story was enshrined in rhyme.

Lizzy Borden took an ax
And gave her mother forty whacks;
When she saw what she had done,
She gave her father forty-one.

Lizzy was acquitted, but her memory lingered on, and by the time the Menendez boys went to trial, sexual abuse—and the sometimes violent and deadly response by an abused child—was a subject whose time has come.

In 1962, after years of research, Dr. C. Henry Kempe of Denver finally defined what has become known as the battered child syndrome. For two centuries, families had kept such things secret, hidden from neighbors, friends, and relatives. Kempe's work eventually would have far-reaching consequences.

But his work was read primarily by the scientific and legal communities. Great literature, such as *Hamlet* and the Greek tragedy of Oedipus, had been written about parricide. Now it would be the media—as it had been in the case of the unfortunate Mary Ellen and the Lizzy Borden incident—that would publicize such a case and put abuse into a modern context. It happened in 1972, in of all places Cheyenne, Wyoming, far from the power and media centers of the nation.

Richard Jahnke, at the age of sixteen, armed himself with a knife, a pistol, and a 12-gauge shotgun and hid in the family garage, ambushing his father as he stepped from his car. At his trial, where he pleaded self-defense, it was proven that Richard had been severely beaten and abused by his father since the boy was two years old, and that his sister had been sexually abused. "I just couldn't handle it anymore," Richard told the jury, which didn't seem to hear him. He was sentenced to prison and only after a shrill reaction from the public did the boy win a gubernatorial pardon.

Clearly, the consciousness of the public was awakening to the possibility of sexual abuse, child abuse, spousal abuse, and other such vile crimes.

As the stigma attached to the victims of such crimes was slowly removed, more and more of them were willing to step forward and document what had been done to them. In the calendar year of 1982, a million cases of sexual abuse were reported. By 1992, as the Menendez trial approached, that number had escalated almost 200 percent, to 2.9 million reported cases.

Companion and shocking statistics showed that five thousand children were being murdered each year by their parents in the United States and that in 1987, of every thousand children, thirty-four would suffer serious abuse of some sort.

The situation of family violence was not new, as shown in ancient literature, nor was it confined to the United States. Elliott Leyton, in his book *Sole Survivor—Children Who Murder Their Families,* described a 1988 case in Tokyo in which a fourteen-year-old boy, tired of parental pressure to excel in a demanding scholastic program, stabbed his father thirty-seven times, knocked his mother in the head with a baseball bat and stabbed her seventy-two times, then strangled his grandmother and plunged the knife into her fifty-six times. The sheer violence of the act would fit the scenario involving the Menendez brothers. Leyton also told of Bruce Blackman, twenty-two, of British Columbia, Canada, who shot and killed his mother, father, brother, two sisters, and one of his brothers-in-law.

And Charles Patrick Ewing's book *Kids Who Kill* pointed out that in most cases of patricide, the father who is murdered has been physically, mentally, or sexually abusing the child who kills him. Ewing states that in matricide, the mother also usually has inflicted psychological or sexual abuse on the child.

The dark past of family violence is being shown more and more often for the evil that it is, and slowly its mask is being pulled away by celebrities such as former Miss Americas, United States senators, and television stars who are willing to speak out as victims of abuse. For those who are abused, it is but a short step sometimes to stopping the problem with a gun or a knife.

By the time the court prepared to pick its Menendez jurors, hardly anyone in the United States was unaware of sexual and child abuse.

That did not mean that all such cases were successfully prosecuted, or even that all of them were believed, and courts have been consistent in ruling that abuse is no excuse for murder. As if to test just how deep that chasm was between "believe the children" and "innocent until proven guilty," as the Menendez case was in progress, Hollywood and the music world were rocked by allegations that superstar Michael Jackson had been accused of molesting a thirteen-year-old boy.

Anyone can *claim* anything, but proving it is an entirely different bucket of worms.

In a case in which abuse is cited as the reason for the crime, the defense must turn the charge around 180 degrees and prove to jurors that it is the parents, not the kids, who should be held accountable. Just because there was not an immediate danger or reason for slaying a parent does not mean, in such a scenario, that there was *never* such a danger or reason. In other words, fear instilled over a long period of time, even reaching back into distant years, could become a defense.

Shrewdly done, the prosecution would have to prove more than that Lyle and Erik simply committed the murders. The prosecutors would have to show that years of abuse were not enough of a reason for a child to protect himself from a parent. Abramson was designing a case that would put the state of California in the position of embracing child molestation.

The jurors would be able to hear Lyle and Erik describe horrible, gut-wrenching instances of abuse, but the prosecution would be unable to call the only two people who could directly rebut those statements, because the boys had killed both of them. Since the alleged abuse took place behind closed doors, and there would be no eyewitnesses or physical evidence, such as a videotape to show jurors, the word of the boys would have to be the primary evidence.

The defense team would have to carefully reconstruct the incidents of abuse. The prosecution would have to prove the boys were liars. The idea that they killed to get millions of dollars could easily become lost in the emotional shuffle.

One expert that Abramson consulted was Paul Mones, a lawyer and children's rights advocate in Los Angeles and author of a book called *When a Child Kills*. His book outlined much of what would be the defense of Erik and Lyle Menendez. According to Mones's research, such perpetrators usually are peaceful kids with successful parents in families that are very private. The children have a low opinion of themselves, and react only after suffering their abuse silently, trying to please their parents in every way. When they explode, according to Mones, they normally strike when the parents are extremely vulnerable, and a single bullet seldom does the job. Just as Lizzy Borden chopped time and again with her axe, the Menendez boys burned plenty of ammunition in the television room.

Instead of having little data with which to work, as might have been the situation only a few years ago, the Menendez team now had a wealth of information and expert opinion from which to draw.

For instance, therapists who deal with incest survivors rely frequently upon a thirty-four-point checklist that outlines aftereffects of childhood sexual abuse. The diagnostic tool, developed by E. Sue Bloom, a therapist and author of the book *Secret Survivors,* contains many points that could handily fit the current profiles of Lyle and Erik Menendez.

Among the checklist items are a fear of sleeping alone, blocking out some period of early life, the feeling of carrying an awful secret, and stealing, all of which were admitted by Erik. Lyle's comments fit checklist items such as a desire to disassociate from his family, creating a fantasy world with his stuffed animals, feeling a demand to achieve in order to be loved, and a rigid control of the thought processes.

Other aftereffects on Bloom's list that might also be taken into account when considering the Menendez situation would be a victim's fear of losing control, guilt and shame, compulsive behavior, suicidal thoughts, depression and senseless crying, and an inability to express anger. The Menendez boys certainly met an unusually large number of such criteria, but so do many normal people.

The defense team would also take the jury into the relatively new legal arena that equates abused children with battered women, whose claims that they killed their husbands in self-defense have been upheld. In a startling comment that would pinpoint the problems in the case, the *Times* interviewed Maryland Circuit Court Judge Vincent Femia, who warned that the law must tred carefully in such cases. "In this day and age it has become *de rigueur* in parricide cases to claim this abuse. The father is gone, the mother is gone. The sympathy now lies with the children, who complain of having their pudding withdrawn."

The jurist was swimming against the tide. His point about the parents being unable to testify was on target, and his concern was well placed that a successful self-defense argument could mean that any child who was mad with its parents, for any reason at all, from not being allowed to drive a car to getting a spanking for low school grades, could kill them first and claim abuse later. But this raft of new cases was not about pudding, cars, or homework. They were about violent and continued abusive behavior inflicted on a child. A new day of abuse awareness was dawning, whether or not the judges and law professors wanted the sun to come up.

The question that would be placed before the court was whether the young Menendez brothers, whom the jurors would see at age twenty-five and twenty-two, were ruthless, greedy murderers after the family fortune, or just a couple of helpless kids swept up in one of the most controversial and popular psychological questions of the day: child abuse.

The outcome of the trial could very well set legal precedent in California and the nation, one way or the other.

16

Court

The San Fernando Valley Government Center, where Erik and Lyle Menendez would go on trial, is a rather sad collection of big, boxy buildings that are almost as seedy as the neighborhoods that surround it. It is in the heart of Van Nuys, a northwest section of Los Angeles that natives pronounce as the single word *Vaneyes* and is a predominantly Latino area filled with people who have Menendez-like names, but who live in small apartments and houses that might as well be on a different planet from Beverly Hills.

Van Nuys Boulevard, on the western border of the government center, is home to an unending stretch of mixed commercial establishments that range from neat banks to fast-food shops. Immediately across from the court complex, you can munch a wiener from Happy Dogs, shop at the army-navy surplus store, or seek help from Leibowitz Bail Bonds, which advertises on a large yellow sign along Sylvan Street that it is AL-WAYS OPEN.

Tyrone Avenue runs in back of the complex and is anchored by the First United Methodist Church, a low building of dull red brick with a parking lot protected by a tall fence of ornamental wrought iron. Not relying solely upon the protection of either a divine spirit or the police station directly across the street in the government center, the church locks its parking lot. Cheap little homes fill the neighborhoods and clusters of them have been converted into what benevolent city administrators refer to as "affordable housing." The cars and trucks of tenants park in skinny driveways and on dead, sun-bleached lawns the size of postage stamps.

Despite being on the downside of the Golden State's economic ladder, the area is not a sad place. Noisy and crowded, yes, but not sad. Songs sung in Spanish and backed by trumpets echo along the boulevards, as large, old American cars, adjusted to the "low-rider" style favored by Hispanic youth, cruise shopping center parking lots. Restaurants teem with excited children and people yell in normal conversation. Living so densely packed, they must be loud just to be heard. Erik and Lyle—products of the gentleness of Princeton and the wealthy communities of Calabasas and Beverly Hills—would automatically feel out of place in such a setting, despite the Latin flavor of their names. Sitting in a little restaurant near the courthouse, it is impossible to imagine the Menendez brothers playing pinball while noisy infants toddle between their tasseled loafers, or eating giant burritos stuffed with *sesos* (beef brains) or *boches* (pork maws) while south-of-the-border music blares on a boombox. This is more the life of the average Angeleno, not the style of rich kids with fancy backgrounds. The Menendez boys wore the mantle of the exiled Cuban elite, not the dirty jeans and baseball caps of Mexican day laborers. They didn't even speak Spanish.

But the setting was very appropriate for the celebrated trial just because of its gritty realness. The two young men would face trial in the North West Superior Court Building, a multistory courthouse that towers above a line of tall trees in the plaza around which the government buildings huddle. A public library, a health building, a post office, and various other structures also share the one square block of official addresses. During the business day, the plaza is filled with attorneys, citizens, officials of various stripes, everyone going about some sort of government business. At night, the focus changes to the police station on the Tyrone Avenue side, which provides an aura of safety for several homeless women who migrate close to it at each sundown, pushing shopping carts packed with their meager belongings. Exciting and pleasant by day, the plaza is a different place at night.

The seediness seemed to fit the situation, for despite the money and glamour and headlines involved in the Menendez case, the trial guaranteed an outpouring of sleaze. The victims and the accused were no longer on some unassailable Beverly Hills pedestal, but were being exposed as a weird family of lowlifes with a bunch of money. In a season that would revive the memory of the popular *Beverly Hillbillies* television show, about the adventures of a family of mountain folk who struck it rich and moved to Beverly Hills, it was appropriate to learn that Jed Clampett and his clan were not the only rubes in town. Jed carried a long rifle, but never actually *shot* anybody. Sometimes, around Hollywood, the line between truth and fiction is very fuzzy.

On Friday, May 14, 1993, just a month before the trial was to begin on June 14 with jury selection, Judge Stanley M. Weisberg had made the unusual decision to marry the separate actions against Lyle and Erik Menendez in the interests of time, cost, and convenience. The ideal situation of conducting individual trials, even if they were held back to back, would probably have consumed a year of work, with almost total duplication of witnesses and arguments. That would simply take too long and cost too much.

A Princeton newspaper, *U.S. 1*, ran this montage.
(*US1* Newspaper/Craig Terry)

A 1988 photo of Jose Menendez, Chairman and CEO of LIVE, a video and entertainment company.
(*Los Angeles Times* photo/Boris Yaro)

Erik and Lyle Menendez in front of the Beverly Hills mansion where their parents were brutally murdered.
(*Los Angeles Times* photo/Ronald Soble)

The Menendez family lived in this house in Princeton before moving to California. (Robin Murphy)

Erik Menendez
in court.
(AP/Wide World
Photos/Nick Ut)

Lyle Menendez
in court.
(AP/Wide World
Photos/Nick Ut)

Leslie Abramson,
Erik's defense
attorney.
(Robin Murphy)

Pamela Bozanich,
Deputy District
Attorney.
(Robin Murphy)

Attorney Leslie Abramson strokes Lyle before he is to face cross-examination. (AP/Wide World Photos/Eric Draper)

Dr. L. Jerome Oziel on the stand. (AP/Wide World Photos/Nick Ut)

Lyle and Erik Menendez in their Los Angeles County Jail denims.
(AP/Wide World Photos/Nick Ut)

Erik Menendez breaks down on the stand.
(Ken Levine/Sygma)

The gravestone in Princeton Cemetery.
(Robin Murphy)

There was plenty of legal precedent for the unusual arrangement of dual trials, a procedure approved by the California Supreme Court. The tactic normally is used only in murder cases where the death penalty is possible for multiple defendants who have confessed to the crime.

So with great reluctance, Weisberg decided on pairing the trials, with one jury hearing the case against Lyle, and the second listening to the evidence involving Erik. The main penalty of doing it this way was a guarantee of a complex and longer single trial. Each time evidence involving only one brother was presented, the other jury would have to get up and leave the court. That sort of shuffling alone would eat up valuable time.

Some eleven hundred people were summoned for jury duty, to be pared down until there would be two distinct panels of twelve jurors, plus an extra six serving as alternates on each jury. The huge number of alternates underlined Weisberg's determination that neither jury would run short of qualified members, even if several jurors had to be excused during the trial for some emergency purpose.

At least one potential juror was easily dismissed. Henry Llanio, of Northridge, was passed over when he identified himself as a first cousin of Jose Menendez. "Can you believe this? There are ten million people in the San Fernando Valley and I get called for this jury!"

It would not be easy to pick suitable jurors. Many candidates said they simply could not give up five months of their lives to sit through the trial. Many others had already made up their minds because of the extraordinary news coverage the case had been given over the past three years. One woman said she didn't know much about the case at all, only that it was alleged that two brothers "shot and killed their rich parents for money." She was not chosen to hear the case. Another characterized Lyle and Erik as "wealthy spoiled kids." He wasn't chosen either. A third wrote, in answer to a question from the court, that "A coworker expressed that the brothers were guilty, and I said, 'You're probably right,' " but the prospective juror insisted that he could still be impartial. The court disagreed and scratched him from the list. The names of all the major tabloid television shows were invoked by some jurors as the source of their information on the case.

Judge Weisberg would hold forth in Courtroom 410, a tiny arena paneled in dark wood, and there would be no vacant chairs. It was about the size of two side-by-side handball courts with no wall to separate them, with dim fluorescent lighting painting everything slightly gray. Weisberg officiated from a tall desk at the front of the court, flanked by the American and California flags, and court stenographers and clerks worked at various desks, while marshals stood in corners, failing in their efforts not to look bored and unpleasant. The witness stand, with a microphone on a flexible arm, was just at the judge's right hand.

In the normal jury box, to Weisberg's right, sat one panel of eighteen jurors, while another eighteen occupied the three center rows where spectators normally sat.

The defendants sat directly before the judge, surrounded by their lawyers, in quarters so cramped that the wooden tables assigned to the prosecution and defense teams were bumped together like flatcars on a train.

The question of where the relatives would sit was simplified by the fact that they were all in the same camp, relatives of both the accused and the deceased, so they could all squeeze together in the right front rows. Directly behind them were a handful of seats for the media, with a lone television camera peering over their heads to where the action would take place. The few spectators who made it in for each proceeding occupied the few remaining rows on the left side of the courtroom. The whole thing looked as much like a crowded bus station as it did a court of law.

Since California was hardly ever without some high-profile case, the legal representation in court had an interesting track record. Judge Weisberg had presided over the first Rodney King beating trial, and while the Menendez case would not ignite riots in Los Angeles, it certainly promised to be just as closely covered by the media. And while it was going on, the city would be going through still another major trial, in which two young black men were accused of beating a white truck driver in the riot that followed the King verdict.

Erik was being represented by Leslie Abramson, a frizzy-haired, high-priced lawyer who specialized in defending murder cases. Like Jose Menendez, one of the people her client was accused of killing, she was a graduate of Queens College in New York. Erik's second lawyer was Marcia Morrissey.

Lyle's team had undergone a change. Since Gerald Chaleff had defended Erik in the Calabasas burglary case, he might be in an ethical bind if he continued to represent Lyle, for he possessed privileged background knowledge of Erik. Chaleff's job would have been to take care of Lyle, which meant that he might have to move against Erik at some point to save his current client. That would be an untenable situation for any lawyer, so Chaleff, whose track record included the unsuccessful defense of Angelo Buono in the famed Hillside Strangler murder case, was replaced by Jill Lansing, who would be working with San Francisco attorney Michael Burt.

The prosecution team had also gone through a

metamorphosis since Alhadeff had been replaced by
Pamela Ferraro, of McMartin Pre-School trial experience. But the case, as it went to trial in July of 1993,
would be prosecuted by a pair of soft-spoken deputy
district attorneys named Pamela Bozanich and Lester
Kuriyama.

All were well tailored, articulate, bright, and capable. All were ready for the fight that lay ahead.

Weisberg knew he was going to have his hands full
keeping this one on track.

There was one final major player in court. Not a
someone, but a *thing* that would come to be as attached to the case as any of the lawyers. Weisberg,
wary of publicity following the King case, reluctantly
allowed a single television camera in the courtroom.

There was intense public interest in the case but
only a handful of courtroom seats available to the
media. So a special pressroom was set up nearby,
complete with TV sets, to house the technicians,
correspondents, and reporters who could not actually
be inside the court. From there, writers could file their
stories and television presenters could run outside to
where their stations' cameras sat on tripods, pat powder on their noses, and give a brief update on developments. But like millions of other people, they
watched the whole thing on television.

Without a doubt, the media star of the trial was not
a big-name correspondent or a beautifully coiffed TV
mannequin, but the new kid on the block—Court TV.

By the start of the Menendez trial, Court TV had
covered 249 trials in thirty-four states and five foreign
countries since being launched in July 1991. Its list of
celebrity trials included such high-profile characters as
William Kennedy Smith, Jeffrey Dahmer, Rodney
King, and Betty Broderick, with the trials of New
York lover boy—mechanic Joey Buttafuoco and Holly-

wood's accused madam Heidi Fleiss waiting in the wings.

Critics say that Court TV has already grown a bit too smug, considering itself an arm of the court when in reality all it does is park a camera in the courtroom while the lawyers do their thing. The Menendez operation was done on such a shoestring that the camera crew was rented and the reporter had to be his own producer.

But on a hot case, it is not unusual for Courtroom Network Television to be the nation's most-watched cable channel, and when the Menendez trial was in full swing, Court TV pulled a nationwide audience of more than fourteen million viewers! The tightness of the small courtroom meant nothing. Millions of people were watching and listening to every word. From doctors' offices and gymnasiums to saloons and beauty parlors, the real-life drama in Van Nuys caught viewers in an addictive web.

17

Pretrial

The prosecution won the biggest part of its case one week before the opening gavel fell on Monday, June 14, 1993, almost four years after Jose and Kitty Menendez had been murdered. During a pretrial hearing on June 9, Leslie Abramson said the defense team would admit that the boys had killed their parents. The reason for dropping the innocent plea was that Judge Weisberg had ruled that the Oziel tapes could be admitted into evidence. Since the jurors would be allowed to hear the damning audio material, which still had not been made public nor even given to the prosecution team, the brothers' long-held plea that they were innocent would be nullified. Therefore, the prosecution could start the trial without having to prove guilt. The defense was now saying publicly that Jose and Kitty were abusive parents and that the shotgun massacre was actually self-defense by a pair of frightened boys.

That development was fine over at the CBS studios, where some preproduction work and even some casting had begun on a television miniseries based on the glamorous, tangled case. Producer Zev Braun had bought the rights to Dominick Dunne's article in *Vanity Fair* and to the story of Judalon Smyth. He had already hired a screenwriter and made a deal with Tri-Star Television to produce the story for CBS. Braun told reporters he had started talking with CBS back in 1989, when the case was still unsolved, but everyone had decided to wait a while to see if the brothers were arrested. Now the screenwriters were going to have to be fast if they were to keep pace with the story that was to come.

Abramson, in an interview with the *Los Angeles Times* three days before the trial began, said a series of increasingly intense confrontations between the brothers and Jose and Kitty had led to the fatal evening. She said Lyle had ordered his father to stop molesting Erik and threatened to go public with the abuse. "If people would just kick back and think for a minute, there are some fundamental precepts of family life. Precept Number One is that children love their parents. Good parents do not get shotgunned by their kids. Period."

In her extraordinary interview, the tart-tongued lawyer laid out her basic case, which would primarily consist of trashing the image of the Menendez family. Over the past four years, most reports, including interviews with relatives and friends, noted that the family was a happy, rich, competitive clan. Abramson intended to rip that picture into a thousand shreds.

"They were objects for the gratification and the aggrandizement of the parents," she said of Lyle and Erik.

"These kids lived in an atmosphere that was like a training camp. Later it was more like a concentration camp once the really ugly stuff began." Already, the defense lawyer was putting her own spin on the story, using terms like "kids" to describe a couple of husky young men and raising the specter of "ugly stuff." She had not proven a thing yet. The trial, in fact, had

not even started, but Abramson was making up for
three years of silence by barking loud and long.

Kitty was a monstress, she said, who branded Erik
stupid for having trouble in school. "She never called
these kids by anything but their names. Never. Not
honey, not dear, not sweetie, not goo-goo, not anything but Erik and Lyle."

Jose was even worse, according to Abramson. He
molested his older son from the ages of six to eight,
and he kept on molesting Erik right up until the
shooting. She said experts would testify that Erik was
a "textbook" example of a sexually molested male,
and that he could recall some three hundred instances
of molestation by his father. When Erik threatened to
run away from home or tell someone about the treatment, Jose would threaten to kill him.

Abramson told the newspaper that Erik had hoped
he would be allowed to live in the dormitories at
UCLA, far from his father's unwanted sexual attention, but that Jose had demanded Erik sleep at home.
When Erik finally told his older brother about the
situation, Lyle demanded that Jose stop molesting
Erik or risk having the sordid tale made public.

A series of confrontations followed in August of
1989, and then it became clear to the brothers that
they were "about to die," she said. After a final
argument on August 20, the boys attacked with their
shotguns, blasting Jose five times and Kitty ten times.

That was to be the defense case. Jose and Kitty
were rotten people, and Erik and Lyle were horribly
mistreated kids who had no alternative but to blow
away their parents if they ever wanted to be free of
their dominating father's wrath. Abramson played the
media well, and would continue to do so, dishing up
quotable material and righteous indignation on a regular basis.

Bozanich, who would be the lead prosecutor, did

not join the verbal barrage. Abramson might get the headlines, but Bozanich already had outscored her more well known opponent. Stripping away the smoke and flash, the boys would sit through the long trial with admissions of guilt on the record.

Abramson and the other defenders could knock balls all over the legal yard in the weeks to come, but they would never again be able to say that their clients, Erik and Lyle, did not kill their mother and father. Reasons, motives could be argued, but not one undeniable fact: They did it! Bozanich did have one comment, however, which sort of summed things up. If you love your parents, "you generally don't kill them," she said.

The end of June came, then the first part of July, and still everyone was stuck on the monotonous chore of picking a pair of juries. Since Weisberg officially began the case on June 14, some 580 prospective jurors had been called for Lyle's jury and 437 for the panel to hear the case against Erik. The lawyers and the court worked through them all, one by one, to winnow the final selection down to a pool of about a hundred persons. As June was torn from the calendar, Weisberg pushed the planned date for opening statements back to July 19. The people being examined for jury duty were getting a glimpse of the long, long road that stretched ahead of them.

The nature of the trial itself became clear in an examination of the detailed questionnaire, thirty-four pages in length, that jurors filled out. They had to answer 122 questions, including the critical one, "Do you think physical, sexual, emotional abuse of children happens in the homes of wealthy families?" There were 15 questions on sexual abuse and violence within families, and one that probed, "Do you have any strongly held beliefs that a child does not have the right to kill a parent in self-defense?"

It went deeper, the questions going after some closely held personal beliefs of those being examined, with queries on whether they had been victims of sexual abuse themselves, or knew anyone who had been molested. It was a somewhat boring process, but the trial wasn't going anywhere until Weisberg, Bozanich, Abramson, and Lansing could hammer out agreements on who would be sitting in the jury chairs. Each side had placed questions on the form in an effort to weed out bias, for to allow even one person to slip past the questions and bring a load of preconceived notions into final deliberations could prove to be a disaster for the case. The last thing anyone wanted was a mistrial.

So the questioning went on and on. "Do you think that family violence is a private problem that should be handled within the family?" "In what ways do you think people can be harmed or damaged by their childhood experiences?" "Do you think boys and men would be reluctant to report or even discuss their experiences as victims of sexual abuse?"

The back-and-forth examination of the men and women whose names a computer plucked at random from the rolls of driver's license holders and registered voters consumed valuable days and weeks of early summer. The trial, which officially had started back on June 14, did not get around to opening arguments until more than a month later, on Tuesday, July 20.

Lyle and Erik had changed dramatically since their first preliminary hearing, when they oozed cockiness and rich-kid arrogance. In their place were two almost entirely different young men. Not only had they aged and matured since they were arrested, their entire manner had changed. When they stepped into the courtroom this time, they were twenty-five and twenty-two years of age, and they had lost their outdoorsy, tanned good looks. The dark eyes that once shone with aggressiveness were dulled, their athletic moves had given way to slouching walks, and they wore the looks of people who knew all too well what the inside of a jail cell looked like. Also gone were the dark, well-cut sport coats and ties that early bespoke of elitism. For the coming weeks, they would wear a succession of colored sweaters, striped shirts, and casual slacks, making them look preppy, neat and clean, and like the sons a juror might want to have.

Whether the changes came from within themselves or from the careful coaching of their lawyers was unimportant; the two young men had cleaned up their act. It is a well-known defense tactic to present a client that is well dressed and mannerly, as if they were stepping out of Sunday School rather than county jail. A juror should be able to look at them and wonder how anyone so nice looking could be accused of such a crime, and they couldn't do that if the brothers waddled into court wearing dowdy prison denim. That was the charade side of it, which was expected by court-watchers. But there was more to it now. The Menendez brothers *were* different. They had changed. Three years in the slammer and dropping the innocent pleas had had an effect. They wore gloom like a dark halo, for the game was over, the posturing done; and they hardly ever looked at each other. At stake in the small courtroom, after the months of legal turmoil and the hundreds of uneasy nights that they spent in barred cells, were their very lives.

The lawyers were arguing right up until the time for them to stop talking to each other and start talking to the juries, as Weisberg pushed opening statements back one more day in order to hear final pretrial motions on Monday, July 19. The judge, Solomon-like, gave something to each side in the case.

The prosecutors won the important point of being

able to play the emotion-laden 911 telephone call that
Lyle had made on the night of the killings. According
to Deputy District Attorney Lester Kuriyama, the lies
that the defendant made during the call showed that
the brothers were carrying out a carefully orchestrated
scenario to provide an alibi, which further indicated a
conspiracy to kill.

But the defense team won the judge's permission to
bring the character of Kitty Menendez before the
jurors. "Her children were afraid of her, that's why
she's dead," declared Jill Lansing, Lyle's lawyer.
Weisberg said the defense could not go into great detail
on Kitty's drinking and drug use, but could show that
the slain woman was obsessive and unstable.

Kuriyama also argued that the two boys had
"bragged" to Dr. Oziel about committing the perfect
murder, and that Erik had told the psychotherapist
that Jose had indicated he might cut the boys out of
his will.

Spicy stuff, all of it. But such shocking statements
were going to be lost in the avalanche of lurid testimony that would pile up in the coming weeks. A
family's deepest secrets were going to be laid bare for
public scrutiny. The lives of Jose and Kitty Menendez
had already been terminated, and now their reputa-
tions were about to be destroyed.

For there was only one way for Erik and Lyle to
emerge from the courtroom without facing sentences
of life in prison or possibly execution. They had to let
their lawyers hang up as much dirty laundry as possible to convince the juries that yes, they had killed
their parents, but they had been pushed into a corner
and had no other choice—either Jose and Kitty had to
die, or Erik and Lyle would be the ones killed.

Abramson and Lansing and their teams had spent
weeks, sometimes including holidays and weekends,
interviewing the brothers; they knew as much about

what had gone on behind the closed doors of the Menendez home as anyone in the immediate family, more than most of the relatives. They were ready for trial.

The prosecution team was also ready to go. They, too, had lined up every piece of evidence the police could find, and already had in their pockets the admission of guilt. And they would point out to the jurors that one very important thing would be missing from the explosive trial. Jose and Kitty were dead and buried; no one could really know whether Erik and Lyle were the violently abused children portrayed by the defense, or just a couple of lying and scheming murderers who plotted to whack their parents with more than a dozen shotgun blasts in order to inherit millions of dollars.

18

Openings

All four lawyers made opening statements on Tuesday,
July 20, 1993—exactly forty-seven months since Jose
and Kitty were slain—finally getting the Menendez
trial off the ground. In doing so, they tore away any
pretense that the trial would be anything but one of
the ugliest episodes ever heard in a court of law.

"But for a few mistakes they made, this was almost
the perfect murder," Pamela Bozanich told the jury,
pointing toward the two young men who looked like
choirboys. Tousle-haired Erik, with large round horn-
rimmed glasses perched on his nose, had on a button-
down blue shirt and a subdued paisley tie. The collar
of Lyle's pink shirt peeked above the neck of a sweater
the color of eggshells. "They nearly got away with
their crimes," echoed Lester Kuriyama.

"The father cried out, 'No! No! No!' [and] the
brothers then began to blast away," Kuriyama told the
jurors. Kitty was "moaning on the floor" and "tried
to crawl away" from the thundering shotguns, and the
brothers ran out to get more ammunition to finish her
off. The last things the twitching Kitty Menendez ever
saw on this earth were the faces of her two sons,
killing her. One of her ten wounds was caused by a

shotgun that was fired in direct contact with her left cheek.

The two prosecutors declared they were asking for the death penalty for the brothers, who showed no mercy or pity in murdering their parents. It was not an act of rage, but one of carefully plotted murder, after which they picked up the expended shotgun shells, hid the weapons off of scenic Mulholland Drive, stuffed their bloody clothing into a garbage dumpster, made up a lie for an alibi, and used the insurance money to take off on a wild spending spree. Bozanich admitted that Jose Menendez was guilty of dominating his family and holding the boys to impossible standards, but that, she said, was not reason enough for him to be brutally murdered by his sons. Erik and Lyle, she said, killed to speed along their inheritance. Money was what it was all about.

Further, Bozanich stressed, the brothers had *admitted* the killings. There was no question about that, and the jurors should recognize the fact. "This is not a prosecution trial. This is a defense trial. The defense has conceded all the prosecution charges. They have to prove that the boys were in imminent danger from their parents. And they have to prove the sexual molestation."

Bozanich and Abramson made their opening arguments before the jury hearing the Erik Menendez case, while Lyle's jury waited outside the room. When they were done, Kuriyama and Lansing gave their statements for and against Lyle, while Erik's jury was sequestered out of hearing range. Such switching of juries—designed to put evidence concerning only one of the boys before the jury hearing that specific case—became a familiar courtroom shuffle.

The small, fifty-year-old Abramson, rising to make her statements, made it plain to the jury that, while there were many other lawyers and officers and a judge present, she was the queen of this particular court. This was her fifteenth high-profile murder case and she well knew how the game was played. Her grandmother had been an organizer for the International Ladies' Garment Workers' Union, and Abramson had inherited those stubborn, make-waves genes. She intended not only to make some waves, but to brew up a tsunami for the jury. From the start, Court TV had found its star.

"This case will take you behind the facade of rich houses, fancy cars, wealthy friends, and impressive social engagements," she pledged. The centerpiece of her argument, and what had caused the killings, was that Jose had molested Lyle from the time the boy was six years old until he was eight, and had sexually abused Erik from the time he also was six until he was eighteen years old and about to enter college.

The sexual abuse by Jose "escalated in a carefully calculated pattern of grooming the child for his father's sexual gratification. This pattern included repeated acts of forcible oral copulation, sodomy, rape, and the intentional infliction of pain by the use of foreign objects upon Erik's person. Jose Menendez's obvious purpose was to use his child's body to satisfy his lust."

Kitty was no better, she said. Instead of being able to turn to their mother for help and solace, all the boys found was a disturbed woman who dished out even more abuse, sexual, physical, and psychological.

"You will hear evidence that she never tended to her son while he was throwing up in the bathroom next door to her bedroom after a sexual episode with his father," the lawyer said. "You will also hear evidence that, up to the age of fifteen, Erik's mother would periodically make her son submit to her physical inspections of his genitals, which she called 'checking you out.' "

Lansing backed up Abramson's statements by branding Kitty as a violent, unstable, drug-addicted, alcohol-dependent, and obsessive woman who knew all along about the molestation and did nothing to stop it. "Cold and distant, some say hostile," Abramson added.

She gave a couple of dreadful examples, things that would never be included in a guide on how to properly raise a child. Lyle had startled her one day while she was slicing vegetables in the kitchen and she cut her finger. As punishment, she painted his face with her blood and made him wear the macabre mask during dinner. Or, Lansing related, Kitty might punish him by ordering him to roll beneath a bed, where the family's pet ferret, Chipper, had defecated and the mess had never been removed.

In short, according to Abramson, the expensive mansion on North Elm Drive was not really a home at all. It was a war zone on a quiet street in Beverly Hills.

The jurors of both panels were enthralled, bewildered, and a bit embarrassed at the deluge of horrible allegations, and they were rather uncomfortable when Lyle began to sob softly and Erik wiped tears from his eyes.

The defense attorneys spun a web of horrid, but fascinating, tales of abuse. The boys, getting older, had been showing signs of rebelling against their parents' domination. Less than a week before the murders, Kitty and Lyle got into a screaming fight and Kitty reached up and yanked the toupee from his head. Lyle had lost most of his hair as a teenager. It had just fallen out. The discovery came as a shock for Erik, who had not known that his brother, whom he considered almost perfect, wore a rug.

Discovering Lyle's secret about being bald, Erik decided to take his older brother into his confidence about a painful secret of his own, and told him that

Jose had been molesting him for years. Lyle stepped
to Erik's defense immediately and told his father to
quit. Jose would not, said Abramson.

After that, the brothers were terrified that Kitty and
Jose would protect the evil family secret at all costs,
including killing the boys. Seeking some protection,
the brothers tried to buy some pistols, but were de-
terred by the required two-week waiting period. They
had no time to waste, so they drove to San Diego and
purchased the shotguns, and on the night of August
20, 1989, convinced their parents were on the verge of
murdering them, the brothers, "in pure terror," struck
first.

Kuriyama outlined for the panel the strange development in which Erik, "having vivid dreams of his
parents being murdered," confessed to his psychotherapist. "He told Dr. Oziel, 'We did it.' " Bozanich
pitched in with one of the prosecution's most important points—that while the brothers had told Oziel
they killed Jose because his harsh treatments "made
them feel inferior," neither boy had ever mentioned
sexual abuse. The same was true in an earlier confession that Erik had given Craig Cignarelli, the prosecutors claimed. Nobody had spoken about abuse until
they had to come up with a legal defense, some seven
months after blowing away their parents.

And Erik and Lyle told Oziel they had decided to
kill their mother because she would have been miserable, possibly suicidal, without Jose. Under such a
bizarre reasoning, they killed her to keep her from
killing herself. Kuriyama also rolled out a more reasonable theory when he added that the brothers had
told Oziel Kitty would have been a witness to the
slaying of Jose.

Yes, Abramson countered, there were talks with
Cignarelli and Oziel, but that did not mean that Erik
had told either of them the true motivation for the

killings. To do that, he would have had to reveal shameful secrets he had spent most of his life concealing.

Lansing added that the brothers had kept silent after they "made the decision they were not going to reveal the family secrets."

Those opening arguments set the table. Public interest was already high, and the day's revelations only turned up the temperature. The very first person not officially connected to the case to get a seat in the courtroom on opening day was a screenwriter.

The opposing lawyers announced that the three key players still alive in the drama—Lyle, Erik, and Dr. Oziel—all would be placed on the witness stand in the weeks to come.

When they did testify, the outpouring of stories about the sordid behavior, the true nightmare on Elm Drive, would shock everyone.

19

Trial

The prosecution always begins a trial, bringing on witnesses and laying out evidence to back up the charges brought against the accused. That portion of the job was made substantially easier in the Menendez case when the brothers admitted their guilt. However, if the state of California wanted to send Lyle and Erik to the San Quentin gas chamber, Bozanich and Kuriyama would have to defeat the quirky defense of child abuse. Therefore, even though the guilty verdict was in their pocket, they would play this just as if the boys were sticking with their pleas of innocent. The jurors needed to be pounded hard on the brutality of the murders, and they were.

Beverly Hills police dispatcher Christine Nye was the first witness called, stepping to the stand just after the opening arguments on Monday. She had fielded Lyle's incoherent 911 call on August 20, 1989, and was able to testify that the young caller had sounded as if he were falling apart. That contrasted sharply with what the jurors already knew—that Lyle's terror was feigned, that he was just putting on an act. A tape recording of the emergency call would be played later in the week to allow the jury to catch the overwhelming emotion evident in the voice. It would leave them wondering whether anybody was *that* good an actor.

The next move by Bozanich and Kuriyama showed just how gruesome the trial was going to be, and made several jurors sorry they had been selected. A pair of bloodstained tennis shoes, the very shoes Kitty Menendez was wearing the night she was slaughtered, was shown to the jurors. This sort of physical evidence usually provokes a mental jolt for those weighing the case, because it demonstrates that they are not dealing with some abstract legal theory. Kitty actually wore those shoes, tennies probably not unlike shoes the jurors had in their own closets. Of course, their shoes were not soaked in blood. They didn't know the victims, but anyone could relate to shoes.

Having won the attention of the court, the prosecutors then set up a bulletin board and displayed a color photograph. It depicted the corpse of Jose Menendez, his white shirt splotched with blood, sitting askew on the corner of the couch. What was left of his head was tilted at an awkward angle. The body of his wife lay at his feet, dead in a pool of blood. The pictures served to introduce Jose and Kitty as people, not just names that had been bandied about in the opening statements. They had been alive, and now, as anyone could see from the photograph, they were quite dead. And their sons had killed them, a fact painfully clear to the jurors.

Naturally, the defense lawyers had put up strong arguments to suppress that photograph and the even more horrific autopsy photos that would soon follow, "meat shots" as they are known in the trade. The stomach-turning portrayals of slaughtered victims always have an impact on jury members who cannot imagine such nightmarish things. But Bozanich would win the judge's permission to hang up five pictures from the murder scene and a dozen closeup autopsy

pictures that would clearly show the damage done to
Kitty and Jose, including one closeup of Kitty's
wrecked face, a dead eye open and staring toward the
camera. The other eye is gone. When a defense lawyer
protested that the pictures were too gory to be shown
to the jury, Bozanich responded, "Those who have
committed crimes like these, it ill behooves them to
complain of the carnage they leave." A deputy medical examiner, Dr. Irwin Golden, would testify later
that the human wreckage had been so extensive that
he was never able to determine exactly how many
shots had been fired.

When the picture of their parents went up, Lyle and
Erik kept their faces empty and betrayed nothing.
Stone cold and staring, they ignored both the photo-
graph and their mother's shoes.

Then the prosecutors produced a tape recording,
not from the now-famous Oziel library of audiocassettes, but from the Beverly Hills Police Department,
where Erik was interviewed shortly after the murders.
Jurors heard Erik, who would not be arrested for
another seven months, tell detectives his version of
what had happened that night, as the prosecution
sought to demonstrate that the boys had carefully built
an alibi to cover their tracks. "I don't understand
why, why there was blood everywhere . . . there was
blood everywhere. I didn't even hear anything and I
don't understand why the hell nobody came out of the
house when I came home," Erik said. In a statement
that would haunt him later, Erik also told the cops that
he had smelled gun smoke when he and Lyle walked
in and found their parents dead.

Bob Anderson, a charter boat captain, came to the
stand to describe the peculiar shark-fishing trip that
the Menendez family had taken the day before the
shootings. The main thing the skipper remembered

was that Erik and Lyle had remained at the bow of the thirty-one-foot boat throughout most of the seven-hour trip, although they were freezing and soaked to the skin by breaking waves and a cold ocean breeze.

Jose and Kitty had stayed in the stern and cabin of the *Motion Picture Marine,* with Anderson, his girl-friend, and a deckhand. Anderson recalled that there was hardly any interaction between the boys and their parents, from the time he pulled the boat out of Marina del Rey until they came back to the dock seven hours later. The brothers climbed down from their freezing perch to stand in the stern only a few times. For almost any other family, such an expedition would have been an exciting foray at sea. For the Menendez troop, it was only a trip filled with tension.

Jill Lansing described the boys' action as an attempt by them to stay beyond the reach of their father. Leslie Abramson, after complaining loudly about continually being ambushed by television cameras, used the pres-ence of the TV lens to state outside of court that Lyle and Erik had been trying to hide on the small boat, afraid that the voyage was part of an elaborate con-spiracy to kill them. The other half of the scenario— why the boys would have gotten on the boat in the first place if they were afraid of being murdered and dumped at sea—was left hanging. She was developing a habit that would last throughout the trial, of com-plaining bitterly about media coverage while unhesitat-ingly using the cameras to put a positive defense spin on whatever had happened in court that day.

ABC-TV had been involved with the story from the first, when Diane Sawyer, a former office aide to Richard Nixon and now a TV hostess, had leafed through the family photo album alongside grand-mother Maria Menendez. Since then, the network had run interviews with both Judalon Smyth and Dr. Oziel, and after the first day of testimony there was an interview with Dominick Dunne. The writer observed that he had been watching Maria Menendez and Jose's two sisters during the opening arguments and that "nothing happened on their faces as they heard these extraordinary charges of oral and anal sex." Marta Cano, Jose's sister from West Palm Beach, retorted hotly, calling together some cameras herself and claiming that Dunne was off base. She said that she and her sister had been fighting to hold back tears as the lawyers made their wrenching statements about the family's behavior, and that Maria was "practically in a fetal position." Dunne did not back down, but cushioned his own response by saying that the women could have felt strong emotions without showing it. It would not be the last time that Dunne, and his work, would be involved in side issues. His personal celebrity status did not mean he was the best reporter at the trial. In fact, one Princeton newspaper observer wrote that "Dominick Dunne is the lesser-known brother of novelist John Gregory Dunne and a man who has experienced the destruction of a crime of passion. His daughter was murdered by her boyfriend. . . . He leaves no rumor untouched."

On Thursday, July 22, the police tape of Lyle's interview at headquarters was played in court, as the prosecution pounded away at the brothers' lies. He described how he and Erik were out of the house, watching *Batman* at a Century City theater, when their parents were murdered. He also gave a hint of how the brothers viewed their powerful father. "His motto is 'A deal a day,' " Lyle told detectives. "If you're weaker, you lose." The tape also disclosed that Jose could be ruthless in business and liked to "squeeze out smaller companies."

Detective Sergeant Tom Edmonds, who had listened to the boys' explanations during the separate interviews, said that both had seemed traumatized by their grisly find and presented police with a decent alibi. Because of that, he had chosen not to test their hands for the presence of gunpowder residue. Still, Edmonds said, he wondered about Erik's statement of smelling gunpowder upon entering the death room. "Smoke dissipates very quickly," the veteran policeman said. It was a point that police had kept coming back to during their investigation, because the timing didn't fit. Neighbors had heard the apparent gunshots about 10:00 P.M., and the 911 call came in at 11:47—almost two hours later and with plenty of time for the smoke to have cleared.

Perry Berman, who had known the brothers for about five years, dating back to their days in Princeton, was the star witness for the day. It was Berman whom Lyle Menendez called the day of the murders, allegedly to ironclad their alibi. An old tennis pal, and one of their many coaches, Berman testified that Lyle had called him on Sunday afternoon and arranged to meet at 10:15 P.M. at the Santa Monica Civic Auditorium, for the "Taste of L.A." festival. When the brothers did not keep that appointment, Berman returned home, only to get another call from Lyle "sometimes after eleven." Lyle, in a voice that seemed anxious to Berman, apologized for not showing up and said he and Erik now wanted to meet at the Cheesecake Factory in Beverly Hills, right after the brothers went home to pick up a fake identification card so the underage Erik could buy a drink. They never showed up there either. What they told police was that when they went home to get the ID card, they had stumbled onto the murder scene.

The prosecution wanted to prove the boys had cobbled together an alibi, complete with Berman, a witness who never saw anything pertinent on the night of the murders. It wasn't really necessary to do so, because the brothers had already admitted they pulled the triggers. What was really on the table here was not that Lyle and Erik were killers, but that they were also liars! Kuriyama and Bozanich hoped to impeach the credibility of the Menendez brothers before they had a chance to testify. If they would lie about an alibi, what else would they lie about?

The Berman testimony was jolted off track on cross-examination as the defense twisted the spotlight away from the brothers and onto Jose. Berman, who had seen the family frequently over the years, described how Jose ran the household with strict discipline, treating Kitty, Lyle, and Erik as if they were a company and he were "chairman of the board." Before he was done, Berman's tour through the Menendez family dynamics made him sound almost like a witness for the defense.

Like the proverbial bad penny, Oziel's name popped up again beyond the courtroom during the first week of trial. The state Board of Psychology accused Dr. Oziel of illegally allowing the therapy sessions of Lyle and Erik to be tape-recorded, and also said he had furnished two women with drugs without prescriptions. The board, in a sixteen-page complaint, further claimed that the therapist had been romantically involved with both women. Oziel's own attorney scoffed at the reports as an attempt to discredit him. The board disclosed only the initials of the women, not their names—J.S. and A.K. The allegations unerringly followed the story line that had been given out by Judalon Smyth.

Inside the courtroom on Friday, Judge Weisberg dealt a setback to the prosecutors, indicating that he probably would not allow the jurors to view the *Friends* screenplay that Erik had coauthored. Prosecutors claimed the story was a blueprint for murder, while the defense said it was merely the rambling of a couple of schoolboys. The judge put off his ruling for a few days, but clearly believed that the screenplay was so remote from the case that it was not relevant. In addition, co-author and best friend Craig Cignarelli testified, with the juries absent, that he did not think the story had anything to do with the killings.

After the first of many weeks of trial, Bozanich gave a brief interview to Alan Abrahamson of the *Los Angeles Times*, in which she declared investigators had found "no evidence of physical or sexual abuse." But on the mental abuse point, the can of worms opened inadvertently by Berman, the prosecutor had to concede that Jose "was domineering, controlling, overbearing and very hard to live with."

"You don't kill people you love," she said, in an explanation that lapsed into the Hollywood banter that stuck to this trial like glue. "We're not saying this family was *Ozzie and Harriet*. Or even a *Leave It to Beaver* family. This was more like *Father Knows Best Meets Godzilla*."

With Godzilla and the Beav now in the story, it was not surprising that the press began to talk about the Three Musketeers testifying the following week. But Craig Cignarelli, Donovan Goodreau, and Glenn Stevens would have changed the Musketeers' motto from "All for one and one for all" to "Every man for himself." Jose would have been proud. They turned on Erik and Lyle like a bunch of snakes.

Craig Cignarelli was a witness from central casting, the sort of good-looking young man who might appear as a witness in a television drama, someone not rough-edged enough to be real. A pair of giggling girls were his escorts to the trial when he testified against his former best pal. The Shepherd and the King were no longer on speaking terms.

Now a twenty-three-year-old student at the University of California in Santa Barbara, Cignarelli told the court that Erik Menendez, during a walk around the grounds of the big Beverly Hills house on September 1, 1989, only a few days after the murders, had flatly admitted killing his parents.

"Do you want to know how it happened?" Erik had asked, and Craig said he did.

"He said he was coming home from a movie and that he was going inside to get his ID, a fake ID, to go out to the bars," Cignarelli testified. "He said that he went back outside and his brother was standing there with two shotguns and said, 'Let's do it.' And they walked inside and Lyle was standing—or Erik went up to the door on the left, which was slightly open . . . Lyle went up and put his shoulder against the door on the right. And Erik said he looked in, saw his parents sitting on the couch. And Lyle swung open the door and shot his father and looked at Erik, and said, 'Shoot Mom.' And Erik said he shot his mom and she was standing up, yelling."

"I wasn't sure if I believed it," Cignarelli said, recalling his own astonishment at the admission. After the confession, the boys went inside for a game of chess.

In court, Erik kept his eyes pinned on Craig, who avoided the stare. It was the first time the defendant had paid such rapt attention to a witness's testimony.

Cignarelli was not in for an easy ride, however, as the defense lawyers took him to task for not having a clear recollection of things that had happened four years previous.

He admitted that in a November 17, 1989, interview with police, he told them Erik had confessed in October. But he also mentioned that a man believed to be a computer expert had been at the house that day, and police said that person had gone to North Elm Drive on September 1, not in October. Cignarelli then changed his story to match the police date.

He also admitted, under cross-examination, that he gave police in November a slightly different version of Erik's confession. At that time, Cignarelli claimed that Erik had told him of a plan they'd had in which Lyle would kill Jose and Erik would shoot Kitty, but that Lyle had opened fire first on both parents. In that version, Erik shot Kitty twice, but only after he thought she was already dead.

"I wasn't sure if he was telling the truth and I didn't want to be the one who turned him in," Cignarelli said. But Abramson shot back, "You were willing to help the police to get your best friend arrested, right?" Her question appeared to put loyalty for a childhood chum above bringing a murderer to justice.

Cignarelli might not have wanted to do in Erik, but he agreed, only twelve days after the police interview, to wear a tape recorder and hope that Erik would again admit to the killings. However, while they ate a seafood dinner at Gladstone's, Erik did not give a repeat performance.

The testimony was interesting but had nothing to do with knocking a hole in the abuse defense. Certainly, if he was trying to paint Erik as a liar, his own credibility was in similar jeopardy. Cignarelli and his girls might have been cute, but from a legal standpoint, he was a waste of time.

The only really important development in court that day involving Cignarelli came when Judge Weisberg handed down his formal decision that the screenplay that Craig and Erik had written would not be submitted as evidence. The jurist claimed the story had been written too long before the shootings to have had any relevance to the crime. The screenplay was written in 1988, and Jose and Kitty were shot to death in 1989, but the jurors would not hear the tale of a rich boy who kills his parents for their fortune, which was exactly the line the prosecution was trying to sell.

Twenty-six-year-old Donovan Goodreau, another best friend, followed Cignarelli to the stand and did not fare much better. He testified that, when he was evicted from the Princeton dormitory room he had shared with Lyle as a nonstudent, he'd noticed that both his driver's license and his wallet were missing. That driver's license, which listed Donovan Jay Goodreau as a six-foot-one white male weighing 165 pounds and born on January 11, 1967, was used on August 18, 1989, as identification by someone to purchase a pair of shotguns from a Big 5 Sporting Goods store on Convoy Street in San Diego. The Mossberg 12-gauge guns, both model No. 50406, cost $199.99 apiece and were used two days after they were bought to kill Jose and Kitty Menendez. Goodreau could prove he was not even in California on that day, and the height, weight, and age listed on the ID were almost a perfect match for Erik Menendez.

Goodreau also testified that he had once confided to Lyle that, when he was a little boy, he had been sexually molested. Lyle, he said, did not respond with any similar sort of remark about himself and never mentioned being molested during the entire time they were roommates.

The defense quickly began to gnaw on Goodreau's credibility, too. Rejecting a freedom-of-press argument, Judge Weisberg compelled author Richard Rand to give up an audiotape that he had made during a March 1992 interview with Goodreau. On the tape, which later was broadcast on television, Goodreau said Lyle had once confessed that Jose had indeed abused his sons. He said Jose Menendez "would take baths with them and stuff like that . . . it's weird."

Which version was the truth? Goodreau self-destructed as a witness for the prosecution.

Next came Glenn Stevens, twenty-three, another "best friend" of Lyle's, and a virtual funnel of information for police. Stevens was also a former roommate of Lyle's at Princeton, was with him in the Jeep the day of the arrest, and continued to manage the chicken-wing business for him while his boss was in the slammer. His primary testimony would show that Lyle had Goodreau's driver's license long after Goodreau had already been booted out of the dorm. Again, it was not only a prosecution attempt to show how the license had ended up being used to buy shotguns, but an attempt to paint Lyle as a scheming thief and a liar.

Lansing and Abramson made quick work of Stevens, the former friend turned police snitch. He, too, seemed to have trouble understanding that pesky Princeton honor code. As the defense lawyers hammered him for discrepancies on his résumé, Stevens defended his actions. "That's the way they taught us at Princeton, to embellish a little on the résumé," he said. He had listed himself as valedictorian of his high school class, said he oversaw twenty employees at the chicken-wing emporium, and claimed he did the accounting for the business. The truth was different; he was never class valedictorian, he managed only five employees, and he just delivered the business receipts to the real accountant. He also confirmed that the business's receipts, which had been averaging eighteen hundred dollars a day, suddenly had dropped to about five hundred a day after Lyle was arrested and Stevens began managing the place. It was also pointed out that when the arrests went down, Stevens was wearing one of Lyle's Rolex watches, which he later sold, pocketing the money.

Still, Stevens tried to portray himself as one of the good guys in helping the cops nail Lyle. "Friendship transcends a lot of things, but homicide is not one of them," he proclaimed. The jurors could well have wondered just what kind of moral compass Stevens owned.

20

The Perfect Crime

There would be a total of twenty-six witnesses for the prosecution's first phase of the trial, but most of them were minor players—ranging from Lyle's former bodyguards to the store clerk who sold Erik the shotguns. All they could do was build a web around the issue of guilt. They did little to argue against the expected defense of abuse. For that, Bozanich and Kuriyama had to reach for their star witness—none other than the beleaguered Dr. L. Jerome Oziel.

Judge Weisberg, on Thursday, July 29, declared that the Beverly Hills psychologist would be allowed to testify in front of both juries. But first the judge would have Oziel brief him on what his testimony might contain, after which he would decide what would be presented to the juries.

There was no doubt that Oziel presented the biggest threat to the brothers, particularly after early testimony, out of earshot of the jurors, directly contradicted the defense theory of child abuse because Lyle and Erik never had said a word about such behavior to Oziel. For the prosecution, the motive was greed.

The psychotherapist was going to testify that the boys wanted to kill Jose because he was a dominating force that made them feel inferior. Kitty was murdered

because they did not want to leave her behind as a
witness, Oziel said in the preliminary session. If unchallenged, his testimony could be damning.

But Oziel, already battered by the allegations made
by his former lover, Judalon Smyth, and the new
attack from the state Board of Psychology, was under
no misconception about what lay ahead for him in that
cozy courtroom. Not only would he be forced to
disclose what his patients told him in privacy, but he
knew that the defense lawyers, particularly Abramson,
were stewing for a fight. She said she planned to use
"every way known to man and God" to ruin Oziel in
the eyes of the jurors. In coming weeks, she would
refer to him as the Great Satan, and claim he had all
the credibility of a doughnut hole.

Only a few days before he was called to testify,
Oziel took his story to a nationwide television audience, explaining on ABC-TV that he was reluctant to
reveal anything at all about any patient, even one who
had threatened to kill him. In a high-minded statement,
he said, "A therapist is like a priest or a minister in
the sense that people come in and confess. I, and any
therapist, carries with him or with her at all times
hundreds or thousands of people's secrets. And it is a
sacred obligation to preserve those secrets, unless the
law mandates that one does otherwise." But later, in
his testimony, he would comment that he would never
"make the analogy that what patients tell their psychotherapist is the equivalent of what they tell their
priest." Even after all of the case law that had been
argued, the point was still unclear, even to the psychotherapist most directly involved.

Still, Oziel spelled bad news for the defense. On that
very first day in court, in his briefing to the judge he
said Lyle and Erik had appeared to be "immensely
pleased with the excitement of pulling off these crimes
without being caught." Although the critical tape re-

cordings remained sealed, Oziel did have a transcript of his notes at hand to refresh his memory.

His summary of Erik's recollections hinted at the icy calculations of which the brothers were capable. When they drew up their plan, they had refused to change it in order to spare Kitty. "If the plan was altered, it wouldn't be perfect, and they wouldn't be able to kill their father at all," the psychotherapist stated.

His testimony, indeed, promised to be poisonous stuff.

On Friday, July 30, as the trial ended its second week, Oziel continued to brief the judge on his future testimony. The jurors were still not in the room as Weisberg determined what the therapist could or could not say. His rulings left both the prosecution and defense holding the half a loaf of victory.

The important point won by the defense was a ban on the therapist's use of the word *sociopath* in front of the juries. Oziel told the court he had described to the boys the difference between a crime of passion and a premeditated assault, and that they had exchanged startled looks and said, "We're sociopaths."

Although the brothers had used the term themselves, the judge said it was just too hot a label to announce to a panel of ordinary people, perhaps even so prejudicial as to prevent the defendants from receiving a fair trial. Instead, Weisberg said Oziel could testify about the definition of the word without actually mentioning it. He could say that the killings had been planned and did not take place as an act of passion.

For the prosecution, it did not seem to be a significant loss, and after court that day, Bozanich said she was confident that by the end of the trial the jury would know exactly what a sociopath was. The lead prosecutor had good reason to be upbeat. The judge had handed her a plum, ruling that Oziel could testify about how the brothers had mapped out the murders.

"We just get turned on by planning the murder. Once we plan it, nothing gets in the way. Once we start, nothing will stop us," Oziel would be able to say the boys told him. "And we can't change the plan because it's already perfectly formed." Not only was it a clear admission of premeditated murder, but the comments did not contain a single word about childhood abuse.

It was time to bring in the juries and let Oziel tell his story to the people who would decide the fates of Lyle and Erik Menendez.

It was Wednesday, August 4, when Dr. Oziel began to pull the curtain aside on the dark confidences that his clients, Erik and Lyle Menendez, had shared with him almost four years earlier. It was a cold, mirthless recounting of murder most foul, and the jurors were shaken by the therapist's tale of horror. Although Oziel and his tape recordings had been at the center of the case for several years, this was his first time to speak publicly about the matter, and Judge Weisberg shuffled the juries in and out of the courtroom throughout the day, depending upon what Oziel was going to say. Some information was meant solely for Erik's jury, other material could be heard only by Lyle's jury, and some information was heard by both.

Oziel described how Erik had contacted him on Halloween day, 1989, and, after a brief walk in the park, admitted that "We did it. We killed our parents." The idea, according to Erik, came to the brothers while they watched a British Broadcasting Company television show in which one of the characters killed his parents. The initials "BBC" would soon become very important.

In the October 31 meeting and a follow-up session on November 2, the brothers elaborated on the crime, saying Jose was "a dominating force and a negative force" who was "impossible to live with." In addition, Erik and Lyle thought their father was drawing up a new will that would cut them out of the family fortune. Lyle insisted to the therapist, however, that the murders were not over money, but out of hatred.

One of the more difficult parts of their plan was that they had decided their mother had to die also. "Although they felt the mother didn't deserve to die, shouldn't die, they included her in the plan," Oziel said.

"Erik told me his father said, 'No! No!' and turned away. The mother was shot second, as she was beginning to stand . . . and she fell to the ground." Then, the younger brother told his therapist, Kitty was "moaning and trying to crawl away," so Lyle reloaded his shotgun and "finished off the job." During Oziel's presentation, Erik showed little emotion, his eyes staring down at the polished defense table, while Lyle slowly shook his head, as if in disbelief.

That was an odd reaction from Lyle, based on what he knew the doctor would testify to next. Not only did the boys pick up the used shotgun shells and hide their bloodstained clothing and the weapons, but they later told Oziel they thought they had pulled off the "perfect crime." In particular, the therapist said Lyle confided that "he knew his father would have been proud of him for killing him" and doing such a good job at the grisly task.

Oziel also testified on the vital point of the threats made against him, the very comments that broke the pledge of confidentiality between patient and therapist. When Lyle stormed into the office on October 31, after Erik had confessed, the psychologist believed Lyle to be a menacing figure and a strong threat. It was not until the next session, on November 2, that it was revealed that the brothers had sat in the car and actually discussed that possibility.

"How do we kill Dr. Oziel?" Lyle had asked, but Erik had wimped out, saying he was "not up to killing anyone else." So they decided, apparently, just to frighten him. "He [Lyle] said it wouldn't look too good if I disappeared too soon. Because if I did, it might begin to cast an unwelcome light on them," Oziel testified. The threat seemed to have worked, to a degree. Oziel only told his wife and his ex-girlfriend, who later took the news to the cops.

After the threat, Oziel was terrified, he stated as the defense began its cross-examination.

"Why did you not call police?" Leslie Abramson asked him.

"I thought I would be killed," Oziel replied.

Instead, Oziel said, he telephoned some lawyers and fellow therapists for their views on the applicable laws and ethics of the profession, but he could not reach the attorneys. It wasn't until three days later that he finally contacted his attorney about the situation, but in the meantime, Oziel had acted on his own. A therapist he had talked to had confirmed the point that he was duty bound to warn anyone who might be in danger, so Oziel telephoned his wife, told her of the trouble, and urged her to take their children and leave the house immediately.

At that point in his testimony Oziel finally had to step into the Judalon Smyth trap, for the defense attorneys left him no choice. After talking to his wife, Oziel said, he went over to Smyth's house, to see the woman that Abramson claimed was his "romantic love girlfriend person."

"I definitely felt that she was in danger," the therapist responded. Although Lyle and Erik didn't even know the woman existed, Oziel said he thought they might raid his house and find her address and notes about his personal relationship with her. The state Supreme Court had ruled much earlier that he did nothing incorrect by warning Smyth, but Abramson was relentless in undermining his credibility, showing the jury that the clean-cut professional man before them was also a man who cheated on his wife.

Under further probing, Oziel said his notes of the October 31 and November 2 sessions were not written down, but had been tape-recorded. Abramson drew from him the fact that he did not even make those recordings until much later, possibly up to two weeks, during which time he had seen dozens of other patients. The therapist insisted that there was nothing wrong with his memory.

Finally, the question was raised as to whether or not Judalon Smyth actually had been in Oziel's office while an Erik-and-Lyle session was under way. She had claimed she had overheard what was said. Oziel maintained that she knew only what he had told her.

Under the harsh questioning of the defense attorneys, the facade of the therapist began to crack. He had insisted that it was Smyth who was the pursuer in their affair, but telephone records proved that he had called her frequently, sometimes chatting for a minute or, on at least one occasion, talking for almost four and one-half hours. He also admitted taking her on a vacation. This was not the sort of behavior expected from a man of his stature, and at one point, Leslie Abramson rolled her eyes in disbelief, a bit of stage-craft that was not unnoticed by the juries or the judge. Weisberg warned her to be more professional.

Still, Oziel insisted he did not think Smyth had overheard any of the vital October 31 therapy session. "I'm positive she wasn't sitting on my desk or rubbing my neck," he said. But he did cough up the knowledge that Smyth had indeed been in the waiting room on

November 2, when Erik and Lyle came back to discuss the killings further, the day they made the threat. Defense lawyers jumped on him for not giving out that detail before. He said he had never before been asked about it while he was under oath. Still, Oziel insisted that he had not told her to be there, and that she had shown up on her own.

He would occupy the witness stand for six days, and while his testimony contained lurid details about the therapist's own life and habits, his history had little to do with the central issue. Unchallenged was the fact that the boys had admitted to him that they had killed their parents. And, even after the parents were dead, the brothers had never discussed the subject of sexual abuse with him. Anything else that Oziel said was rather immaterial. "A cheap edition of *Divorce Court*," sniffed prosecutor Bozanich as the cross-examination dragged on and on and on.

Although his story had some credibility flaws, Oziel finally was dismissed as a witness without having caved in either to Abramson's tantrums or to the subtle, relentless pressure from Michael Burt, one of Lyle's lawyers. The therapist walked out of the courtroom, but not out of the story. The Smyth-Oziel show would return. Amy Fisher and Joey Buttafuoco they weren't, but it wasn't for lack of trying. For the moment, the prosecution's key witness had done his job effectively. He might not be without blemish, but as far as the jurors were concerned, the man had heard what he had heard. The brothers had told him about planning and executing the perfect crime in killing their parents, then laid a threat of death on Oziel. And, maddeningly for the defense, the psychotherapist had backed up the contention of the prosecution that sexual abuse was not an issue in the decision by Lyle and Erik to blow away Mom and Pop.

Embedded in the minds of the jurors was the image

of Kitty Menendez, moaning in pain from multiple shotgun wounds, trying to crawl to safety, as her elder son stepped forward with his shotgun and "finished off the job." This wasn't a case about a psychotherapist and his former girlfriend. It was still about murder.

21

The BBC

The prosecution was nearing the end of its presentation, with one niggling item that still needed clarification—the BBC movie the brothers had mentioned. Investigators believed the boys had been correct when they told Oziel about the movie, and assumed it was a product of the British Broadcasting Company. Scotland Yard had even been brought into the matter in an effort to track it down. After running into many obstacles, they finally stumbled upon the right answer purely by accident.

Lester Kuriyama and his family went shopping for a video in early August, and when his wife reached for *The Addams Family*, she noticed a video box in the rack just beneath it, entitled *The Billionaire Boys' Club*. The movie, also known by its initials of *BBC*, was broadcast on NBC on the final two nights of July in 1989, only twenty or so days before the murders, and the brothers had watched it, entranced. When Kuriyama rented the tape and gave it a preview, he understood their fascination. "It sent chills up my spine," the prosecutor said. While the jury was out of the court, he tried to have it introduced into evidence through heated arguments with Abramson.

The Billionaire Boys' Club bears an astonishing

number of similarities to the murders of Jose and Kitty Menendez.

It is the true story of a group of idle, rich young men from privileged families with the best addresses in Los Angeles, including Beverly Hills, who become entangled in a scheme to get even richer quick, without actually having to do any real work. Led by someone who had been a social outcast during their prep school days, this chic gang that can't do anything right, other than dress in Italian suits and drive fancy motor vehicles, eventually find themselves up to their manicured fingernails in murder most foul.

They think they're con men, but they get outconned by an even smoother operator, whom the leader of the pack, with his muscle man bodyguard, then executes. Finally, with tens of thousands of dollars' worth of inheritances gone up in smoke, and with their BBC organization with its pretty secretaries and fancy offices facing bankruptcy, they plot to help another privileged youngster bump off his oil-rich father to get the man's assets. They are convinced they have committed the perfect crimes, but, like all crooks, they are wrong. The leader, who has suckered the playboys into his web, goes to prison for murder.

Sitting down to watch the movie today, even years after the Menendez slaughter, a viewer is struck by the fact that Lyle and Erik could have found in *The BBC* nothing less than a blueprint for a similar crime. Among the glaring similarities:

- There is a character, a brother, named Eric.
- The young men are all dapper, educated, handsome, suave products of successful families and wise in the ways of the Los Angeles upper crust.
- The leader asks the question, "If you could be absolutely certain you would not get caught, would you kill someone for a million dollars?" When the

question is answered in the negative, he follows up by asking if the person would kill if he saw his mother being raped. The answer then is affirmative, which the leader points out means that the person is indeed capable of killing, and would "cross the line," if the motive seemed proper.

• The leader is an outsider, just as the two Menendez brothers had never fully integrated with their peers.

• The BBC runs an investment from five million dollars up to fourteen million. The estate of Jose Menendez was exactly fourteen million.

• Following a murder, one character asks another, "Who is your alibi?" The answer is, "You." The Menendez brothers also depended upon each other to provide an alibi.

• The first murder victim is shot in the back of the head, just as Lyle shot his father.

• Multiple shotgun blasts are used on the first victim, and the murderer claims that with the body so butchered, it could not be recognized. He adds that it was so cool that, after one shot, the victim's brain actually jumped out of his head and landed on his chest. The violence in the Menendez television room mirrored such a scene.

• The film considers the crime perfect, and one comments that his brother "Eric was right in the middle of it."

• Eric, in the film, says, "Life is getting like a movie." In real life, Erik wore a Rolex watch and had an open-top Jeep, just as the lead character did in the movie.

• During the film investigation, friends lie to protect the murderers. Throughout the Menendez case, investigators would have difficulty piecing together who—the boys, their relatives, their friends—was telling the truth and when they chose to do so.

Kuriyama wanted to show the film to the jury, and Weisberg cracked, "Are you going to sell popcorn?" But the judge was not as intrigued as the prosecutors were with the film. Just as he had barred the screenplay *Friends* from being placed into evidence, he also prevented the introduction of *The BBC*. If the jurors wanted to see it, they would have to wait until the trial was done and go rent it themselves.

As the prosecution neared the end of the first part of its case (it would be allowed to present some witnesses in rebuttal after the defense presented its case), Bozanich and Kuriyama made a few more significant points to further tarnish the clean-cut images of the two young men who sat before the jurors.

The big money-spending spree that the brothers went on was paraded, price tags and all—the plan to buy a condominium costing almost a million bucks, the sixty-four-thousand-dollar Porsche, the chicken-wing business, the twenty-four-grand-per-month apartment rental at Marina del Rey, and more. A hurricane of dollars thrown about. According to Kuriyama, Lyle and Erik had demonstrated an "intent to spend large sums of money shortly after the killing of their parents." Before Jose and Kitty died, the boys were virtually broke. Afterward, they had a mint.

And finally, Kuriyama brought in the matter of the burglaries in Calabasas. He read an official statement that said Erik, while at a friend's home in July 1988, had found a slip of paper with the combination of a safe written on it. He popped the safe open and stole money and jewelry, then two weeks later, and joined by Lyle, burglarized a second house. The net take was worth an estimated hundred thousand dollars. Accompanied by his father and an attorney, Erik had surrendered in September of that year and given a statement admitting his own guilt without implicating anyone else. Authorities had bought the deal and let Lyle skate free, keeping his record felony free, while little brother Erik, a juvenile, got slapped on the wrist.

Whether they looked preppy or not, the brothers who sat in court had been proven to be liars, murderers, and thieves. So Bozanich and Kuriyama had reason to be satisfied with the overall case they had presented, and the prosecution rested against Lyle Menendez on Friday, August 13. The case against Erik would be completed the following Monday, wrapping up a total of four weeks of prosecution evidence.

"We had to fight tooth and nail for every piece of evidence we put in. But we got it in, and it's intact," Bozanich declared after court on Friday. "Now they're going to put the parents on trial. And since the parents are dead, they can't say much about it, can they?"

Abramson naturally had a different viewpoint. "Now we start talking about what really happened," she declared. A family history that was already portrayed as more than a bit warped was about to get downright dirty.

22

Defense

"Every time someone picked his nose and the father slapped his hand, that's not going to be before the jury. This is not a novel, where someone's life history is put before a jury. This is a trial," Judge Stanley Weisberg warned from the bench as Jill Lansing and Leslie Abramson prepared to open their defense.

It was a timely statement, because the heart of the effort to parry the prosecution's claims of cold-blooded murder was to win jury sympathy through allegation after allegation of childhood abuse. Even with the stipulation from the bench, the defense started playing its abuse cards early and often.

But the judge was firm, at least at first, until he, too, seemed to wear down under the barrage of testimony. The first defense witness was Marta Menendez Cano, Jose's sister, whose initial testimony was heard with the juries out of the room. Weisberg wanted a preview. Cano said Jose had told her directly that he planned to be a tough-love kind of father, with the goal of making his boys stronger, particularly Erik, whom Jose described as being "too tender." Weisberg noted that those conversations took place back in the 1970s, were not relevant to the trial, and would not be admissible as evidence. There was a round of head-shaking—

Cano, Abramson, Erik, Lansing, Lyle—as the aunt left the stand, useless as a witness on that Monday, August 16.

More than ninety witnesses were to be called by the defense, however, so Abramson and Lansing were not staggered by the initial setback. In fact, witness number two, University of Southern California psychology professor John Briere, immediately put things right. Briere, as an expert witness, introduced the element of abuse and linked the behavior patterns of battered women and abused children. Eventually, he said, either type of victim may lash out violently at the perpetrator, even years after the abuse took place.

So why didn't Erik or Lyle tell somebody about the problems they were enduring? Briere said that was simple. They were males, and ashamed of what had happened. ''Men abused as children don't tell people about it. They feel they're going to be judged harshly,'' he said.

The lawyers then quickly moved the jury from the theoretical to the practical, real world and brought on Alan Andersen, a cousin from Lisle, Illinois, who had spent several summers in the Menendez home. Now, even as a man thirty-one years of age, Andersen was still uncomfortable recalling the strain that existed within the household, where everyone stuffed his true feelings deeply inside of himself. ''Emotion was something you did not show. It was a sign of weakness,'' he said. And weakness, in the book of Jose Menendez, was almost the original sin.

Still, Andersen testified, he never actually *saw* any evidence of sexual abuse during his visits in the 1970s, and he was never struck by either Jose or Kitty. Punishment was verbal and stern, and sometimes he was locked in his room, a punishment also dealt to the brothers.

However, he brought up the abuse issue, for he had

watched while Jose took off his belt and whipped his children until they were bruised. When the boys were small, they would shower with their father following their tennis lessons, and occasionally Jose would haul one of the boys into a bedroom alone. "As soon as Jose took either one of the boys into their room, the door was locked behind them, and Kitty made clear that you did not go down the hallway."

Andersen said that Jose also enjoyed giving his sons boxing lessons. Andersen, at the age of sixteen, would kneel on the floor holding pillows as the little boys punched him. Erik, only six, had become withdrawn and introverted and was hesitant to hit his cousin, while nine-year-old Lyle would whale away as their father-coach encouraged them to learn to slug the opponent below the belt or in the back, and to surprise the enemy with a vicious blow. In other words, Jose was teaching them to win at all costs, even if it meant having to ignore civilized rules about fighting. Andersen said that he was glad Lyle was able to vent his aggression with the mock battles, because otherwise he would retreat to his bedroom and rip apart his stuffed animals.

The lawyers also turned some light on Kitty, to tear away her motherly surface. First of all, Andersen said, he once found a plastic jar filled with feces beneath the bed of one of the boys, thus indicating Kitty was a lousy housekeeper. She tried to make French toast for Lyle and Brian one morning, but threw eighteen eggs into the mix, so she was a lousy cook, too. She was also prone to flying into sudden rages. The witness stood and gritted his teeth, clenched his fists, and tensed until veins bulged in his neck to show how angry she could become. It was not unusual for her to fling crockery in the kitchen.

Dinner at the Menendez table was not a happy time, he testified, snapping his fingers to imitate how Jose would impatiently demand answers to questions he would toss out. "It was very much like a *Jeopardy* setting, with Jose quizzing the kids."

Jill Lansing cocked an eyebrow. "And if they didn't know the answers?"

"They were instructed to put down their knife and fork and go find the answer in a newspaper or encyclopedia. It was a very tense time. I did not enjoy digesting my food at the dinner table."

The jurors had heard all about the wealth and privilege, Beverly Hills and Rolex watches, tennis championships and Jose's big job. They were clearly uncomfortable as they began to see and hear the darker side of how the accused brothers grew up, and the tale was just beginning.

The next day, another cousin, Diane Vander Molen from Denver, said that during a 1976 visit, Lyle Menendez, only eight years old, had pointed toward his crotch and whispered that he and Jose had been "touching each other down there." The shocked Vander Molen summoned Kitty immediately, whose response was one of disbelief. Beginning to weep on the witness stand, she related how the mother had hauled her little boy upstairs and that the subject "was never discussed after that."

Vander Molen also testified that Kitty was fast with a car, ripping across Pennsylvania "at ninety-five miles per hour," and slow with a broom, leaving piles of pet shit lying around the house.

Weisberg had had about enough of this line of questioning. He had already fired a shot across the defense team's bow, and they seemed intent on parading a series of witnesses on the subject. He was still handling a murder trial, not a molestation trial. "This whole issue is being blown out of proportion," he declared. "That somehow there's a linkage between the molestation, if there was one, and the killings."

"It does not surprise me to hear the court say that," shot back Abramson. "It horrifies me, but it does not shock me."

"The fact that there was a molestation doesn't constitute a legal defense," the judge retorted. The temperature was definitely heating up between the judge and the defense attorney. Later, outside the courthouse, Abramson said that Weisberg apparently was considering this case in the same light as some liquor store heist, when it clearly was not an ordinary trial.

Without being able to play the molestation card, the defense would fail before it began, and the lawyers were not about to give it up. But Weisberg's comments may have given a clue about what his charge to the jury might eventually be—that molestation is not an excuse for murder. Abramson also said the idea of using such a defense had originated with the boys and not with her. Only after they had been jailed did Lyle and Erik finally confide the abuse to a psychiatrist and relatives, and only after that were the lawyers brought in on the secret, she said.

Still, Weisberg was throwing a quick gavel. For instance, he would not allow Vander Molen's sister, Kathleen Simonton, to testify how Kitty had flown into a rage because Kathleen wore a bikini at the Menendez swimming pool. The milder stuff that did get into her testimony, that Jose made her eat caviar unwillingly and how she cut her summer vacation with the Menendez family short, was barely helpful.

Vander Molen stuck by her abuse story during cross-examination, and she actually was able to expand on the theme. But she did admit that she had not told lawyers about Lyle's graphic admission of being groped by his father until June 1991, seven months after she first visited her cousin in jail. Prosecutor Bozanich accused her of rehearsing the testimony in prison, which Vander Molen denied. Bozanich also extracted that Vander Molen, like Andersen, had never actually witnessed any sexual abuse.

She said she had lived with the family during the summers of 1982 and 1983, when she was twenty-three and the brothers were aged fifteen and twelve. Then she testified that, even as adolescents, when Jose was gone from home on a business trip, the boys would take turns sleeping in their mother's bed. Further, she said that at those ages, the boys were sexually curious. Once, they tied her up while wrestling and stripped off her top. "They got me down to my bra, but it stopped there," she said. Another time, the three of them were watching television when Lyle, without warning, suddenly climbed atop her and "began fondling my breasts." She managed to stop that assault, too. The cross-examination had gone a step too far, letting in the specter of a couple of boys who were sleeping with their mother at the precise ages when they were curious enough about sex to grope their cousin.

The defense shifted focus, fighting a pitched battle to get permission for Cynthia Dawn McPhee, a former baby-sitter for Dr. Oziel, to testify. She had lived with the Oziel family for five years and had given defense attorneys a thick document of accusations they could use to smear the therapist's credibility. She'd had sex with him on a regular basis and he had drugged her, the lawyers said she would testify under oath. Weisberg ruled her story was primarily about the bitterness she felt toward the doctor, who had also had her arrested several times for vandalism and theft. It had nothing to do with the trial, he said. The defense had hoped to use her to bolster the idea that the doctor was a philanderer. They failed. McPhee was allowed on the stand for a mere six minutes, long enough to say she knew Oziel intimately and didn't like him.

On August 20, 1993, exactly four years after the

slayings, the march of the coaches began. The defense would bring in a string of people who had been hired to give sports lessons to the boys, only to find that the fat salary they were paid also meant they had to put up with the family's craziness.

Charles Wadlington, the first tennis coach Lyle and Erik had, choked with emotion as he described the training ordeal. But he, too, had to admit that, despite the stern regimen, he never observed any sexual abuse. For five years he coached the kids, competing for their attention with Jose, who would stand on the sidelines and shout orders to them. They practiced constantly, through rain or sickness or holidays. Erik, he said, would sometimes snap during a private lesson, retreat into his own mental world, and start smashing balls against a fence. He described Kitty as a brash, sarcastic woman whom he never saw crack a smile. Within the family, he said, he never saw any sign of "love and kindness and touching and hugging."

As for Jose, who fired Wadlington after an argument, the coach said he had worked with about a thousand tennis parents, all of them eager for their offspring to excel. Jose was the worst, he said. "I just couldn't stand the guy, because I saw him being mean to the boys."

Another tennis coach, William Kurtain, would testify that Jose had displayed the "insulting" habit of yelling at both the students and the coaches during tennis practice.

Swimming coach Meredith Geissler added to the picture of Jose always pushing his sons to do better. As Erik plunged into the pool during a race, Jose would stalk along the poolside, yelling for him to push harder, to go faster. At the finish line, he would yank the boy out of the water and deliver a loud lecture as the exhausted boy, dripping wet, listened with bowed head, humiliated before his teammates.

* * *

Marta Cano returned to the stand on August 24, to testify about abuse, but she stumbled into admitting that she had withheld information from investigating police. While being cross-examined, she said that she had withheld certain information because of pressures from relatives. Prosecutors wanted to know whether, in October of 1989, Detective Leslie Zoeller had specifically asked whether she was aware of problems within the Menendez household, and whether she told him she knew of no such thing. Cano insisted that Zoeller had not been precise enough with his questions to use the word "abuse." At the time, Cano testified, she did not think the inner workings of the family had any bearing on the killings.

Back then she was evasive to protect the family image. In court she was willing to do just the opposite, and said Kitty and Jose were cruel people who mistreated their boys sexually and mentally. "They were very good kids," said Aunt Marta.

While that was going on, Abramson and Weisberg tangled again, with the judge threatening to hold her in contempt if she did not curb her courtroom histrionics. The sparks began to fly when the judge was listening to Cano's proposed testimony that Lyle and Erik were surprised at the size of their father's bank account. As a professional financial planner, she had explained to the boys that the estate would top fourteen million dollars, or about eight million after taxes and expenses.

"I can't believe my father had so much money," she said Erik told her, adding that the brothers thought Jose had scratched them from the will. Cano insisted that Erik—who had robbed houses to steal cash, had hired a private tennis coach, and had paid his own way to fly to foreign tournaments—didn't care about money. She insisted that he probably would have given his inheritance "to homeless kids."

Weisberg quickly said that Cano could not tell that kind of thing to the juries, and Abramson shook her head in disagreement. Weisberg pounced on her. "Ms. Abramson. You tend to shake your head negatively when the court rules against you. You had better stop doing that or the court is going to find you in contempt."

Abramson was not in a conciliatory mood. She crossed her arms and barked, "Well, the court may be finding me in contempt pretty soon, anyway, because I'm finding the court's rulings astonishingly biased."

The judge wanted to know if that was an invitation, a dare, for him to place sanctions against her, and she backed down. "No, no. I'm just saying there's only so much unfairness one can bear," she said.

"You had better behave professionally. I'm warning you at this time, is that clear?" asked Weisberg.

Abramson glared. "I heard you. Yes, indeed, sir."

They both knew they had skirmishes yet to come.

August came to a close with the strange testimony of Alice Hercz, an old family friend from Princeton, who had little good to say about the deceased, although she had taught Lyle at Princeton Day School, attended parties at the Menendez home, played cards with Jose and Kitty, and visited them in Beverly Hills.

She described her pal and neighbor Kitty as "pathetic, kind of suspicious of people, disorganized, spacey." Jose was "abusive and cruel. I found him destructive at times."

In her English and Spanish classes, Lyle was a quiet student who would arrive late for class, still wearing tennis togs, and who several times sat in her office, silent and staring, for half an hour. "Lyle was a robot. Very much like a robot."

The family as a unit was secretive and "hermetically sealed."

If she felt that way, the prosecution asked in cross-examination, why party with them? "They were attractive in the sense that we talked about them. They were going somewhere. They had this quality of power like movie stars or something, they had this aura."

And if young Lyle was so troubled, why did the Princeton Day School teachers not intervene? Hercz said everyone was fearful of a confrontation. "Kitty could be fierce," she said. "You knew that your job could be at stake. They were intimidating people. They intimidated all of us."

Still, none of the witnesses had actually observed any sexual abuse whatsoever. Abramson and Lansing were not worried, for they knew the horrific story would unfold as soon as Lyle and Erik took the stand.

23

Lyle

Twenty-five-year-old Lyle Menendez wore a light blue shirt beneath a navy blue sweater when he went to the witness stand on September 10, the thirty-fifth day of trial. Jurors had heard, in boring encyclopedic detail, of the family's life together, everything from Cookie Monster dolls to pet ferrets, with only the slightest mention of the alleged sexual abuse. In fact, only Diane Vander Molen's testimony from her 1976 conversation with Lyle, in which the boy said he and his dad had touched each other "down there," had any direct bearing on the subject, and the court had not allowed the jurors to hear even that.

When the time finally came for the boys themselves to take the stand, the representatives of all three points of the legal compass thought things were exactly where they wanted them. Judge Weisberg still insisted he was not trying a child custody case, where the characters of oddball parents had relevance. The prosecutors were confident that their theory of deliberate and premeditated murder had not been damaged. And the defense lawyers were certain that the more than thirty witnesses they had put on the stand had sufficiently set the table to show the potential for abuse within the Menendez household. Now it was up to

Lyle and Erik to confess, in public and before the
ever-curious Court TV camera, that their parents had
made their lives a living hell and that Jose and Kitty
had deserved to die. It was a tall order indeed, and the
lawyers had been visiting the brothers in prison for
months to coach them for the ordeal. The prosecutors
also had some secret ammunition squirreled away. The
show inevitably drew more interest than normal, as
word spread that the brothers were about to testify
and spectators lined up for seats outside the courthouse as early as 4:00 A.M. No one who listened to
Lyle Menendez during his nine days on the witness
stand would be disappointed.

It started slowly, as Lyle recounted warm and fuzzy
memories of his parents, of watching his mother care
for sick birds, and of frolicking in the snow with his
dad and their dog. He particularly was fond of visits
to his grandparents, Jose's mother and father, who
stuffed the brothers with food forbidden at their own
table, and he fondly recalled a grandfather who told
them stories.

That was about it for the sweetness and light and,
as the defense lawyers directed Lyle toward the heart
of the matter, he began to weep openly. The careful
composure he had shown throughout the previous four
years shattered like cheap plaster and he cried like a
baby, wiping tears away with the sleeve of his preppy
sweater and burying his face in his hands. Sometimes,
he just could not talk at all, as choking emotion welled
inside of him.

Lyle testified that when he was about six years old,
his father would give him massages after sports practices, and fondle him while spinning tales of how
Greek soldiers had sex with one another to forge
stronger bonds before going into battle. Such "bonding" meant that the relationship between father and
son would be strengthened, Jose said, adding a warn-

ing that Lyle should never speak of their sessions, because "bad things would happen to me if I told anybody."

Two photographs were pinned to the courtroom bulletin board that once had been used to display the shotgunned corpses of Jose and Kitty. This time the pictures were of naked little boys, which Lyle said were of himself and his brother and were taken by their father. The photos were only from the waist down. No faces were shown.

Lyle continued to describe how, when he was seven, things became even more involved. "We would be in the bathroom. He would put me on his knees. He would guide all my movements, and I would have oral sex with him." Within a year, "He'd use objects, like a toothbrush. We had what we called object lessons. He would take my pants down, lay me on the bed and he'd have a tube of Vaseline and play with me." Suddenly, Lyle glanced through his veil of streaming tears toward his brother, Erik, and said that during that same time, he would take his little brother to the woods and molest him in the same manner. "And I'm sorry," he said. At the defense table, Erik also began to cry.

After that, Jose began to force Lyle to submit to anal sex, and the boy begged his father to stop because of the pain involved. Lyle said he also finally went to his mother about the mistreatment. "I told her to tell Dad to leave me alone, that he keeps touching me. She told me . . . that I was exaggerating—and that my dad has to punish me when I do things wrong. She told me he loved me." His mother, he said, was never a paragon of support and often told him that she had ruined her own life by having children.

But not long afterward, when he was eight years old, his father's abuse came to an end, without explanation. It just stopped. He confirmed that the only person he ever told of the abuse was his cousin, Diane Vander Molen.

When he was about thirteen, Lyle recalled, he overheard noises that led him to believe Jose was molesting Erik, and he told his father to "leave Erik alone."

"He told me Erik made things up sometimes, but it would stop." Lyle followed that with the startling comment that Jose had said if the boy told anyone else about his suspicions, Jose would kill him.

The questions and answers that followed were surprising.

JILL LANSING: Did you love your mom and dad?

LYLE: Yes.

LANSING: On August 20, 1989, did you and your brother kill your mother and father?

LYLE: Yes.

LANSING: Did you kill them for money?

LYLE: No.

LANSING: Did you kill them to pay them back for the mistreatment?

LYLE: No.

LANSING: Why did you kill your parents?

LYLE: Because we were afraid.

LANSING: Do you have a lot of nice memories of childhood?

LYLE: No.

LANSING: How did it start?

LYLE: After sports practices, he would massage me. We would have the talk. He would show me . . . fondle me, and I would do the same. We would undress.

LANSING: Did you want to do this?

LYLE: (crying and breaking down): He raped me!

LANSING: Did you cry?

LYLE: Yes.

LANSING: Were you scared?

LYLE: Yes.

LANSING: Did you ask him not to?

LYLE: Yes . . . I told him I didn't want to do this. He said he didn't want to hurt me, that he loved me.

LANSING: Did you tell your mother?

LYLE: Yes. I told her to tell him to leave me alone, that he keeps touching me.

During his second day on the stand, Lyle brought Kitty into full focus as an abuser herself, someone who was so alien to tender feelings that she would not accept his collect telephone calls when he was away at camp and lonely, and would hurl his favorite toy animals out the window when she was angry. It was not unusual for Lyle to find her lying on the floor, aimlessly arranging rubber bands, or outside, staring blankly while she played in the dirt. When one of the pet ferrets died, Kitty took it to the taxidermist to have it stuffed and mounted on a log. The dead beast was then given a place of honor on the television set so Kitty could look at it.

This line of testimony only proved the boy believed his mom to be looney, but it said nothing about abuse from her. So, to validate that claim, he also recounted how she would kick him and drag him about the room by his hair, or even chase him around the house waving a knife.

Then came the bombshell of how his mother was almost as sexually weird as his father. When he was little, Lyle said, Kitty would show him photos of herself wearing sexy lingerie or a bathing suit. Lansing quickly put a photo into evidence to corroborate that, pinning the picture of Kitty in black underwear to the court's bulletin board.

As he grew older, she grew bolder. At age eleven, he remembered his mother parading topless before him, or even walking around naked, or with her bathrobe open, and asking how he thought she looked. Up until he was thirteen, she was still giving him baths. But the real shocker was that she would bring him into her bed, sometimes with Jose lying there beside them, and invite the boy to touch her "everywhere."

Lyle Menendez looked at his lawyer. "I took it to be love," he said. "She was enjoying it." Jill Lansing stopped short of asking whether they had sexual relations. He was the one who had finally brought it to a stop at the age of thirteen, he said, despite his mother's harassment that developed into an ongoing series of arguments. Later, when he began dating, Kitty would brand his girlfriends as bimbos and sluts. In one extraordinarily strange situation, his mother refused to let him eat off of the family china after he began dating a model that Kitty claimed was infected with AIDS. "I ate off paper plates in the den," he explained to the court.

The jurors were shocked, and even Pamela Bozanich was impressed. "I thought his testimony was compelling. Just as watching Laurence Olivier act is compelling."

The next day, in an appearance cut short by the flu, Lyle wistfully remembered how he mentally traded in his real family for his trusted collection of stuffed animals. "For me, it was very comforting. You could have your own family in there and play. As I got older, it was embarrassing to me because stuffed animals are for little kids. But it was very important to me."

He also referred back to the Princeton days, when his father would religiously telephone him to query about the university work. Then Jose would prepare homework assignments and send the material back to Lyle by overnight mail, honor code be damned. This confirmed the lifelong pattern of Jose, and his entire family, being willing to lie, cheat, and steal—do anything—to win. It backfired when Jose dashed off an essay on, of all things, *The Prince,* by Machiavelli. Lyle got a bad grade because Jose, who epitomized much of Machiavelli's back-stabbing theory of success, had never read the classic.

Lyle fired another shot at Kitty when he described how his mother popped thirteen pills one day and wrote out a suicide note saying she could not deal with the shame of having discovered Jose was having a love affair with another woman. Lyle said he suggested that his mother might consider divorce instead, only to be told that "she never regretted a day that she was married to my father."

The centerpiece of Lyle's testimony was to be the night his parents were murdered, and it wasn't long in coming. Lyle was excused from court the next day to be taken, under heavy guard, to a hospital for treatment of his flu symptoms, but he was back on the stand on Friday, September 17, in a light blue shirt and off-white crewneck sweater, looking somewhat shaky.

The week before the murders was a tumultuous one, he testified, starting with an argument between himself and his mother, who was worried about her father being ill. She had often been out of control, he said, but this was worse than her usual tantrums. When the argument reached a fever pitch, Kitty reached up and snatched the toupee from his head, an act so humiliating that he began to shake and cry. Erik, who did not know about the false head of hair, saw his brother bald for the first time.

When Lyle's hair loss had become noticeable a few years earlier, Jose, who thought Lyle might eventually go into politics, decided Lyle needed hair to be photogenic for television. After seeing the wig incident, and Lyle's shame at the exposure, Erik decided to confide in his older brother that he, too, had a terrible secret.

"He told me those things with his dad were still going on," testified Lyle.

Lyle didn't want to believe it, he said. "I had dismissed what had happened to me as something that happened to little boys," he said, and he snapped at Erik. Why didn't you fight back? Why didn't you tell someone earlier? In answer, Erik merely began to cry.

Lyle said he would make Jose stop the molestation. They were almost grown now and he knew that if they told people about the abuse, their father could be ruined. Therefore, Lyle said, "we held all the cards." That bit of bravado was short-lived.

The Wednesday night before the murders, Lyle told his mother about the situation, and she responded, "Erik is lying." Jose was off on a business trip and did not arrive home until Thursday, when Lyle immediately confronted him about his actions, saying the abuse of Erik "had to stop."

"You listen to me," Jose snapped angrily. "What I do with my son is none of your business. I warn you: Don't throw your life away. Just stay out of it."

Lyle didn't back down. He called his father a "fucking sick person" and then threatened to "tell everybody everything" if Jose did not quit bothering Erik.

Although the boys thought they held the cards, they had forgotten they were playing against Jose Menendez, the man who never, ever lost. "We all make choices in our life. Erik made his. You made yours," Lyle testified that his father told him.

Lyle steepled his fingers and peered steadily at Jill Lansing as he continued his testimony. "I thought we were in danger. I felt he had no choice. He would kill us. He'd get rid of us in some way, because I was going to ruin him."

There was no use trying to run away, he said, because his dad was powerful enough to find them no matter where they tried to hide, and the brothers did not think the cops would believe their fears.

Friday came and Lyle and Erik drove down to San Diego, found a gun store, flashed the Donovan Goodreau identification, walked out with a pair of powerful shotguns, and returned to Beverly Hills. Saturday was the shark-fishing expedition, during which, despite the freezing water splashing on them, the boys stayed near the bow because they thought their parents planned to kill them out on the ocean.

His mother was jittery when they returned to the house that night, telling Erik that "if he had kept his mouth shut, things might have worked out in this family." Lyle said the boys interpreted that as a prelude to something happening, that their parents had laid plans to kill them.

Sunday, Lyle had another shock, for when he spoke to his father about attending a tennis camp, Jose looked mildly amused and asked, "What does it matter anymore?" His voice firm now on the witness stand, Lyle testified: "I took it to be my dad's sarcastic way of saying, 'You're dead. You're not going to be around to go to camp.' "

When the brothers announced that night that they were going out to the movies, Kitty barked at them to stay home. Jose led her by the hand into the television room and closed the doors. "I was sure that was it. I just freaked out . . . I thought they were going ahead with their plan to kill us," he said.

As Lansing prodded him with soft, brief questions, Lyle said, "I ran upstairs to tell my brother that it was happening now, and that this was it, they were going to kill us. At some point I said I was going to get my gun, and he said he would get his gun."

LANSING: How did you feel?
LYLE: Like I had to run as fast as I could and my

life was slowly slipping away and that we were going
to die.

The boys went out and got their shotguns from
Erik's car and jammed in buckshot shells, then
stormed through the doors and began shooting. At the
defense table, Erik, leaning his chin on folded hands,
listened closely as Lyle described the death shots.

LANSING: Was the room lit?
LYLE: No, it was dark, the lights were out. I
remember seeing a shadow off to the right, my
brother off to the left. He ran off into that direction.
I started firing immediately in the direction of whoever was standing right there. I realized it was my
dad at some point, coming forward in my direction,
so he was standing. I remember firing directly at
him.
LANSING: Was a lot of firing going on?
LYLE: Yes, my brother was, I guess, firing. There
was shattering and the noise was phenomenal. We
fired lots, many many times, and there were just
glass, and could hear things breaking and could hear
the ringing noises from the booms, and there was
the smoke from the guns and, uh, it was basically
chaos. I really didn't know who was firing at whom,
or what was going on. I was just firing my gun.
LANSING: Do you remember firing a very close
shot at your father?
LYLE: I believe so.
LANSING: Did you reload it?
LYLE: Yes.
LANSING: What did you do after you reloaded?
LYLE (answering in a tearful, breaking voice): I
ran around and shot my mom. I just leaned over and
shot her close.

Leaving the stand, Lyle patted his brother on the back and ran his fingers through Erik's hair as he walked to the defense table. The electrifying testimony had shocked a nationwide television audience and everyone in the courtroom. The defense was ecstatic with its impact, while Bozanich said Lyle's acting had fallen from the level of Olivier to that of Stallone, from Richard III to Rocky.

Before turning him over to the prosecution for cross-examination, the defense team wrapped up a few loose ends, including trying to soften the impact of one particularly threatening piece of news. Lyle, under questioning by his own lawyer, had admitted offering a large amount of money to his former girlfriend, Jamie Pisarcik, if she would appear as a witness and lie to say that Jose had made some unwanted sexual overtures toward her. The girl refused and told police of the bribe offer. Lyle confirmed her statements, in effect admitting that he was still capable of constructing a lie or two if it would help him.

In a further attempt to defang potentially damaging questions from the prosecution, Lyle confessed that he never told Oziel about the sexual abuse, but he also denied bragging about a perfect murder and said it was Oziel, not the brothers, who had said that killing Kitty had "probably done her a favor." He brushed aside the spending spree as merely a way to "focus" after the murders.

Deputy District Attorney Pamela Bozanich, a petite woman with her brown hair swept up, wearing a business suit, pink shirt, and pearl earrings, was not moved, not an inch, by Lyle's emotional testimony. Now it was her turn to question him, and she was merciless. After five days of listening to Lyle present one of the more startling stories ever heard in a court-room, she was now going to hammer him.

For four days the prosecutor peppered him with questions designed to turn his story around, subjecting him to a withering cross-examination about the deaths of his parents.

First, she painted him as a consistent liar, something to which he admitted. Lyle insisted that he was now, finally, telling the truth.

BOZANICH: Isn't it true that you killed your parents because you couldn't stand your father's control any more, and you couldn't figure out any other way to kill him, except to kill your mother too?

LYLE: No, that's not true.

The prosecutor switched on the 911 tape recording, playing its emotional content for the court.

BOZANICH: You told the police that you had just come home and found your parents dead. Is that correct?

LYLE: I think I might have said someone killed my parents.

BOZANICH: They asked you a lot more questions, and when they asked you those questions, you were crying. Correct?

LYLE: Right.

BOZANICH: At the same time, you were lying, while you were crying, correct?

LYLE: Right.

BOZANICH: You learned to lie as a child, didn't you?

LYLE: I would say I did.

BOZANICH: And you almost didn't get caught in this case, isn't that fair to say?

LYLE: Almost didn't get caught?

BOZANICH: Well, the murder occurred August twentieth and you weren't arrested until March.

LYLE: Right.

BOZANICH: You almost got away with it, didn't you?

LYLE: Well, you characterize it that way and you think it's funny. But my brother's and my life was very miserable for six months before we got arrested and obviously wasn't better after we got arrested and isn't any good now. And never really has been great.

With that, Bozanich pounced. Not great, eh? She quickly had Lyle admit that he enjoyed playing tennis at country clubs, never had to hold down a job, attended private schools, and vacationed in Europe without ever having to worry about money. Lyle allowed that his rich life-style wasn't exactly a bowl of cherry pits.

As for the allegations of sexual abuse, she scornfully cut to the heart of the argument, since nobody had yet testified about the allegations of sexual molestation but himself.

BOZANICH: And the two people who could come in and say they're not true, you killed, right?

LYLE: Well, they wouldn't say they weren't true. But then again, I don't really know what they would say.

She slammed him on the shark expedition of August 19, asking him why the brothers thought Kitty and Jose were going to kill them at sea. Lyle replied that there had been an argument because the boys had showed up an hour past the time they were to leave on the expedition.

"You found it nerve-racking that your family waited

for you for a family outing?'' Bozanich asked in feigned surprise. "You found that peculiar?"

"It was a big deal to me," he said.

The prosecutor and her uncomfortable witness returned to the wretched argument that apparently had caused the final schism, and Lyle testified again that he had told his father to leave Erik alone. Jose responded, "I'm warning you, don't throw your life away. Stay out of it . . . I can tell you what's going to happen. You're going back to Princeton and your brother is going to UCLA like we planned. And we're going to forget this conversation ever took place."

"I interrupted him," Lyle told Bozanich, embellishing his earlier testimony. "It was just like the other conversations we had, where he was just dismissing it. I swore and told him he was a fucking sick person and told him, no, he wasn't going to touch my brother again. [If he did] I would tell everybody everything about him. I would tell the police and I would tell the family."

When his father told him that everybody makes choices and got up to leave, Lyle said he panicked. "I thought, oh my God, he thinks I'm going to tell people regardless . . . I started to plead with him before he left. I got up and said, 'Dad, you know, I'm only going to tell people if you don't stop touching Erik.' He just looked at me and said, 'You're going to tell everyone anyway.' And he left."

After that, he said, he was certain Jose was prepared to kill them both.

BOZANICH: You were your father's proudest creation?
LYLE: Yeah, I guess so.
BOZANICH: You were his namesake.
LYLE: Yes.

BOZANICH: You were a Menendez.

LYLE: Yes.

BOZANICH: You really believed your father was going to destroy you?

LYLE: Yes, ma'am.

About 9:45 P.M. on the night of the murders, the family argued about the boys going out to the movies, then Jose led Kitty into the television room and shut the doors behind them. "Closing the doors, to me, was the last thing that caused me to totally freeze and panic and realize it was happening," he said. "I thought they were armed. I thought they were in the process of killing us. I thought they planned this in advance."

But under Bozanich's prodding, Lyle said he had never searched the house to determine if his parents had any weapons. He added the rather bizarre theory that perhaps his mother had a pistol equipped with a silencer, a gun his parents might have gotten from friends in organized crime.

Lyle said that he'd lived in fear of retaliation because he had stood up to his father, something that people just did not do. "I didn't confront my father at all," he said.

"When you had a gun, you confronted him just fine," snapped the prosecutor.

"We were afraid. We didn't know what was going on. We thought they were going to kill us."

LYLE: I loved my mother.

BOZANICH: When you put the shotgun up to her left cheek and pulled the trigger, did you love your mother?

LYLE: Yes.

Bozanich bored in on why Lyle had gone after his mother in such a remorseless manner.

LYLE: In my mind, she was sneaking around the coffee table.

BOZANICH (in a voice of shock): Was she going to be crawling, trying to get away from being shot to death?

LYLE: Something I saw, or something that I heard, freaked me out even more. I was afraid.

BOZANICH: You were afraid she was going to live, weren't you?

LYLE: It was a kind of caving in kind of fear. I was not really in control.

The police came, but the boys did not say a word about sexual abuse, he admitted. "I didn't think they'd understand," said Lyle. "We had just shot my parents and regardless of the reason, we were going to go to jail and our lives would be ruined."

As the hours and days of cross-examination wore on, Lyle admitted that his parents did not have guns, had made no direct threats, and he conceded that his story "sounds awful" in some of its parts, but then "a lot of decisions don't make sense."

Bozanich jumped to the spending spree. "What you did was you killed your parents and began to spend their money, right?"

"Well, that's something that happened. But I don't think characterizing it that way is putting it in the right context," Lyle replied.

She pointed out that he bought a money clip for fifteen thousand dollars and a Rolex watch four days after the murders.

"I realize, I look back, it sounds awful, and I wish I hadn't bought them. It is . . . a bad thing. But it wasn't for any specific reason. I was just wandering in a store. And I was feeling down, so I bought them."

"So you thought that a nine-thousand-dollar eighteen-karat-gold Rolex would go nicely with your funeral suit, is that right?" Her manner dripped with scorn.

"No. I didn't. Again, I really didn't think much about money in my life. I just bought things spur of the moment all the time. This was just another thing."

They would go over the same horrifying scenario several times, and each trip was just as gruesome as the ones before it. Lyle, exhausted by the sharp questions, was hit one last time on September 24, as he wrapped up nine grueling days on the witness stand.

Answering a question by his own attorney, Jill Lansing, Lyle said his parents had controlled their sons at times through subtle gestures, the same way Jose used to cheat during tennis tournaments by coaching him with hand signals.

"What hand signals did you father give to you before you put a gun to the back of his head and pulled the trigger?" asked Bozanich in another cross-examination period.

"He didn't give me any," replied Lyle.

"What signal was your mother giving you when she was sneaking away near the coffee table before you went out and reloaded?"

"Nothing," he said. "I was just afraid at that point."

When he was finally released from the witness stand, court adjourned for the weekend, to the relief of everyone. There had been more than enough excitement for a while. Asked how things had gone for the defense, Leslie Abramson said Lyle had stood up during the tough grilling quite well, for a "severely abused and psychologically traumatized youngster." Bozanich had a different slant, obviously relieved to be done with the ordeal herself. "I don't think his cross-examination was any more unique than any other defendant's," she said. Then she paused and added, almost with a giggle, "Perhaps he was better dressed."

24

Erik

After Lyle's testimony, the line of people waiting to get into the increasingly popular trial began gathering long before dawn. One chill morning, when Erik was ready to take the stand, five young people had driven over from Palm Desert, arriving at the courthouse shortly after midnight to be the first in line, camping out on the stone floor beside the locked doors with the same enthusiasm they might show for a rock concert. They were part of a legion of Menendez junkies, hooked by Court TV. "We just sit and watch it like zombies," said one. They made a day of it, as if they were at a theme park, getting into the courtroom for Erik's morning testimony, then checking out the mansion on North Elm Drive, where they interviewed the mailman, and returning to the courthouse at day's end to attend the lawyers' news conferences. It was better than Disneyland or Universal Studios, they insisted, because it was substantive, not a bunch of animated gewgaws and costumed characters. This was *real!* "This is a historic trial . . . it could be the trial of the decade!" one declared.

When the trial first began, a spectator could show up at 9:00 A.M. and get a seat. But before long, as it

gained popularity, if you wanted a seat you needed to
arrive hours before the doors opened at 7:00 A.M. The
Van Nuys Superior Court did not convene until 9:30,
and it was not unusual for a latecomer to wait eight
hours before being allowed in for the afternoon session. The early birds gathered at one end of the
terrazzo-tiled corridor on the fourth floor, suspiciously
eyeing anyone who might try to break into line. Courtroom 410 wore a sign: NO SEATING AVAILABLE. DO NOT
ENTER. DO NOT KNOCK. A marshal would distribute
numbers inked on little squares of paper at 8:45 A.M.
for the morning session and at 11:45 A.M. for the
afternoon session, and it was strictly first come, first
served. Perhaps ten spectators could get in for each
session, because the court was so crowded with lawyers, juries, press, and family that there simply were
not enough seats for the public. Hopeful spectators
could have fared just as well by turning on Court TV.
"It's not the same," insisted one regular. "You gotta
be *in* there."

Certainly, as Erik Menendez came to the witness
stand on Monday, September 27, he was the center of
attention. As an amateur actor at Beverly Hills High
School, he had delivered a Shakespearean soliloquy,
but now he was going to appear before millions. Neat
in a blue shirt with a maroon tie, the tall and slim Erik,
very pale and obviously nervous, was in the spotlight
of notoriety. Judge Weisberg was watching not Erik,
but his lawyer, Leslie Abramson, whom he had
scolded the previous Friday for her habit of gently
stroking Erik's back or putting an arm around his
shoulders during particularly harsh testimony. The
judge did not like the juries to see such things, believ-
ing it might influence the sympathy vote, and told the
lawyers to be professional and not act "as nursemaids
or surrogate mothers." So Erik, an athlete strong

enough to play on the tennis circuits of the world, found the strength to walk to the witness stand by himself. But Abramson would be his questioner for the first phase of testimony, and he could expect gentle, sympathetic treatment, although the subject matter would be difficult.

She walked him quickly through the preliminaries, having him note for the jury that he had returned from Israel to surrender voluntarily, knowing he would probably stand trial for murder. That he had skipped free for seven months was not mentioned.

Then Abramson quickly switched gears and dove straight to the sexual abuse angle that was the basis of the entire defense. Her careful questions were met by Erik's soft, wavering voice. Before the day was done, he would frequently break down in tears, his face twisting into a mask of anguish.

His shocking testimony would corroborate that of his brother, Lyle, and Abramson lofted the questions to him in a soft voice, pushing him through the tortured memories, as she followed the major points that she had written down to make sure he covered every dirty detail.

LESLIE ABRAMSON: Mr. Menendez, you've heard the testimony of your brother that you and he killed your parents on August 20, 1989, did you not?

ERIK MENENDEZ: Yes, we did.

ABRAMSON: And what do you believe was the originating cause of you and your brother ultimately winding up shooting your parents?

ERIK: Me telling . . . Lyle that, uhhh . . .

ABRAMSON: You telling what? You telling Lyle about something that was happening?

ERIK: My dad, my dad . . . (Erik stopped talking, his reddening face covered with his hand as he openly wept) . . . had been molesting me.

ABRAMSON: And did you want something from your brother? Is that why you told him?

ERIK: Yes. I just wanted it to stop.

ABRAMSON: Were you seeking help from your brother?

ERIK: Yes.

It had begun when he was about six years old, and his father had been brutally frank about what would happen if the boy told anyone about what went on between them, Erik testified. "He told me he'd tie me to a chair and beat me to death."

ABRAMSON: Mr. Menendez, during the summer of 1989, were you being sexually molested by your father?

ERIK: Yes.

ABRAMSON: Were there patterns to the behavior, so that there were actually different kinds of sexual incidents with your father?

ERIK: Yes.

ABRAMSON: And did you come, over the years, to give those different kinds of sexual incidents names?

ERIK: Yes.

ABRAMSON: And would you tell us, what were the names that you gave to the different types of incidents?

ERIK: Umm. Knees.

ABRAMSON: What was another term?

ERIK: Nice sex.

ABRAMSON: What was another term?

ERIK: Rough sex.

ABRAMSON: Rough sex. And was there still another kind?

ERIK: Yes.

ABRAMSON: And what name did you come to give that kind?

ERIK: Just sex.

The courtroom was totally silent, as if a dark blanket had been thrown over it to muffle the sound. Here was a young man baring his deepest secrets in public, before reporters and a television viewing audience of millions. He testified that, during oral sex, his father would stick him with sharp pins and tacks, and that he had engaged in a sexual act with his father as late as May 1989, just before graduating from Beverly Hills High. He said he had sworn to himself to bury the secret deep, never to let his friends know. "I didn't want to be humiliated."

But Erik added that he felt partially responsible for the incestuous abuse because he never put a halt to it. "I thought I was a coward. I hated myself for it."

He did try, once, with disastrous results. He testified that when he was seventeen, his father came into the room and "I said no." Jose flew into a fury, went to get the large, ragged-edged knife that had been given to him as part of a *Rambo* film promotion. Then he came back to the bedroom, threw Erik on the bed, put the sharp blade at his throat, and forced the boy to have sex, Erik testified.

He said the single hope for breaking the cycle was that he was going to live in a dormitory with other kids when he went to UCLA. But Jose gave him the news that, several nights a week, Erik would sleep at home.

ERIK: He was telling me I was going to be living at home and, basically, the sex was going to continue.

ABRAMSON: Did he say the sex was going to continue?

ERIK: No, he didn't say that, but that's what I knew he meant.

ABRAMSON: And how did that make you feel?

ERIK: It made me feel like the hope that I had was gone. Suddenly, this was going to continue, throughout college. I felt like I was crumbling, I couldn't . . . I felt like nothing mattered anymore, that it was going to continue.

ABRAMSON: How did you feel at eighteen, the fact that your father was having sex with you?

ERIK (his voice beginning softly and trailing off to a whisper): I hated it . . . I hated it . . . I hated it.

ABRAMSON: What did you think your options were with respect to sex with your father?

ERIK (looking up in surprise): Options? I had no options.

There were thoughts of suicide—hanging himself, driving off a cliff, slitting his wrists. Why? his lawyer coaxed. "Because it would end the sex, and that's all I wanted," Erik declared.

The jurors would weigh whether the emotional statements were true or not, but it was obvious that some strange things had been taking place behind those polished doors in Beverly Hills.

Erik confirmed that he had been surprised to see his mother rip off Lyle's "always neat, always perfect" hair on August 15, and suddenly felt the baldness made his older brother, his protector since their days at Princeton Day School, seem more vulnerable. And he told Lyle about the abuse.

After Lyle confronted Jose, Erik said he had a physical fight with his father, escaped from his grasp, and ran downstairs to tell his mother.

ERIK: She said, "I know. I've always known. Do you think I'm stupid?" She was real snide and I think . . . she had been drinking, she was real . . .

ABRAMSON: Sarcastic?

ERIK: Yes.

ABRAMSON: So what did you say, when she said she knew all along, she wasn't stupid?

ERIK: I didn't know what to say. I just said, "I hate you."

ABRAMSON: What did you do?

ERIK: I ran out the back door.

ABRAMSON: And what did your mother do?

ERIK: She immediately got up and started chasing me outside.

ABRAMSON: Was she saying anything?

ERIK: Yes. She was saying, "Get back here, you bastard. Don't every say that to me, how dare you say that to me?"

ABRAMSON: Had you ever heard your mother tell you or your brother, "I hate you, I hate you," over the course of your life?

ERIK: Yeah.

ABRAMSON: Had she said it once, twice?

ERIK: No, she said it often.

ABRAMSON: Had you said it to your mother before?

ERIK: No.

ABRAMSON: Did you hate your mother, Mr. Menendez?

ERIK: No, I didn't hate my mother.

ABRAMSON: Had there also been discussions about your mother poisoning the family?

ERIK: There had never been too much discussion about it, but that's what she had said.

ABRAMSON: She said that?

ERIK: Yeah.

ABRAMSON: Did that develop any sense of fear in you about your mother?

ERIK: Sort of. I had a lot of fear about my mother.

During the following day of testimony, Abramson, her client's incredible story gathering momentum, brought him to the night of the murders. Jurors and spectators were riveted to their seats. They had heard

Lyle tell of the shootings, and now it was the turn of
the younger brother, who allegedly wanted to break
free of the father's sexual bondage and needed his
older brother's help. Instead of getting in the car and
driving away, they had picked up their shotguns. A
shaken Erik, eyes wide with remembering, took the
jury into the room, which was lit only by the flickering
television set and distant lights in the hallway.

ABRAMSON: At that point then, you had a loaded
gun, correct?

ERIK: Yes.

ABRAMSON: So why didn't you just wait and see
what your father and mother were going to do?

ERIK: Because I was thinking they were coming
out [of the family room]. I only thought I had
seconds. I thought that as soon as they came out of
that room, I was going to die, I had to get to that
room before they came out.

ABRAMSON: Now, after you entered the den, what
do you remember happening?

ERIK: I just remember firing.

ABRAMSON: And, did you *aim* in any particular
place?

ERIK: I was just firing as I went into the room. I
just started firing.

ABRAMSON: In what direction?

ERIK: In front of me.

ABRAMSON: What was in front of you?

ERIK (his voice barely audible): My parents.

ABRAMSON: When the shooting ended, could you
see either your father or your mother?

ERIK: Yes.

ABRAMSON: Who could you see?

ERIK: My father.

ABRAMSON: And where was he, at that time?

ERIK (with a coughing sob): He was on the couch.

ABRAMSON: Could you see your mother?

ERIK: No.

ABRAMSON: Now what was it that happened after the shooting ended?

ERIK: I heard a noise from my mom.

ABRAMSON: And what was your reaction to that noise?

ERIK: I just ran out of the room.

He would later add that he heard Lyle fire the shotgun again while he waited outside. When he returned to the room, it was filled with smoke that was sliced apart by the light from the television set. "It was real, real eerie."

ABRAMSON: When you saw them in the den later, didn't they appear to be dead?

ERIK: Yes.

ABRAMSON: And did you accept it then, that they were dead?

ERIK: Yes . . . Well, I accepted that they were dead and they were gone, but I still couldn't believe that. It just seemed too . . . impossible to me.

But indeed Jose and Kitty Menendez were dead, their bodies savaged by shotgun blasts and resting in pools of blood. Lyle and Erik had both admitted to the murders before the trail had even started, and now they each had given the juries absolute proof that they did it. The reason, as put forward by the defense teams, was that the boys had no choice.

Erik, snuffling through his testimony, had said that his father had initiated the "knees" form of sex, which meant oral copulation, when Erik was about eleven years old. The "nice sex" started about a year later and included both hand and mouth massages. Anal sex came the next year, and the sadistic "rough sex" began when he was thirteen: Jose would stick pins in him while Erik performed oral sex on his father, with Jose telling him it was a good lesson in how to endure pain without crying out. It happened two to four times a month, he said.

Lyle's sudden intervention had brought an immediate surge of fear in both brothers, he said. When Lyle screamed, "You're not going to touch my little brother!" Jose had yelled back, "I do what I want with my family. It's not your little brother. It's my son!" During that critical episode, Kitty just stood by with a vacant look on her face.

The law in California states plainly that, in trying to prove self-defense, defendants must show they were in immediate or imminent danger. According to the Menendez defense team, the overwhelming fear that pervaded the boys' lives was more than an immediate threat, it was something that they had to endure daily.

In his following testimony, Erik said he had given himself a nickname—the Hurt Man—but had hedged whenever anyone asked why. "I just told them I got hurt a lot," he said. He also said that his father, who detested homosexuals, used to bait him by calling him "faggot." Erik was too scared to shout back, but silently asked himself, "Then what the hell are you?"

There was one particularly obscene drill that he had to go through when his father wanted to be certain the boy understood what would happen if he divulged their secrets.

"I said, 'You'll hurt me,' " Erik told the court.

"Wrong," Jose would reply.

Then Erik would have to hit himself on the head for giving the wrong answer, and the question was asked anew. "I said, 'You'll kill me.' "

"Right," his father would declare.

He also backed up his brother's testimony of the bizarre behavior of their mother, who would slap him for biting his nails, throw food at him, and lock him in a closet.

Abramson also wanted to use Erik as a foil to discredit Dr. Oziel, and the young man calmly explained that he had gone back to the therapist when he began having nightmares about the killings. "Whenever I'd hear a car engine and smell smoke or fumes, sometimes when someone was cooking, I smelled it and thought about it," he said. "Anything could spark it. Anything would remind me, and I would see them in the room.

"It was confusing, the guilt. Thinking about what kind of person I was tore me apart and gave me a lot of pain."

Abramson asked why he never told the therapist about the molestation. Erik replied that he could not handle such humiliation, so he kept quiet.

On the crucial Halloween visit, Erik said he tried to talk about his suicidal dreams, how he would see things as being peaceful after he died, but Oziel was not able to understand because Erik had not yet revealed his part in the murders.

Once Erik did make his confession, he said, Oziel acted strangely, not wanting to talk about his patient's depression but pushing to learn the details of the murder. And Erik said it was Oziel who had announced that the reason for the deaths could have been that Jose was so controlling and "nobody could live under those circumstances."

It was a story of extraordinary sadness, but prosecutors Pamela Bozanich and Lester Kuriyama weren't buying a nickel's worth. On Thursday, September 30, they set out to prove that the quivering, distraught young man the jurors saw was not only a burglar and a killer, but a liar to boot, and not a very good one.

As Kuriyama brought his legal pads to the small

podium, he looked like a Japanese professor preparing a lecture on quality control, giving no clue whatsoever that the trial of Erik Menendez was at a critical point. The soft-spoken prosecutor was about to let Erik step into a trap that could turn the whole case on its ear.

On the first day of a cross-examination that would go on for days, Erik replayed the assault, said he remembered mostly shooting at his mother, and added, "I didn't think we'd get away with it—from the second it was done."

Kuriyama was soft-spoken but ruthless, serving notice that he wasn't going to give Erik any softball questions. Instead, he threw fireballs, phrasing his questions in vivid forms, such as: "Now, you surprised your parents while they were watching television and blasted them until your pump shotguns were empty of ammunition, correct?" Such questions leave little room for a witness to maneuver.

Erik had tried to portray himself almost as a bystander after he ran from the room. "You were so freaked out that you went to your car and you had ammunition in a box and you handed that ammunition to your brother?" Kuriyama wanted to know. Erik confirmed that he was scrambling for shells and gave one to Lyle, knowing that his brother was going back to finish off Kitty.

Later, he confirmed that he had lied to many people—from relatives to police—about the murders, but suddenly accused Oziel of lying, too. It was the therapist, he said, not the brothers, who had coined the phrase "perfect crime." Kuriyama wanted to know why Erik had not told Oziel of the abuse.

"I was just much too ashamed to deal with it. I wanted to keep it as secret as possible, bury it, throw it in the ocean, make it disappear," he said.

The next day, Kuriyama, having gotten Erik used to his pattern of asking questions, led the witness into a cage and slammed the door. The prosecutor went into great detail about the purchase of the shotguns, particularly having Erik describe in detail his and Lyle's visit to a sporting goods store in Santa Monica in search of a handgun on August 18. Erik confirmed the details, every step of the way. The pistols he looked at were in the top row of a two-shelf glass counter, and he recounted "specifically" that the clerk handed him one but that they chose not to purchase it when the man said there was a two-week waiting period. He and Lyle discussed the weapon, an automatic, together. Erik's comments were confident, detailed, and unwavering.

"You're telling the truth about everything in this case, aren't you?" Kuriyama asked.

"I'm telling the truth the best that I can," Erik replied with a sincere look.

"Even though you lied in the past, you're telling the truth now, aren't you?"

"Yes, I am."

"Did you truly go to the Santa Monica Big 5 store on the morning of August 18 to buy these handguns?"

"Definitely. Without a doubt, we did."

Kuriyama paused a few beats and rearranged his notes, letting the jurors soak up Erik's comments. He put his elbows on the podium, located just behind where Lyle sat at the defense table, and stared at the witness. "Mr. Menendez, did you know the Big 5 stopped carrying handguns in March of 1986?"

Erik looked as if he had been punched in the gut. His eyes went wide and he leaned forward at the waist. "No, I didn't know that." He paused, his mind racing. "Uhh, Mr. Kuriyama, there were guns there and we did look at them and he did say we could not carry them anywhere."

The prosecutor had no more questions on the subject for the moment, but his question stood in the middle of the courtroom like some big elephant, staring the jurors straight in the face and trumpeting. Erik, who had lied to so many people so many times, had just told another one, a whopper, this time under oath in a court of law where he was on trial for his life.

He had been so detailed in his recall of shopping for the guns, so precise in his comments, that when he was found to be totally wrong, jurors had to wonder about the same kind of detailed remembrances Erik had testified to about sexual abuse. Were those lies too?

Not only was Erik caught off guard, but the elephant also stomped on the toes of his attorney, Leslie Abramson, who had not known about it in advance. When court closed for the day, she brushed off the account as being no big deal. But everyone else who heard the stumble thought it was a very big deal indeed.

On following days, the opposing lawyers would come back to the issue again and again. The day after his cloak of credibility was ruined, Erik protested that perhaps it may have been another gun store, and he just thought it was a Big 5. "What is your story today?" mocked Kuriyama.

But there were other subjects to be covered, and it was obvious that the witness was traveling the same ground repeatedly. Just as Weisberg had spurred Abramson, he now told Kuriyama to speed things up.

Kuriyama took Erik back to the scene of the shooting, asking him to go through what happened "step by step" or "one shot at a time." Throughout the methodical questioning, however, Erik insisted that he had a "red blank" about what exactly had happened in that room, despite undergoing intensive therapy. "I must have shot my mother, and I guess I shot my dad. I just don't remember," he said.

Kuriyama laid down his hammer on Wednesday, October 6, and the state rested its case against Erik Menendez after an intense six days of cross-examination. Rebuttal questions, and challenges to them, would keep Erik on the stand for another week.

Abramson now had an opportunity to respond, and swiftly moved to attack the point about the boys looking at handguns in Santa Monica. The subject she had dismissed as being "no big deal" had apparently been elevated to top priority. She could not let the jury see only one side of the elephant.

First, she let Erik paint a couple of alternative scenarios—that he might have been looking at BB guns instead of automatic pistols, or he might have been in the wrong store.

She showed him a set of photographs the defense had snapped in the Big 5 store in Santa Monica *after* his stumble on the witness stand, and Erik said the BB guns and pellet-firing pistols in the photos still looked real to him. Abramson established that Erik was frequently confused, and gave the well-educated young man a pop quiz in geography. He placed Louisville in Tennessee instead of Kentucky, and said Quito was in Peru, not Ecuador. He testified that he had thought the gun store was a couple of blocks from the San Diego Freeway, but now realized it could have been a mile away.

"At this point, do you know where you were when you had the discussion with the man about buying a handgun?"

"No," replied Erik. He shook his head. "I'm not sure I know anything anymore." Why a clerk might have told him there was a waiting period before a BB gun could be purchased was not pursued.

Kuriyama was not amused, and sharply responded, "Now that you know the Big 5 didn't have real handguns, you're coming up with a different story, aren't you?"

"Sir, I described exactly where the Big 5 was to you. I described exactly where it was. I knew you could easily go and check it out. I mean, I wasn't lying to you."

"You had a week to think about what you were going to tell these juries, to explain how to get out of this."

"I didn't lie," Erik responded.

Moments later, Abramson asked Erik what he had been thinking during the days since he had been found in error. "I was thinking about how I could be wrong when I was quite sure I was right," he said.

In other words, the kid who had prepped at the expensive and private Princeton Day School, had carried a B average at Calabasas High and Beverly Hills High, and had been on the verge of entering UCLA wanted the jurors to believe that he wasn't a liar, he was just dumb.

Perhaps UCLA was not that much of a stretch. For on that very day, former junk bond king Michael Milken, having served jail time for securities violations, began teaching a class on money at the Westwood University.

25

The Tape

In early November, after 16 weeks of trial, Judge Weisberg cleared away the final arguments on the crucial tape recording, made by Doctor Oziel on December 11, 1989, in which Lyle and Erik discussed the murders. It was a serious setback for the defense, for the jurors would be able to hear the shocking words from the boys, including Lyle's astonishing analogy that he missed not having his parents around any longer, just as he missed his dead dog. Not once during the long and emotional session, which would take up 47 double-spaced typewritten pages of transcript, did either Lyle or Erik mention physical abuse of any sort.

For four years, the defense teams had contested admission of the tape as an invasion of the psychotherapist-patient privilege. However, Weisberg ruled that the defense had waived that protection by making the mental state of the brothers an issue in their trial, claiming the brothers killed out of fear. Until that decision was handed down, the prosecution knew only that the tape contained important information, based upon documents released earlier by the State Court of Appeal. Bozanich and Kuriyama had not yet heard it. Weisberg denied a delay request to allow still another defense appeal, but acknowledged that, "I think all counsel would agree this is a unique situation that has not been addressed by any other case in any other court.'' The Menendez case was about to break new legal ground, and the judge told the jurors they could forget being released before Thanksgiving. It would now stretch into December, he said.

In an attempt to blunt the tape's impact, the defense won legal arguments that allowed them to play it before the jury. They would attempt to show it contained no evidence of murder for money or a perfect murder. ''It talks about a very crazy, dysfunctional family,'' said Abramson. ''And is, in my opinion, clearly orchestrated by the Great Satan,'' her latest sobriquet for Oziel.

Forty-seven months had elapsed since Lyle and Erik had sat in the office with Doctor Oziel and, unknowingly, had their voices captured on audio tape. Their words would now come back to haunt them as both juries listened to the tape that lasted less than an hour. To say that it rambled aimlessly would be an understatement, for Oziel let the two brothers talk at length and jump from subject to subject, spiraling and repeating at will.

A primary point, however, was their description of the marriage of Jose and Kitty, giving a heretofore unseen side of the relationship.

Lyle, on the tape, said that his father ran the relationship with an iron hand. ''That was my dad's general feeling. When she was crying, which was, 'Hey, you know, I want my life the way I want it. If, if I have to do things I don't wanna do to satisfy the marriage, that's not the way I wanna live. We'll go our separate ways.' And my feeling was very strong. That's not the way it is. I told him flat out. 'You know, you make sacrifices in order to have a relationship. You make compromises. That's the whole point of a relationship.

You're each not gonna get exactly what he wants. So you've gotta come to, you know, you go to a dinner party, even if you don't want to, because she hasn't been able to go to one in a week because you've been working late.' It was not his feeling at all that he should do that."

On the tape, Oziel asked how Jose reacted.

LYLE: He responded by saying, "Well, I'm not prepared to do that. My feeling is that you have a relationship. One person controls the show. If I have to do things I don't wanna do, even the smallest things, then I don't wanna be a part of the relationship."

OZIEL: So it was his way or no way.

LYLE: It's his way or no way . . . And I was shocked by the statement. 'Cause I realized that if I pursued it, it could lead to a divorce.

He further said that his parents had convinced people outside the immediate family that they were genuinely in love, but that letters Kitty had written and arguments the boys overheard showed differently. "On the outside, everyone thought that their relationship was all passion, all-consuming," Lyle said. "Everyone was crazy." It was only a sham, because "the whole family worked behind closed doors . . . It was all a closed game."

As a result, Kitty became increasingly miserable, knowing that Jose was seeing other women, and was "rushed to the hospital" once in New Jersey because she "took the wrong pills or something."

Lyle said that one tennis coach, Brad Werner, told him, "God, I really feel sorry for your mother. She opens up to me a lot. She's just tormented by your father, and I would hate to live her life. Her life is terrible."

In one extraordinary story, Lyle related how Jose made Kitty believe "that they had no money."

LYLE: He had her convinced that they were poor, and that she could literally not afford to take tennis lessons, and do different things for herself, and buy herself nice stuff, and even get a leather jacket for a couple hundred. I was buying leather, hundred-dollar jackets on my allowance I was getting easily, and she said she couldn't afford one. She wished she could get one. And I remember a day when I said, "Come on, Mom." 'Cause I had bought something. "How can you say 'I can't afford this,' when Dad just got a stock bonus of, worth six million dollars?" . . . and his salary is a million-three. And she had no idea. She said, "What stock? What do you mean? His salary is three hundred thousand." Or whatever it was . . . "Because we're cash poor. We're cash poor."

Lyle added that it made him mad that other family members did not intervene to stop Jose's mistreatment of Kitty. Hearing this statement had to come as a shock to some family members who had stuck by the boys from the moment they were arrested. "I had a lot of anger toward my relatives," said Lyle. "And my uncles and my aunts. My Uncle Carlos and Aunt Terry, he knew about what was happening to my mother and did nothing. I just think that they were cowards."

The boys said they considered their father to be a genius, but one whose star was set on success, not on the family. It was one thing to sit and watch the Super Bowl with him, but an entirely different matter to discuss inner feelings. Although Jose had a slight heart condition, he simply would never show any sign of weakness.

"Men don't cry," said Lyle, describing how Jose would close up when a discussion brushed close to emotions. To cry was to show weakness. However, Jose did show "a chink in the armor" after the Calabasas burglaries, when he wept, the first time Lyle had ever seen him cry.

There was another side to the way Jose reacted to the Calabasas issue, too.

LYLE: He told Erik that . . . he handled it terribly. If he were in charge of it, he would have handled it way better than Erik. "You made all kinds of mistakes, and you don't know how to do that even."

OZIEL: It wasn't even so much what you did. It was more that you were stupid in how you did it.

LYLE: Right.

Much of the tape was consumed with Lyle discussing his mother's miserable marriage, and how she faced only the prospect of more problems with her husband. "She at least felt comfortable in Princeton . . . she had her friends, and she had a bonding . . . He took her out of that and brought her to California, and Erik and I knew it was devastating for her. I mean, it was really her death there, and if he went into politics, it would be another one . . . moving to California was just the worst thing in the world, and he knew it."

Even if Jose quit chasing women and pursued a political career, the result would have been much the same for Kitty, a mistress of the flesh being replaced by something that would consume even more of Jose's time and energy. Erik and Lyle would be off at college and she would be alone "in a relationship where she had no identity."

Lyle said, "It was her doom . . . there was no escape." The boys had overheard their parents argu-

ing, had heard Kitty crying, and knew that divorce
was not an option for their mother.

Such observations provided jurors with even more
background of recent familial life within the dysfunctional Menendez household, but what of the actual
murders?

First, Lyle said he would have considered it "murder" if Jose's dictatorial rule at home had forced Kitty
to commit suicide, because "there was no way anyone
would ever find out about it."

With that in mind, "We had to make a decision. It
was one of the harder ones . . . He's the reason. My
father should be killed. There's no question. What
he's doing is, he's impossible to live with for myself
[and] based on what he's doing to my mother."

At this vital point in the discussion, Oziel mentioned
that Jose was talking about disinheriting the boys, and
later the therapist would repeat that comment, claiming that Kitty had talked to him about it, too.

"That didn't enter into it too much, 'cause I felt like
Erik and I could handle it," responded Lyle.

But could they actually carry out such a thing?

LYLE: [It was almost as if] he had raised us to be
able to handle doing this thing that was necessary,
and that we could deal with it better than any other
eighteen- or twenty-one-year-old in the country.
'Cause he had trained us like basic training. My
twenty-one years were a basic training course."

OZIEL: To do what?

LYLE: On how to survive. And how to do what
was necessary.

And . . .

OZIEL: To survive by living without him, or by
killing him . . .

ERIK: To survive.

LYLE: By living without him.

This statement erased any lingering doubts about whether the brothers actually pulled the triggers, an issue that had been decided long ago. But did they plan to do so, as the prosecution claimed, or did they react out of fear, as was the defense position?

"What Erik was feeling that I wanted to say that we, you know, it would be great if we were able to work on it, 'cause even, you know our relationship, because even the planning out of this, the reason it took such a short period of time to figure it out was one, because it could have happened at any moment," said Lyle.

OZIEL: Huh, uh.

LYLE: All the thinking . . .

OZIEL: Huh, uh.

LYLE: . . . Beforehand was done.

OZIEL: Yeah. You already knew what you felt.

LYLE: Ah, we knew what we felt . . . Honestly, I never thought it would happen. Even though I had thought about it. But it was done so quickly, and sort of callously almost, because one, we, if you thought about it too much, the feelings of not having your parents around, and so on, would get in the way of what was more important, which was helping your mother really, and thinking about that . . . and go, "I don't wanna deal [with] my mother's agony." And . . . it [was] sort of a coward's way out. And for one moment before I went back to school, I had a chance, even though my life was going really well. And to show some courage, I felt. And help Erik and I. Help my mother, and we got together and it was the fact that we can't communicate, couldn't communicate together, and sit down and face each other, and talk about the real issues. That it was almost done looking in different directions. It was a little word here, a little word there, and a little word here. And this sort of thing doesn't, you don't kill your parents based on a little word here, and a little word there. It was obvious that we felt a tremendous amount of emotion . . .

And it was just a meeting of the minds. The time is now. It's not a great time. I'm doing well. You're ready to go to UCLA. We're starting to buy a lot of things. But we can't ignore the fact that my mother has to live with this.

Later, Erik was asked by Oziel if they had to kill Jose. He replied that he loved his father, but at the same time hated him for what Jose had done to create the "amazing tragedy" of Kitty's life.

ERIK: Eventually, it had to happen. It was basically ruining my life, and I guess Lyle's. And he was putting my mother through torture, and it got to a point where it . . . he was amazing . . .

Erik continued, saying that he wished he could have lived with an idealized family, and would have been able to discuss everything openly and freely with his mother. Oziel asked if he felt he could not be close to either parent, and Erik replied, "From an early age . . . I guess I was taught, both Lyle and I, that you just don't."

OZIEL: You just don't what?
ERIK: Have a close relationship.
OZIEL: You just don't talk about feelings and what's going on.
ERIK: We keep it inside.

* * *

Shifting gears, he spoke of the murders, saying that to escape his situation, he had to "face the fact that my mother had to be killed. And it was the only way out. It was the only way out for her."

Looking back on the incident, Lyle said he is convinced that the death of his mother was not murder, but a suicide. "I still think Mom's was a suicide, because . . . in her letters to Erik and I, she gave me the permission . . . she had given me permission to please carry out her suicide, and it was obvious that she had decided in her own mind, she wants to die."

According to Lyle, Kitty "couldn't have lived, she wouldn't want to live" without her husband and family, and divorce was out of the question.

"It was a very dangerous situation," he said. "Where Erik and I realized that at any point, sort of subconsciously, the go-ahead was given 'to kill us, to kill me, before you leave.' "

The aftermath of the murders left the boys confused, tangled in a web of love and hate for their father and pity for their mother. Lyle said he was "pissed off" that his father was so cold and stern, but at the same time "I'm glad he made me such a strong person [and] I really can't say whether I would have wanted another kind of father."

Erik was plagued by dreams, including one where he tried to convince two friends to shoot him, but they refused. "So I took the gun that was in my hand and shot myself several times in the heart, and then I died, and there was a moment where there is just immense pleasure, that I was happy and there was no tension on my mind. There was no stress and everything was calm, everything was great." He said when he awoke, he was upset at still being alive and having to surrender the feeling of "no more sadness." Lyle, too, said he had considered suicide, and wished that "somebody would be good enough to have me killed."

Finally, Oziel tried to calm a weeping Erik and have the brothers express their love for each other, no matter what had happened with their parents in the past. "You can now create something between the two of you that is supposed to be there to begin with," he said.

Lyle and Erik resisted. "There's no reason to," protested Erik. The therapist got them to admit they loved each other, but that was as far as they would go. "Oh God, come on," Oziel teased them, laughing. "You can do this. I know you can do this."

"We hate that hugging shit, by the way," snorted Lyle. "We fucking hate that!"

As the tape rolled to an end, Lyle spoke realizing that the family was finished. No more tennis tournaments. No more enjoyable interludes with Mom and Dad. Such thoughts had really gotten Erik depressed, he said.

"I think one of the big, biggest pains he has is that you miss just having these people around," said Lyle. "I miss not having my dog around, if I can make such a gross analogy."

The tape clicked to a stop and silence was thick in the Van Nuys courtroom. The prosecution could not have asked for much more. The boys had clearly spelled out for the court that they killed Jose because of the way he treated Kitty, and that they killed Kitty almost as a favor. Erik said Jose had ruined his life, and Lyle complained that living with his father was "impossible." In a big admission, they said they planned the murders. In their bizarre thinking, their mother gave them permission to kill her in such a hideous fashion. And Lyle said he missed his dog.

The defense lawyers had their work cut out for them, putting a good face on the tape by saying it did not contain anything about killing Jose and Kitty for money, nor did it mention that the brothers plotted a perfect crime. And Lyle had said that money was not an important factor.

But they also had not uttered one single word about being sexually abused. Who was the jury to believe? The Lyle and Erik before them now, who claimed that they acted out of fear for their lives after years of being abused by their domineering father? Or the Lyle and Erik of 1989, who claimed they killed their parents to be free of their dad and, at the same time, be mommy's little helpers by assisting her to commit suicide?

26

Defense

The testimony of other witnesses was sandwiched around the tape, and the Menendez brothers' defense lawyers reached for their experts. To follow the momentum established by the tearful testimony of Lyle and Erik, the lawyers wanted to show the boys were following a tragic pattern established by other victims of abuse. And, according to at least one well-qualified outside observer, the defense still had a long way to go.

"I think the jurors are going to be outraged," declared famed defense attorney F. Lee Bailey in a Court TV interview. "I think the only thing that may puzzle them is, 'Why?' I don't think the money alone explains it. I don't think these boys look like they're insane. But why? I think the jurors are going to have to grapple with that for a while, but I think the defendants are in some pretty big trouble."

Throughout October, momentous events were afoot. Toronto beat Philadelphia to win its second straight World Series; Nelson Mandela and F. W. de Klerk of South Africa shared the Nobel Peace Prize; and Southern California erupted in wildfires. In Judge Weisberg's courtroom, Ann Burgess—a mild-looking University of Pennsylvania professor who consults with the FBI on crime scene investigation—testified as an expert in child abuse and mental health.

She said psychologists generally believe that people who are frequently punished pick up clues of impending violence that an outsider might not notice. Because the boys were so "hyper-vigilant," they considered the closed doors of the television room, following the argument, to be a danger sign.

In addition, Burgess, answering Leslie Abramson's questions, said that the number of times that the victims were shot indicated the killers were reacting to something more than anger. They were probably afraid, too, she said. As a result, the crime scene in which Jose and Kitty were found dead had a "disorganized" look about it, and the use of shotguns in a quiet neighborhood indicated a lack of advance planning. The number of shots was a definite pattern of overkill. "A large number more shots were fired than were necessary," Burgess told the court.

Burgess testified that the years of sexual abuse, in effect, "rewired" the brain of Erik Menendez in such a way that he was imminently fearful of being killed by his father. She said that after spending fifty hours interviewing Erik and reading hundreds of documents, she was convinced he was telling the truth about the mistreatment he allegedly endured.

She recalled a specific nightmare that Erik had also described on the witness stand, in which a cow and a horse and a green face appear with him in the dream. As he shrinks, the face grows in size—becomes his father's face—and chases him: a typical nightmare of a traumatized child, Burgess testified. Following the horrendous argument on the night of August 20, 1989, Erik's brain began sending him signals of fight or flee. The defendant, she said, picked up the shotgun and fired without thinking.

Prosecutors fought back strongly, but yawning ju-

rors obviously felt the trial was slogging through a
rather uninteresting swamp of minutiae. Compared to
the wild stuff that had come before, this was boring. If
the defense was hoping to electrify them with expert
testimony, it wasn't working. Pamela Bozanich
pressed Burgess on her testimony that the crime
seemed disorganized, which meant that the brothers
had not planned it in advance. "Your definition of plan
is not everyone's definition?" asked Bozanich. "I
don't know," replied Burgess, who said she had been
paid $9,000 by the defense for her expertise. "I
haven't checked it out with everyone."

Bozanich, a master of reducing complex arguments
to terms that a juror could understand, attacked the
idea that the murders were not planned in advance.
The brothers had used a fake ID to buy the shotguns
and waited until the maid had a night off to commit
the crime, she said, building to her analogy. She
framed it for Burgess in the guise of a wedding story.
She said, just suppose, that a bride-to-be spends
months planning for her wedding, but on the special
day, the whole thing flops because the preacher arrives
late and the caterer serves up a disastrous meal.
"Does the fact that my wedding did not go well mean
I didn't plan it?" she asked.

The professor answered in typical lecture tones.
"One could say there were certain factors that were
checked and double-checked, and carefully outlined,
which usually goes into a good plan. That's not to say
that extraneous factors can't occur." Jurors could
easily understand a goofy wedding. By using big words
and fragmented concepts, Burgess lost the argument.

The Menendez story was suddenly and totally wiped
from the news headlines by another Los Angeles trial.
A jury had returned a series of acquittals and reduced
charges against two black men accused in the severe

beating of truck driver Reginald Denny, during the L.A. riots that followed the police beating of motorist Rodney King. It had absolutely nothing to do with the Menendez trial, other than demonstrating the eternal truth that juries can reach very peculiar decisions.

Ann Tyler, a psychologist from Salt Lake City, was quizzed carefully by Abramson about Erik's behavior, and said the young man had no reason to lie about being abused as a child. Bozanich pounced, pointing out that Erik had continually lied about many things. "The fact that he lied about not being involved in killing his parents doesn't mean his whole life is a lie, or that the abuse is a lie," Tyler insisted. The psychologist, who had run up a bill in excess of $13,000 for the case, shocked jurors when, on cross-examination, she brushed aside Erik's Calabasas burglaries of more than $100,000 in cash and jewelry as merely the "acting-out behavior" of an adolescent.

On Sunday, October 17, author Neal Gabler wrote in *The Los Angeles Times* that the Menendez saga might be as much a sign of modern times as "Ozzie and Harriet" reflected the tamer values of the 1950s. His analysis noted that Americans were watching the Menendez trial as avidly as any favorite television show, because real life was outstripping fiction as a source of horror and shock. His interpretation of the Menendez case was that "No one is really responsible anymore. If we are unhappy, if our lives seem unfulfilled, if we fail to function as we would like, we have merely to ransack the past for an excuse—just as the Menendez brothers did. The past shall set us free."

Defense expert Ann Burgess, who spent several days on the stand, stuck by her theory that Erik's long history of abuse led him to commit murder instinc-

tively. When Bozanich asked if Burgess thought Erik's
story about looking at pistols in Santa Monica, which
the prosecution had shown to be false, actually meant
the boy was lying, Burgess dismissed the incident as
merely a "peripheral detail." Bozanich also asked if it
were peculiar that, when Erik moved out of the Beverly Hills mansion, he hauled along the bed that was
allegedly the scene of his child abuse. "Furniture had
to be taken to set up a new place," replied the witness.
"I don't see that necessarily as inconsistent." The
purchase of the shotguns with a fake identification did
not indicate planning, just self-protection, Burgess
said. And, while Erik may have told a stream of lies
after the murders, the witness said she felt the boy
was telling the truth now. "It's my theory that this
was a crime born of fear," she testified.

The final expert was Jon Conte, a University of Washington professor of social work, who had spent about
sixty hours interviewing Lyle in jail and a total of
about 500 hours in research on the case. He came
away convinced that, not only was Lyle telling the
truth about being sexually abused, but that many
memories remained deeply buried in his psyche, not
yet ready to surface, even though he was on trial for
murder. One indicator was that Lyle had a little ce-
ramic leopard that he kept in his bedroom, always
adjusting its stance so that the little glass cat could
watch over him while he slept. Lyle's story, said
Conte, contained shame, embarrassment and a reluctance to talk about what had happened. Bozanich, on
cross-examination, asked Conte how he could believe
anything that Lyle said, after all of the lies that had
been told. "I find nothing to suggest he was dishonest
with me," replied the expert, who had also been hired
to testify by the defense. Bozanich made sure the jury

heard the price tag of each of the defense's expert witnesses.

Several family members were sworn in as witnesses, following the experts' parade, but added little to the existing knowledge. Carlos Baralt, an uncle, testified that his nephews broke down and wept during an emotional meeting in prison in 1990, about a year after the killings, admitted the murders and told him of being sexually molested by Jose. It came as a shock to Baralt, who said he had always thought the Menendez family was "normal" and considered Jose to be "a great guy."

Southern California continued to burn in an onslaught of wildfires in late October, and the Menendez trial simmered. Delays were common, charged to everything from Erik having to be hospitalized for kidney stones to Abramson getting some time to attend the birth of a baby she and her husband planned to adopt.

Of course, there had to be at least one more performance of the Smyth–Oziel road show, a subject that would not remain at rest if you put a stake through its heart. Actually, there were two more appearances, each as strange as the other.

In early November, Oziel went to a law office to settle his suit against Dominick Dunne and *Vanity Fair*, where he encountered Smyth, whom he also had sued in connection with the article. Things apparently did not go well between them, and *The Los Angeles Times* reported there was "considerable yelling among lawyers, Oziel and Smyth." A few days later Smyth filed still another suit against her former lover, this time accusing Doctor Oziel of battery, negligence and intentionally inflicting emotional distress. The *Times* reported that Oziel allegedly told the woman, "You slut. You know you still want me." The newspaper said Oziel commented, "Her whole life is now devoted to trying to punish me."

And a few days after that, Smyth finally appeared in court—as a witness for the defense! The woman whose chat with police had brought about the biggest break in the case, resulting in the arrests of the brothers, was now on the stand to assist them. She told the court and the juries that she had lied when she had said during an ABC-TV interview, "I heard from their own mouths that they killed their parents."

Her purpose as a witness now was not to help convict the Menendez boys, but to discredit Jerome Oziel, the prosecution's key witness. Prosecutor Bozanich bombarded her with detailed questions on things she had said earlier, under oath, and Smyth responded, "I don't know what I was concerned with or thinking of at the time."

Her newest version of the story was that she was not responsible for her earlier answers. "I have been brainwashed. I had been told over and over what I did hear, what did happen. I was confused. I wasn't aware that I was so confused . . . I didn't know the difference between what I heard and what I didn't hear."

To attack the credibility of the audio tape that had been played, the defense elicited testimony from Smyth that Oziel carefully stage-managed the recording because "He needed to get them to say incriminating things on a tape, so we would have the tape to protect us." Smyth spent several days on the witness stand telling her incredible tale, including relating an IOU she once gave Oziel that promised 500 sex acts. By the time she was done several days later, jurors seemed to have trouble taking her seriously.

After calling forty witnesses, the defense rested its case in late November, and the trial entered its final phase, as the Thanksgiving holiday passed.

* * *

The prosecution's rebuttal witnesses were aimed at discrediting the boys' emotional stories, and particularly damaging testimony was given by Marlene (Marzi) Eisenberg, who had been Jose's assistant for eight years. She recalled a "fairly bizarre" exchange she had with Lyle following one of the memorial services. They were seated in a limousine and Lyle crossed his legs and wagged a tassled loafer.

"Hey, Marzi," said Lyle. "Who said I couldn't fill my father's shoes?"

Eisenberg said she told him not to try to fill Jose's shoes, but to "make your own tracks in life."

"You don't understand," Lyle explained. "These *are* my father's shoes."

The defense countered with rebuttal witnesses to support the validity of the alleged abuse, hoping to show the jurors that it was not just some scheme dreamed up to create an alibi. Doctor William Vicary, a psychiatrist who examined Erik in jail, said the young man was a virtual "basket case . . . a pathetic, wimpy, hopeless mess," who was fearful of admitting his father's molestation, even while he was behind bars. Vicary, who prescribed therapy and antidepressant drugs for Erik, said his jailed patient finally began telling him of the abuse in August, 1990, a year after the slayings.

Vicary said Erik felt the admission would ruin what remained of the family reputation. Further, Erik was personally ashamed and afraid of how the news would portray him. "Everybody in the whole world would think he was a homosexual, and his girlfriend would leave him, and for the rest of his life he would be [living in seclusion] like the 'Elephant Man.' "

As the trial inched into December and closing arguments, Judge Weisberg had more bad news for the jurors, who had been sitting in his courtroom for nineteen weeks. If verdicts of first-degree murder were returned in either case, more witnesses might be called to determine the issue of life imprisonment or a death penalty. That meant the jurors might still be in their chairs well into 1994.

Appropriately, in the final days of testimony, the actual estate of Jose and Kitty Menendez was discussed. From the beginning, the trial had centered on money, and at the time of the murders in 1989, the estate was estimated at $14 million.

Four years later, as 1993 and the trial drew to a close, many checks had been written on that account. Details of the disbursements were not given, but after probate costs, taxes, the fees of private defense lawyers and the cost of some high-ticket experts charging rates of $200-an-hour and higher, it was announced in court that the estate was now worth only about $800,000 and owed almost exactly that much in taxes and court costs.

Lyle and Erik Menendez, the one-time rich kids from Beverly Hills, who had money to burn before they murdered their parents, could now truthfully say they were penniless orphans.

27

Judgment Day

Judge Weisberg handed the jurors four choices, and their decisions would literally spell life or death for Lyle and Erik Menendez. If found guilty of first-degree murder and special circumstances, they could be headed for the two-seat gas chamber at San Quentin. At the other end of the spectrum lay a possible conviction for involuntary manslaughter, if jurors felt the brothers truly feared for their lives at the time of the slayings. Such a decision could bring as little as a two-year sentence, and, since the boys had already been in jail for more than three years, it could possibly set one or both of them free.

Between those extremes were second-degree murder, which carries a 15-year-to-life sentence in California, and voluntary manslaughter, with a sentence of three, six or 11 years.

Each brother faced sentencing on three counts—the death of Jose, the separate murder of Kitty, and conspiring to kill them. With the additional wording of "lying in wait" to commit the murders, the charges met the "special circumstances" criteria that could bring the death penalty.

So, in reality, there was a multitude of combinations.

A verdict of not guilty was not an option, as the jurors prepared to weigh what they had heard from 101 witnesses and what they had seen in 405 exhibits. Nobody said this was going to be easy.

The trial had stretched for five long months and had grabbed national headlines and television coverage at an unprecedented rate. Even President Clinton had said he was a bit hooked on the case, and millions of Court TV addicts now worked their Christmas shopping around the finale of the Menendez drama.

Closing arguments were heard first for Lyle, with his defense counsel, the cool and methodical Jill Lansing, and her co-counsel, Michael Burt, squaring off against the composed but lethal Pam Bozanich. Later, Leslie Abramson's bombast would oppose the soft but never-back-down style of Lester Kuriyama in the battle for Erik's future. The juries heard the closing arguments separately, and would make their deliberations in guarded rooms on different floors of the Van Nuys Courthouse. Weisberg planned to keep the first verdict sealed until both cases were decided, then announce them simultaneously. Appropriately strange, the tangled case might end with one brother going to the gas chamber, while the other was set free.

Bozanich, Lansing and Burt began their contest of wills and words on Thursday, December 9, and although every single thing they said had been heard before during the previous months, the arguments were still mesmerizing. It was the last chance the lawyers had to possibly sway a juror.

Burt took the floor first and, sticking close to the actual wording of the law involved, argued that the jurors must consider that the shootings were carried out while the brothers were in a state of "fear and panic that followed year after year after year of abuse by bullying parents." He contended that Lyle was operating like an unthinking robot on the night of the murders and that he shot his parents on "instinct" and not as part of some careful plan. That, said Burt, was not enough to meet the legal standards for first-degree murder, and he asked the jury to return a verdict of involuntary manslaughter.

Bozanich responded with quick force and pinned the photograph of the slain parents, lying in their blood, on the bulletin board for the jurors to see. "This is not a hard case," she declared. "This is not a complicated case. These two people were watching TV and they got slaughtered by their sons."

She challenged Burt's idea that there was no planning involved, pointing out that the boys drove to San Diego and used a fake identification card to buy the shotguns. She also pointed to the taped transcript of the session with Doctor Oziel, in which Lyle was quoted as saying there was "no way" he would have carried out the shootings alone, and decided to let Erik "sleep" on the plan "for a couple (of) days."

Bozanich said that planning was clearly evident, from the out-of-town trip to purchase the 12-gauge shotguns on August 18, to the purchase of ammunition on August 20, to Lyle's telephone call to a friend to set up an alibi. "Implicit in that is that the decision to kill was coldly and carefully arrived at," she declared.

With the legalese out of the way, the defense team moved into the roiling, uncharted waters of emotion to bolster their argument that ongoing sexual abuse by Jose forced the boys to kill their parents.

Lyle, wearing a soft yellow sweater over a striped shirt, listened solemnly as Lansing, impeccably professional in a dark suit, verbally walked the jurors through the murder scene and asked them to look not at the gory incident, but instead at the reason: *Why* there were killings in the first place? "It may be hard for you to believe these parents could have killed their children," she coaxed. "But is it so hard to understand these children believed their parents would kill them?"

The jurors knew the details of the crime and the allegations of sexual abuse, but Lansing won points when her cool demeanor frayed, and her voice cracked as she described Lyle's terror beneath the ruthless rule of his father, Jose.

This proved too much for Lyle, who began to sob himself when Lansing described the wracking guilt the young man felt at finally deciding to go public with the family's evil secret in order to stop the abuse. She read his final words from the witness stand—"I felt I betrayed my dad."

Lyle and Erik had been conditioned since they were little boys to "read cues" about the mercurial temperaments of their parents, she said. On August 20, 1989, after a week of escalating confrontations, the brothers believed they read cues about what Jose and Kitty intended, "and they read them wrong," she said.

Lansing asked the jurors to consider the entire event, dating back to Lyle's childhood sexual molestation, and put the violent explosion on that balmy August Sunday night in 1989 into full perspective. Lyle acted as he did because he felt trapped and threatened with his own imminent death, and there was no other option, she said.

She asked the jurors to remember the months of horrific testimony and return a verdict of involuntary manslaughter.

Bozanich, returning to the fray, was openly scornful of the tears shed by the defendant and his lawyer, and charged that child sexual abuse, as an excuse used in this case, would taint such a defense in some future, more worthy case. "For all those children who were severely abused and who became useful members of society, this defense is an offense," she said.

With her brown hair swept up and wearing a tailored red suit, Bozanich said that some victims of abuse choose options other than murder. Then, playing a surprise emotional card of her own, she looked the jurors in the eyes and told them that her own father had been badly abused when he was a little boy, but instead of killing the perpetrators, he joined the Navy and shaped a life that was useful and productive.

That same kind of choice was available to Lyle and Erik Menendez, she said. Instead, she belittled them as being merely "spoiled and vicious brats" who blew away their parents and then used the family fortune to erect "the best defense daddy's money could buy."

Putting more pictures on the bulletin board—one showing a vibrant and alive Kitty and the other showing her savagely butchered face, with a shotgun-blasted hole in her cheek—Bozanich dismissed as "not real" the allegations of sexual abuse, and said that Jose and Kitty were "slaughtered in the prime of life for no reason other than perhaps they were bad parents."

After hearing the final arguments, Lyle's jury was taken to a room on a different floor to begin their deliberations, and Erik's jury returned to the courtroom.

The arguments in the Erik Menendez case began on Monday, December 13, with a two-hour presentation by Kuriyama, who strolled the courtroom before a line of bloody photos of Kitty and Jose. The defendants, charged Kuriyama in his soft voice, were not mistreated children, as the defense tried to claim, but "arrogant men."

"The defendant and his brother viciously and mercilessly attacked their parents," he said. "The defense is no less merciless and malicious to the victims. They have tried to place the victims on trial."

Sexual abuse was not the issue. Murder was. Kuriyama heaped scorn upon the allegations that the defendant was mistreated. In the prosecutor's view, Erik slaughtered his parents because he wanted the money, but "didn't want to toe the line" as demanded by his father. "Erik feared all right. He feared he'd have to get off his butt and work like the rest of us."

And he wasn't about to let the jurors forget that Kitty was also "blasted all over that room" in Beverly Hills, because the brothers thought that was the "only way" to carry out their plan. "That is a choice the defendants made. They should be held responsible for making that decision."

Erik sat frozen at the defense table as Kuriyama hammered away at him for being a liar, a thief and an admitted killer. "Smile," she ordered him as she began to make her own arguments. He managed a sheepish grin.

Abramson, whose final appearance had the trappings of a movie lawyer trying to snatch victory from the jaws of defeat, began by tacking her own set of photographs on the bulletin board—of faceless, naked little boys—and said the prosecution's death scene pictures were merely a sad attempt to deflect the jury's attention from "the important question: Why did this happen?"

She deliberately and dramatically pierced the pictures with pins as she recounted Erik's testimony that his father stuck him with tacks, while forcing the boy into "rough sex." Finally, she said, Erik was "driven over the edge" by "extensive and severe" sexual abuse and "went to his frankly equally screwed-up brother for help." Then she pointed to the death pictures of Jose and Kitty. "And this is what happened."

She stalked the courtroom, a cat on the prowl, pounding on the "constant, chronic, high-level and low-level cruelty" that was endured by her client. She was loud. She was sarcastic. She was unrelenting. She slammed the reputation of Doctor Oziel again, saying he was "manipulative and two-faced," and said the jurors should disregard both him and his tape recording. She told them not to engage in "a certain kind of discrimination . . . called 'Hate the Rich.' "

On Wednesday night, as the case was drawing to a close, ABC-TV ran an hour-long documentary, entitled "Murder in Beverly Hills: The Menendez Trial." It included photographs of a happy family, the parries and thrusts of the opposing lawyers, shots of Abramson stroking Erik's hair, pictures of the naked children, and a partial rendition of Doctor Oziel's off-key singing of an Elvis Presley ballad to his paramour, Smyth. But it was a peculiar story, the sort television loves, for it had no ending. The jury had not returned a verdict on either case and there was little reason to broadcast the episode without a finish, other than to show some shocking pictures. But it did introduce one important concept to its millions of viewers—that when it comes to murder, "the law doesn't care about sad childhoods."

That was the very nut that Abramson and Lansing were trying to crack. Perhaps the judge might not care about abuse as a possible excuse for murder, but they wanted to make certain the *juries* took the tormented childhoods of Erik and Lyle into consideration.

Abramson continued her bombast through several more days, watching the body language of the jurors and realizing she had not yet won. "I can tell some of you are very resistant to what I'm saying. You must entertain the possibility that I'm telling the truth," she urged at one point.

She also drove a wedge between the brothers, saying, "There's no evidence in this case that Erik killed anybody." It was Lyle, she said, who delivered the

final shots to the heads of both Kitty and Jose. That
was a stretch, and she must have known it, for her
client had already admitted participating in the killings.

It was the sexual abuse, the fact that Jose experi-
mented with his boys like "laboratory animals" and
trampled upon "the fundamental rule of father, God
and nature," that finally created a crisis that could not
be overcome. "Only the revelation of the molestation
secret makes sense with why this happened then,"
she declared.

At the end of her exhausting three-day performance,
Abramson asked the jurors to place themselves in the
shoes of a terrified Erik Menendez, who grew up in a
"family environment run by fear," and return a verdict of involuntary manslaughter.

The prosecution now had the final shot, and Kuriyama spent little more than an hour disparaging
Abramson's arguments, relegating them to a "fantasy." He said that Erik had no right to be the "ac-
cuser, prosecutor, judge, jury and executioner" of his
parents, no matter what the family history might have
been. And he once again pointed the case away from
abuse allegations and at the target—murder.

There was one final bomblet. Kuriyama, noting that
the defense made so much of the relationship between
Jose and Erik, introduced the possibility of Erik being
homosexual. The prosecutor reminded the jurors that
Erik testified he and some pals discussed "how to
make semen taste better" and that he even flavored
Jose's coffee with cinnamon in an attempt to improve
oral sex. "We know that . . . he is homosexual,"
Kuriyama stated.

Strangely, the issue had not played a major role in a
trial that had centered so much on the subject of sex,
even though the jurors knew that Kitty had once given
her son six months in which to find a girlfriend. Even

when questioned by his own lawyer, Erik had said Kitty "made it seem like it was worse than death to be gay, and I didn't think I was, I just—I don't know." Abramson had quickly followed up by having Erik state that he liked girls.

Kuriyama, in his closing statement, suggested that Jose had not actually forced Erik into homosexual acts, but was in fact furious that his younger son was a "faggot." The prosecutor was putting the impression of homosexuality squarely before the jury, outraging Abramson, who fired back with a personal attack on Kuriyama. The lawyer, whose entire defense was based on aberrant sexual behavior, said Kuriyama was "disgusting" for mentioning homosexuality in connection with her client.

"Things got turned around in this case," Kuriyama said, quoting Shakespeare's witch in *Macbeth*, saying that, "Fair is foul and foul is fair." He urged the jury to set things straight again and to "bring the murderers of Jose and Kitty Menendez to justice."

Finally, all the words had been said. Christmas was coming, and so were the jury deliberations.

Sandi Gibbons, spokeswoman for the office of the district attorney, said the verdict coverage by the news media was both justified and overdone. "The greatest drama in the world happens inside a courtroom. And this is 'Beverly Hills 90210' gone berserk."

Berserk is right. The entire trial was almost a parody of a legal proceeding. As *The Los Angeles Times* put it, the trial was "a whiny, finger-pointing, name-calling circus." Outrage became the norm, insults fashionable, and the amount of misleading information that came out in the investigation was incredible. The sideshow between Oziel, who steadfastly maintained that he had done nothing wrong, and Smyth, whose erratic course throughout the story left things totally confused, was soap-opera drama, not a high point for the legal profession.

The media and its readers and viewers couldn't get enough of the story. For months, their attention stayed glued to the courthouse. Shopping days counted down to a precious few and Erik and Lyle Menendez spent the time huddled in courthouse cells, awaiting their fate. They might get a Christmas present of life. Or death.

But Christmas arrived in Los Angeles with sparkling lights and 71-degree temperatures, and there were no Menendez verdicts. The *L.A. Times,* however, did feature a color photo of Erik and Leslie Abramson and quotes from Abramson and Lester Kuriyama in its listing of "stories that had everyone talking" during 1993.

Amid the after-Christmas sales, courtwatchers adjusted their anticipation, guessing the verdicts would come in before the Rose Parade and Rose Bowl football game that ushered in 1994. Although the jurors deliberated during the holiday period between Christmas and New Year's Day, they did not reach any decisions.

As the days ticked past—one week, two weeks, three weeks—anxiety was palpable. After five months of trial, the jurors were taking a very long time to make up their minds. That meant, to courtwatchers, that there was a lot of turmoil going on behind those closed doors. The emotional upheaval in evidence outside the court obviously was reflected inside the jury rooms.

The surprising first break came on January 10 when the foreman of the Erik Menendez jury came back into the courtroom with bad news. "We are deadlocked," he told Judge Weisberg on the 16th day of deliberations. "Positions have essentially not changed after three weeks of discussion and debate." Weisberg nodded sympathetically, but instructed the jurors to take up their deliberations once again to see if they could break the deadlock. The foreman was not optimistic. "I see no hope for reaching a decision on any of the counts," the juror said.

The admission of a deadlock after 16 days of discussion brought quick reactions from both sides. Erik's lawyer, Leslie Abramson, was outraged at the judge's instruction because she was not given an opportunity to argue on the record for a mistrial. A no-verdict was as good as a win for the defense, since it meant no murder or manslaughter charge would be returned. But District Attorney Gil Garcetti left little room for elation in the defense camp when he stated that the prosecution would rather have the jury deadlocked than have them return a lesser verdict of involuntary manslaughter, a decision which could conceivably allow Erik to go free because of the time he had already served in prison.

As Erik's jury returned to its private sanctum for further debate, the jury trying to reach a verdict in Lyle's case asked the court stenographer to read back some 400 pages of testimony that centered on Lyle's emotional state just prior to the shooting, when he said he thought his parents were plotting murder. "I was feeling like a ghost, like we were already dead," Lyle had said at one point. Lyle sat in court during the long re-reading process. It was his 26th birthday and the jury had been deliberating for 18 days.

Erik's jury came back to court on January 13, and as Erik, dressed in a striped shirt and maroon cable-knit sweater, listened without emotion, the foreman gave the judge another note. They still had been unable to crack the stalemate. "We remain deadlocked," reported the foreman. "Since our last report to you, we have been unable to move closer to agreement on any counts. If anything, we have become more entrenched in our positions."

Weisberg asked if he could do anything at all to help them reach a conclusion and was told it was impossible. The jury went back for a final effort to see if it could agree to acquit Erik of the most serious charges, which would prevent a retrial. No agreement on that point either.

A reluctant Weisberg announced, "The court finds, based upon the statements of the foreman and all of the jurors, that there is no reasonable probability that a verdict can be reached in this matter, as to any count and as to any verdict. And therefore, the court finds that the jury is hopelessly deadlocked and declares a mistrial in this matter."

Erik Menendez, at least temporarily, had escaped conviction. The six men and six women jurors had not been given the option of finding him not guilty, but the fact that all of them could not agree in finding him guilty of anything was seen as a major victory for the defense. Not only had Erik dodged the gas chamber, but he had not been convicted of anything at all!

It did not mean freedom. Sandi Gibbons in the office of the district attorney gave the official word: Erik Menendez would be retried, and the charge would again be first-degree murder. Erik, his sharp sweater contrasting with his prison paleness, was returned to his cell to await the next act in his long drama. The interest in the Menendez saga had suffered during the long deliberations. The story of Erik's mistrial verdict shared the front page of *The New York Times* alongside President Clinton's historic trip to Russia and the incredible assault on figure skater Nancy Kerrigan.

Meanwhile, Lyle's jury was still out. They had been negotiating for 21 days without a decision, and only a fool would bet on the outcome.

After a year of fires, mud slides, riots and a series of goofy jury verdicts in major cases, Los Angeles was thrown into convulsions early on Monday, January 17, as a massive earthquake measuring 6.6 on the Richter scale throttled the metropolis like a terrier shaking a rat. It naturally had an impact on the long, long deliberations by Lyle's jury. Several jury members sustained damage to their property and the quake jarred the Van Nuys courthouse enough to cause officials to worry about asbestos contamination. The jury now faced the extraordinary task of just getting to the courthouse through a labyrinth of destroyed highways and crushed buildings, and once there, they had to meet in temporary quarters.

In the week following the quake, the jurors were able to meet for only a few hours, crammed inside a trailer beside the courthouse. Finally, their efforts, too, seemed to come to an end. On Tuesday, January 25, 1994, the foreman notified Judge Weisberg that after twenty-four full days of deliberation, ''We regret to inform the court that we are unable to come to a unanimous decision on any of these three counts.''

After the no-decision in Erik's case, the shock value was gone, but this development in Lyle's case nonetheless packed a wallop. Weisberg, in a question seldom asked by any judge, wanted to know if the earthquake had influenced the jurors. They answered that it had not. Against all hope, he did as he had done with the Erik panel and asked them to deliberate further, to see if they could come to any agreement whatsoever.

The sensational trials of Erik and Lyle Menendez had apparently come to whimpering, indecisive conclusions. The previous week, in another highly publicized trial, Lorena Bobbitt was found not guilty by reason of insanity for the mutilation of her husband, who had been found not guilty of marital rape. The day the jury told the judge they were deadlocked in

Lyle's case, entertainer Michael Jackson paid millions
of dollars to settle the sexual molestation charge
brought by a 14-year-old boy. And separate juries
struggled to reach verdicts on Lyle and Erik Menendez, who admitted shooting their parents in a frenzied
shotgun barrage. It was getting hard to convict anyone
of anything.

The mansion on Elm Street has become a hidden
estate, almost isolated in a neighborhood of grand
homes. The sprawling Spanish-style house where a
family with a proud Cuban heritage was destroyed in
the midst of Beverly Hills has become a symbol of
infamy, a stop on the tourist trail, a dot on the maps
of "Star Homes" that are peddled for seven dollars by
street corner vendors. Star-spangled vans loaded with
curious customers cruise Elm Street and halt for a
moment to give the folks from Idaho and Tennessee a
good look at the site of the famous "Hollywood Menendez Murders." But the current resident, an Ara-
bian sheik, wisely let the big trees and tangles of vines
and bushes grow high to provide some privacy, and
the tourists seldom see more than a black wrought-
iron fence, a locked gate, and a portion of a beautiful
white house with gleaming automobiles parked out
front. Then they move on to ogle other homes of the
rich and famous.
The house is the most tangible monument to this
unfortunate case, but certainly the Menendez crime
will live on in the lawbooks, because it was a celebrated test of childhood sexual abuse. The murders
were foul and the two brothers were without significant
sympathetic traits.
The "children"—Erik and Lyle—were already
grown men, not a couple of brutalized tots, when the
abuse came to light. Advocates contend the agony of
childhood abuse never ends, no matter what the age,

but in the Menendez case, the mature, athletic, wealthy and intelligent brothers seemed to have had many more options to escape their alleged plight than others would who were materially less fortunate. The Menendez defense decided nothing. It only muddied the crucial issue of child abuse.

Examining the testimony, the evidence and their lives, it seems the boys simply lacked the ability to go out and face the real world, to get into their fancy cars and leave with a wallet filled with cash and credit cards, to get a job and do what the vast majority of Americans do—live within a modest income. The extraordinary spending spree demonstrated how much they loved having the kind of money they would never earn working at minimum-wage jobs—the only level for which the handsome, pampered young men were qualified.

But could they simply have walked away? Experts say the resolution to prolonged abuse problems never ends smoothly, and that victims often act irrationally. But to believe the Menendez brothers required an ability to pilot on emotion alone, set aside Lyle and Erik's propensity to bend the truth, and believe everything they claimed. For some, it was simply too big a jump, considering the background of the brothers included not only wealth and privilege, but a history of theft, cheating and lying. Over the years, with the help of their parents, they learned how to dodge harsh punishment for their actions, to buy their way out of trouble, and perhaps they thought they could beat the system once again.

Certainly, the Menendez brothers exhibited unusual behavior, including the slayings, consistent with indicators of sexual abuse. The dysfunction of the family, the isolated lives the boys led, and the love-hate relationship with their parents all pointed to an environment in which sexual abuse could exist.

Erik and Lyle grew up in a family that seemed to have no moral compass. Winning, at all costs, was everything. The parents taught the brothers well—the end always justified the means—and Jose and Kitty ultimately suffered the most drastic consequences of such lessons.

There were no sympathetic characters in the Menendez case, even the murdered victims. There is no doubt that Jose was overbearing and intolerant, a father who drove his sons without let-up. The emotionally troubled Kitty was not an innocent bystander, for mothers also play a vital role in child abuse cases by simply letting it happen. But character flaws should not merit shotgun slaughter. The laws remain strict—murder is rarely an acceptable response to child abuse.

One cannot automatically believe any child who claims abuse, no more than one can ignore those claims and let such alleged situations go unexamined. Fortunately, as a society, we are more aware than ever of abuse, and are demanding that our governments intervene earlier.

More than any case before in American jurisprudence, the Menendez trial would cast a shadow on sexual abuse as a defense.

If there is any merit whatsoever in the Menendez case, it is that the long-avoided issue of child abuse was pushed into media headlines and television shows, and perhaps we will be more likely to heed a cry for help by a youngster, or step in to help, before someone reaches for a shotgun. Perhaps that is all we can hope for.

There was one final, extraordinary irony in the Menendez case.

Among the motivational sayings contained in Jose

Menendez' favorite book, *The Greatest Salesman In The World* by Og Mandino, is one that perfectly defines the Menendez tragedy.

"I will live this day as if it is my last," declares the scroll. "Today I shall fondle my children while they are young; tomorrow they will be gone, and so will I. Today I shall embrace my woman with sweet kisses; tomorrow she will be gone, and so will I."